POPULATION EDUCATION

POPULATION EDUCATION

H.D. Kamat

A.David

CRESCENT
PUBLISHING CORPORATION

[The responsibility for the facts stated, conclusions reached and plagiarism, if any, in this book is entirely that of the Author. And the Publisher bears no responsibility for them, whatsoever.]

Population Education

Edition 2024

ISBN 81-8342-046-X

Published by :

CRESCENT PUBLISHING CORPORATION
4806/24, Mathur Lane,
Ansari Road, Darya Ganj,
New Delhi - 110002
Mob : 9711991838, 9999021668
Ph. : 011-23244131
e-mail : crescentbook@gmail.com

Website : www.crescentpublishingcorp.weebly.com

Typesetting by :

Arjun Computers
Delhi - 110051

Printed at :
Roshan Offset Printers
Delhi

PREFACE

Population Education is said to be the process of developing awareness and understanding of population situations as well as national attitudes and behaviour toward those situations for attainment of quality of life for the individual, the family, the community, the nation and the whole world, or Population Education can also be defined as the process of understanding population issues and enhancing the life skills for empowerment to improve the quality of life of self as well as that of the others at family level, community level, country level and world level. 'Population Education' as an educational innovation being experimented in India since early 70's can play a potential role in addressing population problem.

Over-population has been one of the burning problems in India. Efforts have been made by the Government to solve the problem through various measures. Population control the freedom of choice has to be left to individuals. There is only one acceptable way to slow down population growth and that is through freedom of choice. That means paying close attention to individual needs, reproductive health, education and equality between women and men. The economic justification for birth control emphasised enlightened self-interest as the stimulus that would in time bring families and nation to lower fertility. Ecological justification almost demanded individual birth control for good of society. Population explosion, mortality role of government, birth control, ecology, equality, ethics, nutrition status are extensively discussed in the present volume.

The present work was planned in consultation with experts who know the nerves of the field. Workshops were organised for development of the outline and guidelines for writing the book. It is hoped that the book will prove useful for teacher-educators, school teachers, student teachers and other interested in the field.

H.D. Kamat
A. David

CONTENTS

1

THE POPULATION EXPLOSION

A NEW PROBLEM

Human population growth in the last half of the twentieth century is proving different in degree, if not in kind, from any previous population trends. Although the number of people on earth has multiplied from 250,000 persons estimated to be alive at the time of Christ to nearly 4 billion in 1972, more than one-third of that increase has occurred since World War II. (See Chart 1.1.)

Moreover, before 1950 population growth took place primarily in those portions of Europe, North America, Asia and Africa settled by Europeans. Since 1950, however, approximately 80 per cent of world population growth has taken place in Asia, Africa and Latin America. Population increase in those regions has jumped from a decennial rate of about 12 per cent in the 1930s and 1940s to 20 per cent in the 1950s and 22 per cent in the 1960s.

To describe the full impact of this phenomenon, even the sober, dispassionate reports of the UN Population Division seem at a loss for words.

> If the speed-up appearing in the more developed regions after 1950 can be called a "revolution," a more forceful term seems appropriate to describe the far greater acceleration, since about 1950, in the population trend of less developed regions. In fact, so strong a word as

Chart : 1.1

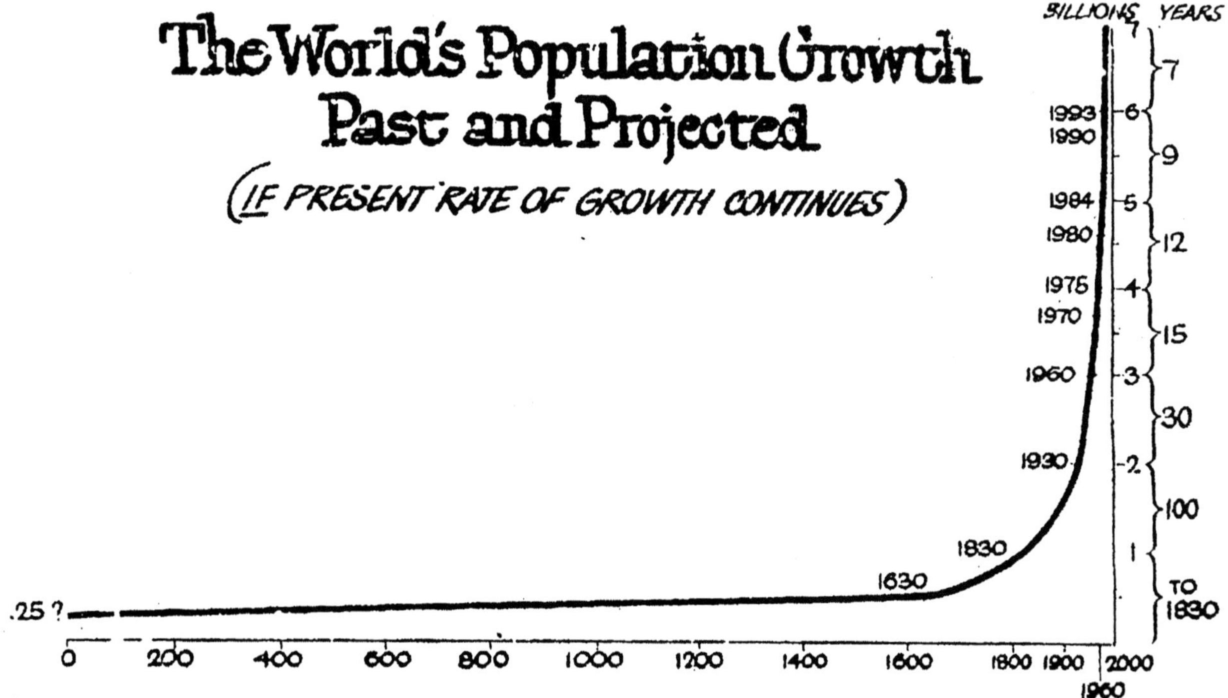

Source: U.S. Department of State.

"population explosion" has gained much currency, and this should be no cause for surprise because the unprecedented magnitude of this new phenomenon is indeed baffling.

Basically, population increase represents the difference between births and deaths. Throughout most of recorded history, human birth and death rates have been high, often in the range of 40 to 50 per 1,000. But at various times and most consistently beginning in the eighteenth century in Europe, death rates declined. Life expectancy, estimated to be 20 years at the fall of the Roman Empire, probably did not exceed 40 years until the nineteenth century. In other words, over the last two and a half centuries, influenced by a combination of factors – better nutrition, reduction of epidemic disease, better sanitation, potable water, improved public health measures, immunisation, and finally antibiotics – death rates gradually fell to a point where life expectancy in the United States and most of Europe is now close to 70 years.

Similarly, but usually after a time lag of several generations, birth rates also have declined. By 1970, birth rates in the developed countries ranged from about 10 to 20 per 1,000, whereas death rates had fallen to about eight to ten per 1,000. Whatever specific factors were the most influential in this long-term demographic transition, there is no dispute that – except in Japan – the dual decline of death and birth rates was the product of European culture, influenced by economic and social change within those societies and carried out in accordance with indigenous attitudes and technology.

Postwar population growth, however, although equally a result of declining death rates and therefore greater life expectancy, was not equally an indigenous product of the peoples affected. The techniques – ranging from DDT and penicillin to massive shipments of food and fertiliser – that conquered many epidemic diseases and mitigated the impact of famine and malnutrition in Asia, Africa and Latin America were not the result of slow local development and adjustment but rather represented a windfall of foreign largesse. Although death rates responded, often with astonishing speed, to this externally supplied technology, birth rates, still the result of individual action and decision, did not. (See Chart 1.2.)

In a notable early (1945) discussion of the approaching postwar situation, Frank Notestein wrote:

> The more rapid response of mortality than of fertility to the forces of modernisation is probably inevitable. The reduction of mortality is a universally acceptable goal and faces no substantial social obstacles. But the reduction of fertility requires a shift in social goals from those directed toward the survival of the group to those directed toward the welfare and development of the individual. This change, both of goals and of social equipment by which they are achieved, is at best a slow process. As a result, the period of modernisation is virtually certain to yield rapid population increase.

In strictly demographic terms the postwar population problem was easily defined as a temporary imbalance in birth and death rates, most acute in Asia but potentially serious in all the underdeveloped areas. Historical and statistical research had by the end of World War II further established that the declines in European fertility resulted not from any physiological changes in human reproduction but rather from deliberate fertility control–primitive methods of contraception, abortion and even infanticide. In his classic *Medical History of Contraception*, Norman Himes offers evidence through virtually all times and cultures of a strong desire to control childbirth and an extraordinary variety of measures to do so.

THE BACKGROUND OF U.S. CONCERN

Nevertheless, despite the widespread private use of various birth control techniques a public policy of disseminating birth control information was not a welcome topic for debate in the United States. As the scientist Harrison Brown, writing in the mid-1950s, pointed out, "The extent to which human

Chart : 1.2

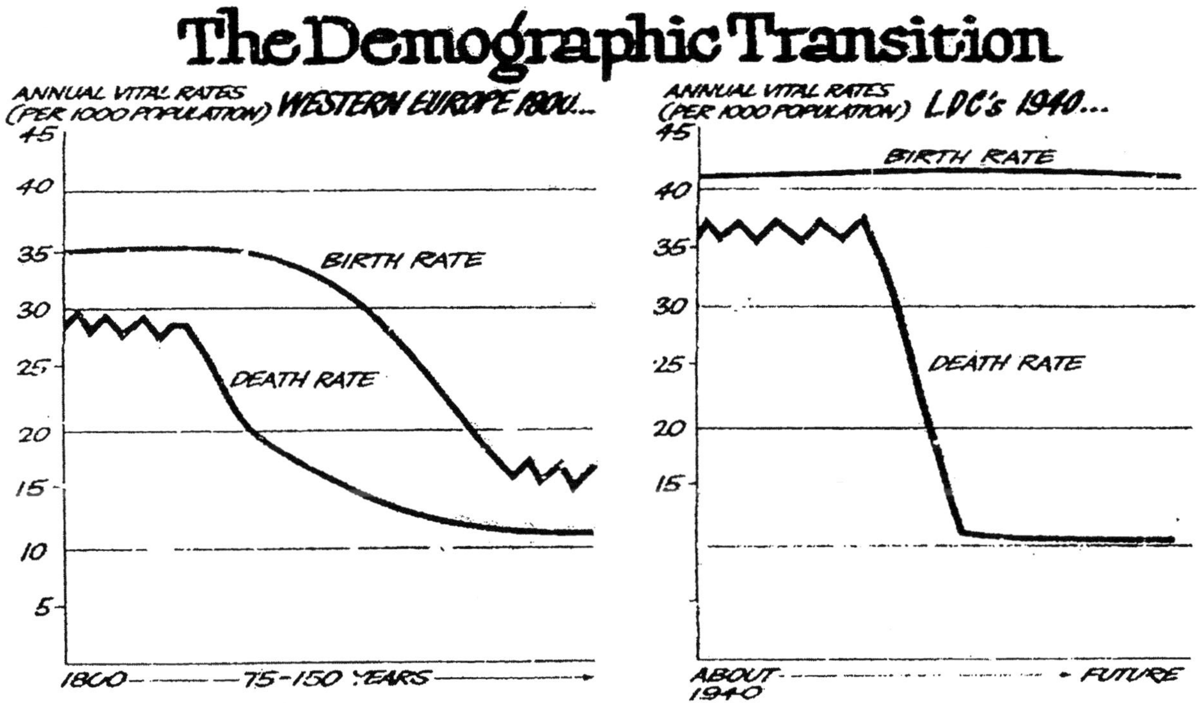

Source: U.S. Department of State.

beings avoid discussing conception control is truly incredible." Not only was birth control intimately involved with sexual practices and religious beliefs – neither considered appropriate for government concern – but also, in the words of one sympathetic official, "The high emotionalism necessary to get this issue going as a social reform worked for a long time against the willingness of government to undertake it."

Two very different elements were involved, almost from the start, in the promotion of birth control and population as issues of U.S. public policy. On the one hand, the activist line of birth control promotion was symbolised in the career of Margaret Sanger, who literally invented the term, who publicised the issue in the United States, and who for many years determined the way in which birth control advocates would approach the government and challenge their adversaries. On the other hand, the professionals – physicians, scientists, demographers – wanted to study the implications of the issue quietly in terms of their own professional values without becoming embroiled in public controversy. The activists needed the theoretical base and factual data of the scientists to make their case. They needed the support of the professionals to give them legitimacy. The scientists, on their side, benefited from the increased public interest that led to a greater demand for their technical output, even as they sometimes shuddered at the uses to which it was put.

In a relationship somewhat like Gresham's Law in reverse, the wide dissemination of bad data stimulated the search for good data. Similarly, the spread of inadequate theories and poor contraceptives by non-professionals promoted the search for better approaches by those technically competent to develop them. In many ways the story of the development of birth control policy is a story of the professionalisation of the activists and the activation of the professionals. In the prewar years, however, the gap between the two was still wide and sharp.

On the activist side, Margaret Sanger founded most of the birth control clinics and educational groups now combined in

Planned Parenthood. Her legacies, many of them still controversial, include a determined feminism, an emphasis upon birth control as a panacea for virtually all sexual, social and economic ills, and an unrelenting struggle to eliminate legal barriers blocking access to birth control. She also had "an unfailing instinct for showmanship and newsmaking." Time and time again, by vividly defining her own role as support for maternal and child health, for freedom of information, freedom of speech, freedom of religion, and privacy of medical records she forced her opponents into a position that most Americans could not easily support. This confrontation technique was valuable to the birth control movement, as it has been to other social reformers who have tried to alter community attitudes. But it was a double-edged weapon that could also cut its most effective wielders out of any role as conciliators of professional opinion or participants in government policy making.

In fact, despite Margaret Sanger's claim that "the Birth Control Movement has allied itself with science and no small part of its present propaganda is to awaken the interest of scientists to the pivotal importance to civilisation of this instrument," doctors and demographers both held aloof from her activities. The physicians, newly imbued with a sense of their own professional standards, were suspicious of lay medicine. Not until 1937 did the American Medical Association endorse birth control at all and then only for therapeutic reasons. Most medical journals avoided the subject.

But the publicity that Margaret Sanger aroused did in fact force medical attention upon the question. Certainly an important factor in the 1937 resolution of the American Medical Association approving birth control was the desire of the doctors to check the proliferation and widespread advertising of useless and even harmful birth control techniques that had developed to meet the growing public demand. As she had predicted, "Just as supply and demand are related to all economic questions, so is propaganda a related part of scientific research in the realms of sex psychology. The medical profession will ultimately meet the issue on the demands of public opinion."

The demographers and others concerned with population on a large scale were at first no more eager than the physicians to take "Sangerism" seriously; many were reluctant even to mention birth control. When in 1927 Margaret Sanger initiated, organised, and largely funded the first World Population Conference in Geneva for scientists of international repute in order to impress the League of Nations with the importance of the population issue, the scientists were uneasy. Delegates to the conference – mainly statisticians, biologists and economists – disputed the use of her name on the programme, "granted her no official recognition, and barred the topic of contraception from the agenda." Despite lively discussions and complete freedom in the exchange of ideas and information, one of the demographers present recounts that "the scholars at this conference deemed it inappropriate to form a continuing organisation under the sponsorship of a proponent of action in a controversial field, and they arranged to meet for this purpose privately in Paris the following year. The International Union for the Scientific Study of Population Problems (I.U.S.S.P.) was organised there in 1928."

The most eagerly sought and acknowledged funding for professional and scientific activities in the field of population came from the foundations. Through the Scripps Foundation for the Study of Population, established in 1922 at Miami University in Ohio, Warren Thompson and P.C. Whelpton became virtually the first academic demographers in the United States, joining the very limited number of population analysts in the Census Bureau and life insurance firms. The Milbank Memorial Fund was encouraged by a determined board member to look at the impact of birth control in a public health context and in 1936 provided funds for an Office of Population Research at Princeton University, under Frank Notestein. The first large foundations to make grants in the population field were the Rockefeller Foundation and the Carnegie Foundation. Influenced by the strong interest of one or two trustees, both foundations supported professional organisations and research but avoided a large direct role.

But even though the researchers and foundations tried to keep at arm's length from Margaret Sanger and her crusade for birth control, they could not avoid some of the same liabilities. Research on sexual problems still carried an aura of witchcraft and was hardly a prestigious scientific field. Catholic opposition remained a perennial source of embarrassment. Frank Notestein recalls friends shaking their heads and wondering how he would ever be able to make a living in such a new and precarious field.

The low status of population activists and scientists alike was reflected in their minimal impact on national government policy. The activists, with Margaret Sanger in the lead, vigorously urged and organised for repeal of the federal "Comstock laws" that barred mailing, shipping in interstate commerce, and importing contraceptives. They tried to amend state laws to permit the operation of birth control clinics. But even with medical support, state legislatures and the U.S. Congress refused to act.

Judicial action brought the first changes in government policy. Lawyers and physicians united in a series of cases of urge the removal of arbitrary, outmoded restrictions upon the prescription of contraceptives for health and welfare. In the critical decision, Judge Augustus Hand ruled that none of the existing Comstock laws should be construed "to prevent the importation, sale, or carriage by mail of things which might intelligently be employed by conscientious and competent physicians for the purpose of saving life or promoting well-being of their patients." Thus only in the courts, where the activists and the professionals could cooperate and, above all, where the political pressures were reduced, was government action possible.

Two other elements weakened the position of those involved in birth control or population work in the immediate prewar and postwar years. First, the state of technology was clearly inadequate. The birth control methods in common use – coitus interruptus, condoms, diaphragms, douching, and various jellies – were not considered effective, esthetic, acceptable, or even safe. They were least practical for those people and nations that most needed help to reduce fertility. Furthermore, because of their immediate link with sexual relations, the methods did not lend themselves readily to public discussion.

Secondly, the Great Depression had a curious and complex influence upon birth control and population studies in the United States. Economic conditions during the 1930s persuaded many couples to have smaller families. As a result the practice of birth control increased even without fully satisfactory methods. Yet as birth rates remained low, especially in better-educated and higher-income families, many demographers forecasted a declining quantity and quality of population for the United States and Western Europe. Such predictions hardly encouraged government enthusiasm for birth control as a national policy.

THE OPPOSITION TO BIRTH CONTROL

The most conspicuous barrier to government policy in the birth control field, however, lay not in the differences between activists and professionals, nor in the temporary exigencies of economics, but rather in the opposition of the Roman Catholic Church. The sexual orientation of Christianity was historically hostile to onanism or birth control, but in the whole compendium of Christian writings up to the nineteenth century, contraception had actually occupied little more than a footnote. Organised, articulate opposition to birth control characteristic of Protestant churches in the nineteenth century and the Catholic Church in the twentieth, was, like population growth, a relatively new phenomenon.

Birth rates had been declining in Western Europe for centuries. That decline was widely recognised and publicised during the late nineteenth century at the very time when the birth control advocates issued their first public appeals. The various national bishops, not the Vatican, responded first to the challenge. From France, after defeat in the Franco-Prussian

War, came objections on patriotic as well as moral grounds to a practice that seemed to be depleting French armies as well as endangering French souls. The first theological work devoted exclusively to the subject appeared in France in 1876. Contraception and declining birth rates seemed to be associated with declining power.

In the United States, too, the militancy of Catholic opposition to birth control had political and ethnic overtones. By 1900, just as the birth control movement was beginning, millions of poor, ignorant, but prolific Irish had immigrated to Massachusetts and other northeastern states. Then came the Italians. By force of numbers and political machines the Irish dispossessed their Anglo-Saxon predecessors. Not altogether welcome in their new home and led by priests and bishops who equated English origins with Irish subjection, the Irish were Catholic in culture and politics as well as in religion. When the ladies of Planned Parenthood tried to offer help, the Black Irish reaction was "What business do those thin-lipped Boston Brahmins have telling us how to behave in bed?" When Harvard graduates argued for repeal of the nineteenth-century Massachusetts and Connecticut Comstock laws in order to propagate birth control, the Irish and Italian Catholics voted "No" at the polls even if they practiced a measure of birth control at home. The emotional revulsion that contraception aroused among Catholics was often an ethnic revulsion against the people who were promoting it. As Father John Ryan put it in testimony against one of the Sanger bills, "We simply cannot subscribe to the idea that the poor, . . . instead of getting justice from the Government and more rational social order, are to be required to reduce their numbers. . . . That is Toryism." At the same time Ryan was perfectly willing to cooperate behind the scenes in drafting legislation that would place control of contraception more fully in medical hands.

The tactics that the Catholic Church in America used to fight against birth control were ambivalent. As a religious institution the church was fighting heresy; error had no rights and did not deserve a hearing. But in the political environment of U.S. government policy-making the right to equal time and the principle of majority rule could not be dismissed as heresy. As the Catholic Church and American Catholic politicians began to demand their share of national resources and their turn at national leadership, they were increasingly compelled to abide by political rules.

When Margaret Sanger began her educational campaign, the Catholic Church had tried to cut off all public discussion. Hotels, meeting halls, even political leaders were threatened with boycotts and reprisals if they offered a public forum. But measures such as these only provided confrontations Margaret Sanger needed to publicise her cause. "Hostility aroused against the Roman Catholic community by these tactics," one Catholic complained, "would be hard to overestimate. In proportion to their ill effect their good effect is small."

Meanwhile, Protestant churches were beginning to break away from their traditional prohibitions on birth control. The 1930 Lambeth Conference of Anglican bishops hestitantly proposed that "where there is a clearly felt moral obligation to limit or avoid parenthood, the method must be decided on Christian principles." As the issue in the United States shifted from a conflict between birth control and religion to an internal skirmish among different religions, the Catholic hierarchy was increasingly isolated.

By the late 1930s the Catholic Church was already looking for a way to accommodate its blanket prohibition with the exceptions required by political, professional, economic, and individual circumstances. Doctrinally, the encyclical *Casti Connubii* issued by Pope Pius XI on December 31, 1930, had denounced contraception and the permissive Anglican bishops in no uncertain terms; yet at the same time it declared sexual relations licit "even though, through natural causes either of time or of certain defects, new life cannot thence result." Though the research that would establish a fair degree of reliability for the "rhythm method" was not yet publicised, the pope's brief reference opened for married couples a doctrinal escape route that soon became a well-travelled highway.

Despite the efforts of Margaret Sanger to promote it and the Roman Catholic Church to prohibit it, birth control before World War II was basically a private practice, not a social issue. Most of those who practiced it were not prepared to preach it. The success of the lawyers in drawing the sting from federal statutes removed rather than stimulated the need for legislative action. The U.S. government even during the Great Depression had few economic and social responsibilities at home and fewer still overseas. Birth control was not relevant to any immediate objective. Even those directly involved were very far from agreement in their definition of the issue. Activists like Margaret Sanger saw birth control as a panacea for social, economic and sexual ills. Doctors and demographers wanted to consider it only as a single, narrow substratum of their larger fields. On the other side, the Catholic Church was publicly determined to exercise the broadest moral and religious prerogatives that were politically feasible. For a government caught among these currents, the only prudent policy was no policy at all.

2

SCIENTISTS AND ACTIVISTS IN THE 1950s

After the Second World War, victory overseas and world power, tempered only by continuing cold war competition, replaced the pessimism of the depression. A new U.S. prosperity was fueled by consumers who wanted more of everything, including children. In the immediate postwar years, birth control had little appeal for those who had been waiting to start or continue their families. Without a pressing social need, with women returning happily to home and cradle, the birth control movement in the United States lost what little momentum it had.

THE SCIENTIFIC APPROACH

Nevertheless, the professionals in the field of population study had an initial advantage over the activists in the postwar era. They possessed the technical skills necessary to identify the new overseas population problem and a recognised institutional base (the Office of Population Research at Princeton) under qualified leadership (Frank Notestein). When in 1946 the Economic and Social Council of the United Nations established a Population Commission representing member governments, a Population Division also was set up in the UN Secretariat under Notestein's direction. The first UN demographic yearbook appeared in 1949 and was followed almost annually by volumes summarising census data and studying specific problems in detail. Influential for their public impact were the UN projections of future population growth. In 1952, for example, a world population of 3.6 billion by 1980 was forecasted. By 1957, the projection for 1980 was revised upward to 4.2 billion; the median estimate for the year 2000 was 6.3 billion.

As a rough measure of the low public attention and interest in world population growth, the *New York Times* index entries for population and vital statistics increased from barely one inch in 1950 to a little over two inches in 1958, but about one half of the total coverage was directly or indirectly related to UN statistical reports and meetings.

A high point in UN concern during the 1950s was the 1954 World Population Conference in Rome, jointly sponsored by the International Union for the Scientific Study of Population and UN specialised agencies and attended by some 600 participants from nearly 40 countries. The largest scientific meeting on population held to date, the Rome conference also considered relationships between population and economic development, but Catholics and communists together blocked recommendations for action. In 1955 when Dag Hammarskjold succeeded Trygve Lie as Secretary-general, population and other research-oriented activities of the United Nations were cut back. The UN Population Division was downgraded to a Population Branch for the next decade.

Apart from the statistical work at the United Nations, the principal boost for increased scientific and professional attention to the population problem in the 1950s came from John D. Rockefeller 3rd. Returning from the Far East in 1948 very much concerned about population growth, especially in Japan, and not satisfied with the token support provided by the Rockefeller Foundation, he arranged for a four-member team – including a public health physician, a social scientist, and two demographers – to report on the status of public health and demography in Asia. Emphasising the difficulty of reducing birth rates, the complexity of social change, the threat of political upheaval, and the need for better contraceptive techniques, their report recommended "study rather than action in the years immediately ahead." They cautiously observed that "the role of the private agencies lies in encouraging teaching, research, experiment and demonstration to increase knowledge and ultimately to foster its wide dissemination." Yet the Rockefeller Foundation hesitated to make interdisciplinary population studies a major programme. Private soundings indicated continuing Catholic disapproval; the foundation's institutional biases were toward public health and agriculture; conservative lawyers feared to jeopardise its far-flung work by entering such a controversial field; and most of the board of directors did not share Rockefeller's feeling of urgency.

In June 1952 at the suggestion of Rockefeller and under the sponsorship of the National Academy of Sciences, a high-level group of experts in public health, conservation, planned parenthood, agriculture, nutrition, demography, and the social sciences was convened in Williamsburg, Virginia. The conference recommended establishment of an international council to concern itself exclusively with the scientific study of population in all its related aspects. In November 1952 the Population Council was organised with Rockefeller as Chairman of the board and Frederick Osborn as executive Vice-President. Its stated purposes were:

> To study the problems presented by the increasing population of the world; to encourage and support research and to disseminate as appropriate the knowledge resulting from such research; to serve generally as a center for the collection and expansion of facts and information on the population questions; to cooperate with individuals and institutions in the development of programmes; and to take the initiative in the broad fields which in the aggregate constitute the population problem.

The founding of the Population Council was a significant start in mobilising the professionals for action. For the first decade or so, its activities were largely research and training, channelled through a relatively small academic community. The universities and the professions both needed this kind of moral and financial encouragement to take up a sensitive multidisciplinary issue. The Population Council provided a heretofore-lacking respectable base from which to influence professional and academic norms and to finance a more specifically problem-oriented approach to population.

The difference the Population Council made in helping to reorient professional behaviour can be seen in the case of the National Committee on Maternal Health, headed by Dr. Chris Tietze. The committee had refused in the late 1940s to become openly associated with Planned Parenthood's work, but by 1957 the committee accepted a considerable grant from the Population Council "to undertake under the best medical auspices an important programme of research to evaluate the effectiveness, acceptability, safety, and cost of various methods and materials of fertility control." By January 1967 the committee's staff and activities were transferred to the Bio-Medical Division of the council–a classic example of professional cooptation.

Yet despite the insistence, as late as 1965, that "the scientific and technical fields are those in which our kind of organisation can be most effective," the Population Council was drawn very quickly into a more active role, mainly because its professionals were among those best qualified to advise developing countries on what action to take. The Indian government, spurred on by the newly opened Ford Foundation office, asked for help from the Population Council. Frank Notestein and Dr. Leona Baumgartner, then New York City Health Commissioner, visited India in the fall of 1955. They recommended to the government an interdisciplinary programme – emphasising a public health approach, including contraceptives – with strong demographic support from a national center. Marshall Balfour of the council participated in a second technical assistance mission to Pakistan in 1959, to help General Ayub Khan establish a government birth control programme. Notestein hoped to develop university-centered public health advisory units and Balfour was accompanied to Pakistan by Dr. Paul Harper of the Johns Hopkins School of Hygiene and Public Health.

During 1955, 1956 and 1957 the Population Council sponsored a series of meetings that included Planned Parenthood officials as well as physical and social scientists to develop and define general principles for promoting birth control overseas. The importance of indigenous leadership, the need for economic planning as an approach to the elite, and the use of public health programmes as an approach to the masses were emphasised. These guidelines were to influence not only the programmes of the Population Council but also the policy advice given to foreign governments and eventually to the government of the United States.

Another project, encouraged by Notestein at Princeton and partially supported by the council in the 1950s, was influential in later government policy-making. Economists like Joseph Spengler and Harvey Leibenstein were developing a theoretical framework to show that population growth, usually considered an impetus to economic growth in the industrial age, could be an impediment in underdeveloped countries. The demographer Ansley Coale and the economist Edgar Hoover applied these arguments explicitly to India to demonstrate that expenditures on family planning would, over various periods, increase per capita income more than any other type of government investment. The heart of their argument was applicable to all developing countries: namely, that a reduced rate of population growth would always mean additional funds for capital investment because it would produce fewer dependents and smaller expenditures for consumption and social needs. This approach turned attention away from the troublesome questions of population size or density (where European history always disproved the Malthusian argument) and focussed the spotlight instead on population growth rates in the developing countries as barriers to economic growth rates. The Coale-Hoover thesis eventually provided the justification for birth control as a part of U.S. foreign aid policy.

The creation of the Population Council had a further impact in the philanthropic area. As an avowedly professional scientific organisation that sought to avoid and not to provoke controversy, it was more acceptable for foundation support than were the active birth controllers. The first two Ford Foundation grants of over $ 500,000 were to the Population Council, which received nearly 80 per cent of all Ford population grants in the 1950s.

Ultimately, as both a grant-making and an operating foundation, the Ford Foundation was to develop population into a major programme under Oscar Harkavy, an economist. But at first, and until 1959, support was only for demographic and educational activities and the Population Council was the preferred intermediary.

Thus, the activity and funding channels in the field of population spread from a few individuals and universities before the war to smaller foundations, and from smaller foundations to larger foundations (with the former often acting as retailers and the latter as wholesalers). By the late 1950s, although no solutions to the population problem were in sight the professional and scientific community had developed a base of expertise and funding to react independently of U.S. government policy to the problem of population growth overseas.

At the same time the implicit justification for organised philanthropy in the United States was not to solve economic and social problems but rather to act as a catelytic agent, providing seed money for innovative projects until such time as others, most frequently governments, would assume responsibility. Only the government could provide to researchers, laboratories and universities the continuing support they needed after initial foundation grants had expired. Despite a deliberate refusal to seek any direct influence upon U.S. government programmes, the foundations were an indirect but powerful force impelling the American government toward recognition of the population problem.

THE ACTIVISTS ORGANISE

The institutional base for the birth control activists was the Planned Parenthood Federation of America, formed by the merger of the American Birth Control Federation and the Clinical Research Bureau in 1939 and given its present name in 1942. But it was considerably weaker than its professional and scientific counterparts. In fact, the organisation had fewer field workers, fewer patients at the main New York clinic, and fewer affiliated local groups in 1959 than in 1939. The transition from a one-woman social reform crusade to a community-based, professional service organisation – the classic "routinisation of charisma" process – was clearly difficult for Planned Parenthood.

During the 1950s the principal aim of Planned Parenthood was to win acceptance – acceptance from the medical profession, from prospective donors, from community leaders, from the mass media, and from the general public. A staff member who joined in 1955 described the whole first decade of his Planned Parenthood work as "trying to persuade people that the roof will not fall in on them if they mention or support birth control." Trying to live down its radical, feminist reputation, Planned Parenthood wooed men, doctors, Protestant and Jewish clergy and business leaders.

One element of Margaret Sanger's special concern that remained strong was the search for better contraceptives. Diaphragms and the medical, clinical, female-oriented approach that they required were not entirely satisfactory for low-income patients. Condoms depended on male motivation and were associated with prostitution and venereal disease. Margaret Sanger personally and later the Planned Parenthood Federation actively encouraged the search for "the pill". In 1951 the federation provided a small grant to Drs. Gregory Pincus and M.C. Chang at the Worcester Foundation for Experimental Biology to study hormonal contraception and later helped to arrange additional private funding, not available from foundations or the National Institutes of Health. In 1958, with the pill only two years away, Dr. Alan

Guttmacher, President of Planned Parenthood, predicted "We are on the threshold of a new era in birth control."

The main public attention the movement received during this period stemmed from confrontation and conflict as, for example, when various state laws were challenged or when in 1953 Catholic agencies resigned from the New York City Welfare and Health Council because Planned Parenthood was elected to membership.

A confrontation that Margaret Sanger herself could not have designed better came in New York City in 1958. Unwritten city policy prevented the otherwise-legal prescription of contraceptives for indigent patients in municipal hospitals. Dr. Louis Hellman in Kings Country Hospital directly challenged the policy, which had been publicised by the *New York Post*. When ordered by the commissioner of hospitals not to fit a diaphragm for a diabetic woman, he called reporters. The controversy raged and received full coverage in New York papers for six months. Planned Parenthood, working behind the scenes, lined up near-unanimous religious and medical support from the non-Catholic community. The issues were carefully and repeatedly defined: medical judgment in a life-threatening situation was being arbitrarily overruled by a religious minority; freedom of medical practice, freedom of religion, freedom of information, even majority rule were threatened. Administrators and elected officials tried to evade the issue but could not. Planned Parenthood and its supporters would not compromise (despite urgings from embarrassed friends).

When the smoke of battle cleared, by late 1958, New York City had a new policy of providing birth control through health and welfare departments. City officials had a different sense of the balance of power on birth control; Planned Parenthood had a renewed confidence in standing up for its position. Perhaps most important, many Catholics specifically redefined their public and political role as a result of that confrontation. "It should be clear," a *Commonweal* article lamented,

> that there are many sound and compelling reasons why Catholics should not generally strive for legislation and directives which clash with the beliefs of a large portion of society. In doing so, they not only strain the limits of the community and actually lessen the persuasive force of their teachings but they almost inevitably strengthen in the minds of non-Catholics the already present worries about Catholic power.

The success of the 1958 confrontation resulted in part from the increased professionalisation of the national Planned Parenthood headquarters. In contrast to many local affiliates, where the part-time volunteer board members (and physicians) were unwilling to risk their community and social status over an awkward controversy for Planned Parenthood, the national staff was fully committed to the cause of birth control and extremely skilful in developing and defining the issue. They deliberately forced the conflict to an unexpectedly successful conclusion.

Planned Parenthood's main effort and also in the long-run its greatest impact on U.S. governmental policy, both domestic and overseas, was through its work in the United States. Nevertheless, the massive growth of population in the developing countries was not ignored by Planned Parenthood speakers and publications.

The United Nations was an early target for the internationally minded birth control activists, as it was for the demographers. As early as 1948, voices were raised suggesting that birth control be included in the activities of the World Health Organisation (WHO). The government of India, also much concerned about population growth, asked for UN assistance. Dr. Brock Chisholm, first director-general of WHO and a Canadian, wanted to respond to India's request for technical help. A Norwegian resolution to study the relationship of health and population growth was dropped, however, after a number of Catholic states threatened to boycott the organisation if any such work were undertaken. Under Catholic pressure, WHO's role was restricted to sponsoring a study of the rhythm system. Several Planned Parenthood consultants were dispatched to India but even by the mid-1950s it was clear that the rhythm system, birth control without contraceptives, would not work there.

Margaret Sanger, who was not always at ease with the more cautious U.S. groups she had organised, saw the drama of the world situation. In 1952 at the third conference of the International Committee on Planned Parenthood in Bombay she helped to organise the International Planned Parenthood Federation (IPPF) to link birth control groups now springing up in a number of countries. An IPPF conference in Stockholm in 1953, a regional one in Puerto Rico in 1955, and a large and well-publised conference in Tokyo in 1955 attracted increasing publicity as well as the participation of an international contingent od doctors, demographers, and sociologists. By 1958 nearly 500 foreign visitors a year were coming to the Planned Parenthood offices in New York to see what kind of help was available for overseas work.

From a political point of view, however, Planned Parenthood activists remained voices in the wilderness. In February 1955 IPPF's application for membership as a consultative organisation with the UN Economic and Social Council was voted down with seven abstentions (including the United States), two negative votes, and no votes in favour. From a financial point of view Planned Parenthood resources were minimal. The headquarters U.S. Planned Parenthood budget in 1959 was only $ 340,000; the International Planned Parenthood Federation budget, only $ 35,000. But every year brought more public attention to the issue and more converts to the cause.

An important recruit to the activist ranks in the 1950s was Hugh Moore. The enterprising and successful founder of the Dixie Cup company, he had established the Hugh Moore Fund in 1944 to promote world peace. Overpopulation, he concluded, as the greatest threat to world peace. His initial strategy was to alert businessmen to the crisis. A deliberately provocative pamphlet entitled *The Population Bomb* was distributed to 10,000 American leaders whose names were taken from *Who's Who*. Letters, dinners and meetings were organised to win over influential people by a polite equivalent of shock tactics.

Demographers and others who wished to approach the problem quietly and scientifically were appalled. Frederick Osborn of the Population Council, for instance, wanted to prevent distribution of *The Population Bomb*. But Moore was not deterred. As he told one irate demographer, "You've been raised in academic halls. I've been raised in the market place. I'm used to presenting facts dramatically. Students of demography have talked for years and nobody listened.

A controversial figure whom most of the large, professionally oriented foundations were reluctant to assist, Moore "spun-off" half a dozen important organisations or activities that eventually played a role in the establishment of government policy. In each case he would seize an issue or opportunity before it was respectable, then fund, encourage, and promote it to a legitimate status. Then just as his flamboyant methods began to embarrass his own organisational protégés he would move on to something else. In the 1950s his influence was a first step in lining up business support and contributions for Planned Parenthood; his attention to the International Planned Parenthood Federation provided staff and the first serious fund-raising campaign; his interest in the Population Reference Bureau, a small information service in Washington, was a catalyst in expanding its horizons. Later he supported voluntary sterilisation, birth control advertising campaigns, and the beginnings of the environmental issue.

Unique in his salesmanship, Moore was in other respects typical of a new breed of activists in the population movement. Male, active in the business world, and more concerned with economics than biology, the new activists included men like John Nuveen, Eugene Black, John Cowles, Cass Canfield, Lammot DuPont Copeland, and William H. Draper, Jr. The experience of the war and European recovery increased their basic confidence, as it had that of many Americans, that most problems are soluble. Economic development was the solution to poverty and communism in Asia, Africa and Latin America just as the Marshall Plan had been the solution in Europe. However, as economic development lagged and as increasingly persuasive statistics suggested that population growth was a reason for the lag, a few of these internationally minded businessmen and bankers began to speak out.

They, like the Planned Parenthood activists, were distinguished from the professionals – both medical and demographic – by wanting, above all, a solution. The lowering of birth rates, in other words, was a definite project to be undertaken, like winning the war or rebuilding Europe; it could be achieved by the appropriate application of the right resources. Rockefeller saw these resources in the form of professional skills, new technology, and scientific data to be developed; Moore saw the resources more in terms of public awareness and federal expenditures; Draper saw them particularly in the form of leadership and government priority.* More organisationally oriented than the Planned Parenthood volunteers, these men thought in terms of building new institutions to extend continuing pressure.

The activists, male and female both, wanted to solve a problem and knew that they needed the help of professionals to do so. The professionals on their part refused to be harnessed so easily to someone else's project. Essentially, to be a professional is to seek and value complex professional outputs for their own sake, not just as a means to some other

* These are the attitudes sometimes described as "elite positivism". Cf. "Americans have developed a strong conviction in their capacity to solve problems though the application both of common sense and of scientific knowledge. Even though these two methods often are at variance, Americans believe that virtually all problems can be solved either by ordinary people cooperating with one another on the basis of commonly accepted ideas, or by groups of experts equipped with the latest scientific know-how and ample funds."

end. To be an activist, on the other hand, is to look for the simplest, most direct means to the specified goal and to apply it as quickly as possible. To the professionals the problem of high birth rates called for definition, study, research and knowledge or practice for its own sake. To the activists, the population problem was much more likely to call for money, good management, and removal of the most obvious bottlenecks.

3

PUBLIC AND GOVERNMENT ON POPULATION

What impact did the studies and practice of the professionals plus the agitation of the activists have on public opinion and government policy? What difference did the opposition of the Catholic Church make? What was the reaction, in terms of public awareness, private practice, and government action, to the new issue that was developing?

Measured by press and periodical coverage – a rough measure, at best – concern for the national or international issue was not great during the 1950s. Periodical coverage reached a peak in the early 1930s, receded through the 1940s and 1950s, and did not exceed the level of the early 1930s until after 1960.

During the 1950s the *New York Times* had a most sympathetic editorial policy and covered local city disputes thoroughly in 1953 and 1958. Excluding these, however, even the *New York Times* averaged only 15 stories, letters, or editorials annually on birth control from 1950 through 1958 and of these only three were on page one. Under the index heading "population" the *New York Times* carried an average of 17 stories annually and of these four (relating mainly to U.S. growth) were on page one. Between 1950 and 1958 inclusive, the *Readers' Guide* listed an average of 13 periodical articles per year on birth control and contraception, or slightly more than one per month. By any reckoning, the amount of publicity before 1959, although rising gradually, was not very great. (See Charts 3.1 and 3.2)

CHART 3.1
Periodical Coverage of Birth Control, 1915 – 69
(as measured by number of entries in Readers Guide under "Birth Control" and after 1951 "Contraception.")

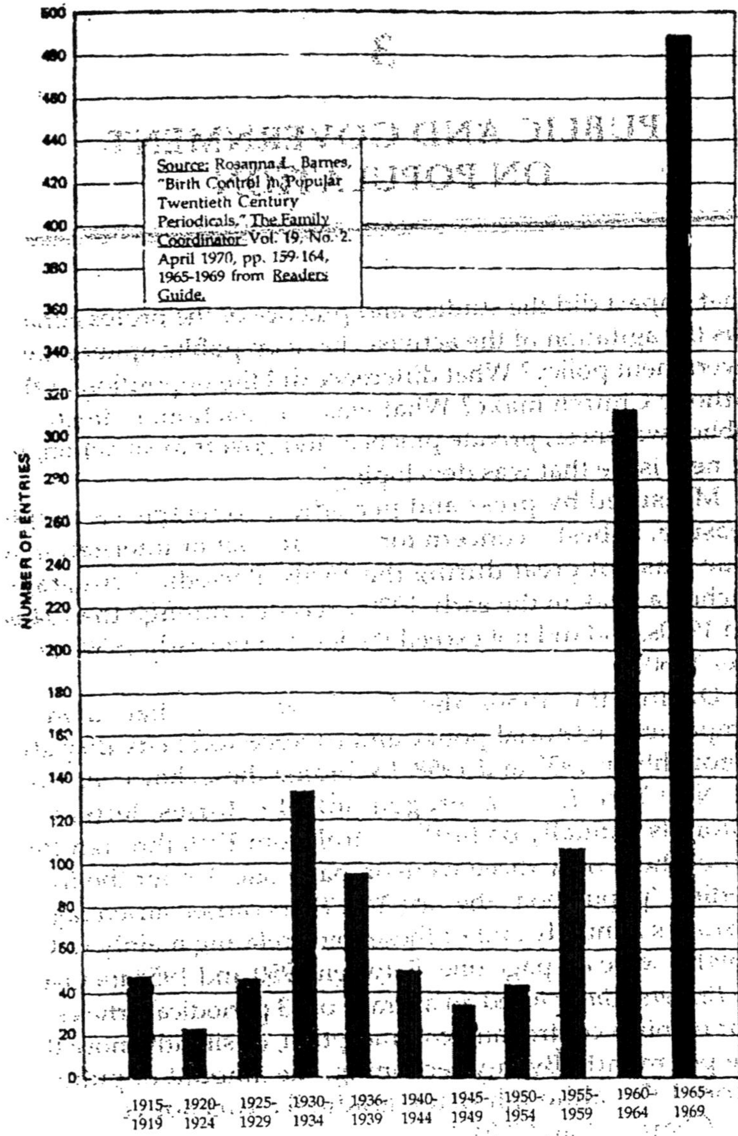

CHART 3.2
New York Times Coverage of Birth Control and Population, 1950 – 70
(Number of inches in Index)

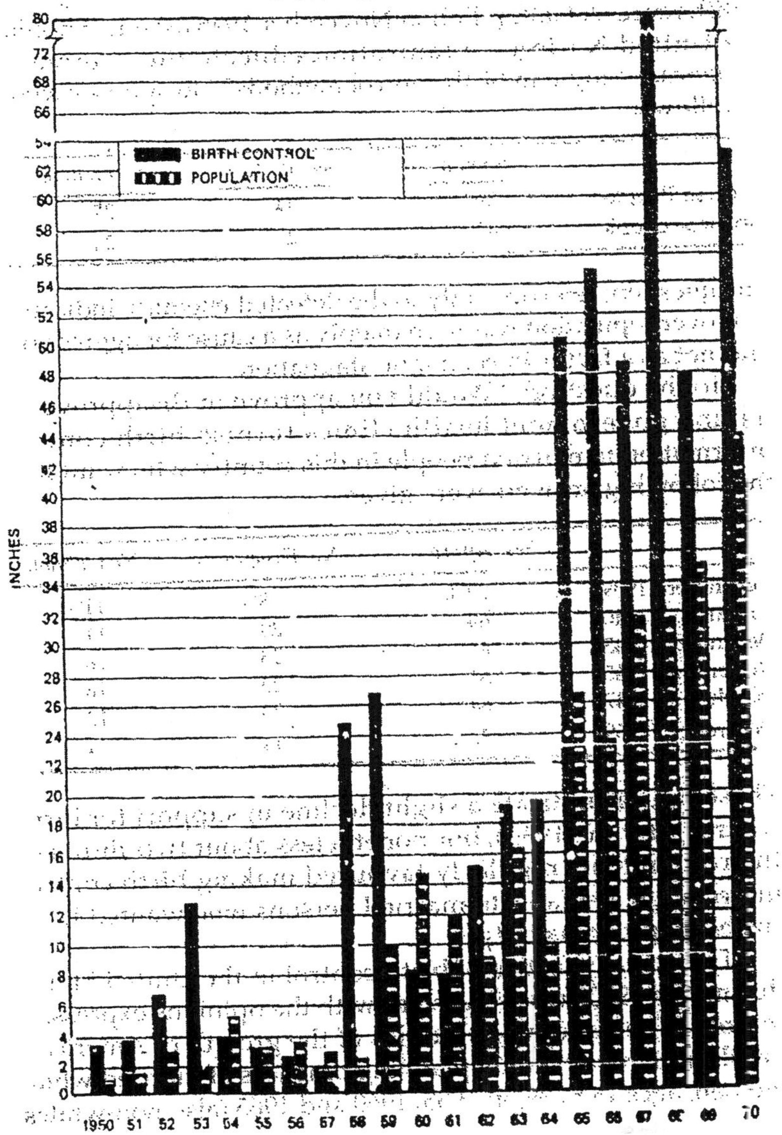

Public attitudes and opinions are reflected in the available poll data. However, between March 1947 and December 1959 no nationwide polls included any question directly on birth control or population – in itself, a measure of public indifference. A Gallup Poll in November 1945 asked, "Should the United Nations organisation educate the (German) (Japanese) people in birth control methods?" Responses were as follows:

	Should	*Should Not*	*No Opinion*
German People	39%	34%	27%
Japanese people	47	29	24

The question, referring only to the defeated enemies, indicates that overpopulation was seen mainly as a cause for aggression and not as a factor in economic stagnation.

To the question, "Would you approve or disapprove of having government health clinics furnish birth control information to married people in this country who want it?" the following answers were given:

	Yes, Approve	*No, Disapprove*	*No Opinion*
December 1939	72%	18%	11%
January 1940	69	20	11
December 1943	61	23	16
November 1945	61	23	16
March 1947	64	23	13
December 1959	72	14	14

These figures indicate a slight decline in support for birth control after the 1930s, but nonetheless about two-thirds of the respondents regularly favoured making birth control information available to married persons who wanted it – a sizable popular majority.

The actual practice of birth control in the United States during the 1950s was consistent with the opinions expressed in polls. The nationwide studies of the growth of American families surveyed family planning practices of married white women, ages 18 to 39, in 1955, 1960 and 1965 (also non-whites in 1960 and 1965). In 1955, 70 per cent of the white wives had used contraception and another 9 per cent expected to. By 1960, 81 per cent had used contraception and another 6 per cent expected to do so. In 1960, when non-whites were surveyed, 59 per cent had used contraception and another 17 per cent expected to. Although combined use and expectation of use were higher for non-Catholics and for upper socioeconomic levels in both years, the increase in use and expectation of use was greater among Catholics and women of lower socioeconomic status. (See Chart 3.3)

With respect to the type of contraception used, approximately half of the Catholic wives practicing birth control had used prohibited methods and half had not at the times of both surveys. But by 1960, 38 per cent of all Catholic wives had used prohibited methods compared with 30 per cent in 1955. To put it the other way around, the percentage of Catholic wives conforming to church teachings declined from 70 per cent to 62 per cent between 1955 and 1960. Yet despite the increasing use of contraception and of methods condemned by the Catholic Church, even by Catholics, public policy lagged behind both private practice and public opinion.

The poll evidence, plus the advantages of hindsight, suggests that one barrier to more rapid development of a birth control policy during the 1950s was the inhibitions of birth control supporters in not forcing the issue to national attention sooner. Agnes Meyer, one of the bolder voices, may have been at least partially correct in 1955 when she told a Planned parenthood meeting:

> The Catholic Church has the right to defend and promulgate its ideas on birth control as much as any other group. If non-Catholics were as honest and forthright in advancing their theories, the influence of the Catholic Church would be confined to its own members and the fog of obscurity, vacillation, and cowardice which surround the need for a nationwide contraceptive programme would be dissolved.

CHART 3.3
Attitudes toward Making Birth Control Information Available, National Polls in Selected Years, 1936 – 71

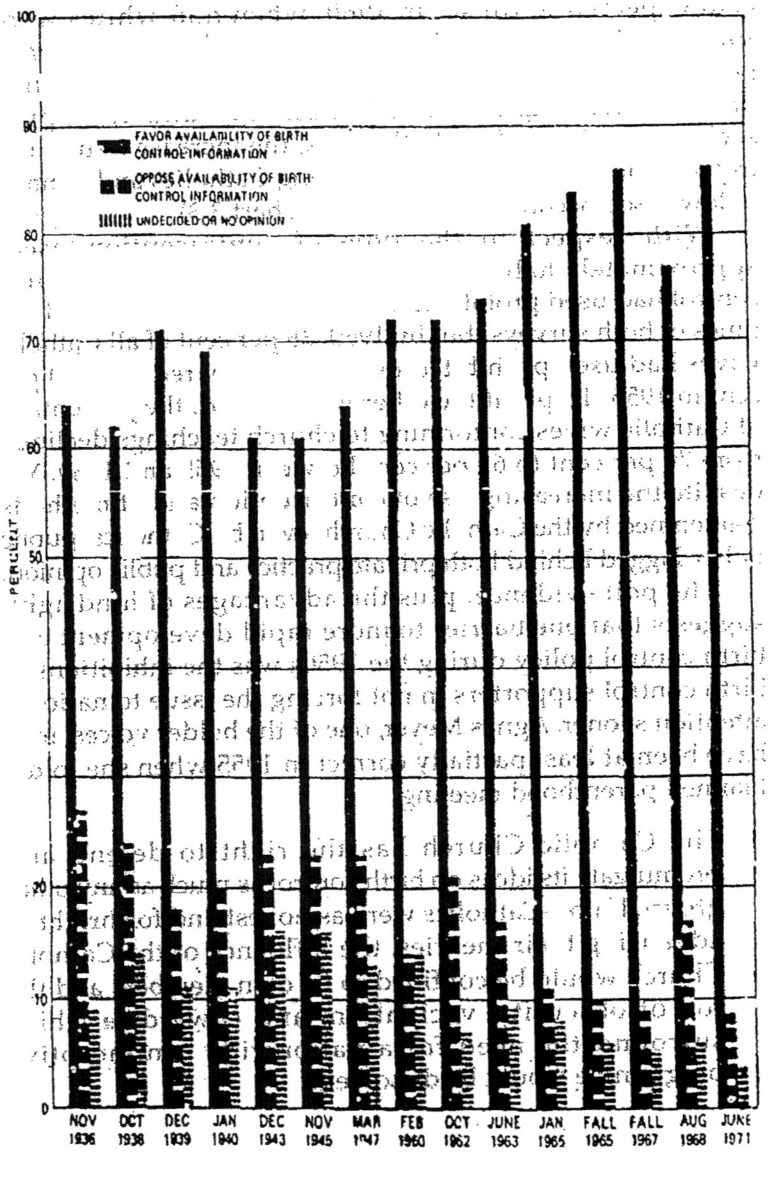

Note: All polls charted are nationwide surveys conducted by the American Institute of Public Opinion (AIPO), Princeton, New Jersey. Although these polls give a general overview of American attitudes toward making birth control information available, they are not precisely comparable because the question asked was rarely asked in exactly the same form as before. The questions asked at each date were as follows:

November 1936:	Should the distribution of birth control information be made legal?
October 1938:	Would you like to see a government agency furnish birth control information to married people who want it?
December 1939 to March 1947:	Would you approve or disapprove of having governmental health clinics furnish birth control information to married people who want it (in this country)?
February 1960 to January 1965 and August 1968:	Do you think birth control information should be available to anyone who wants it or not?
Fall 1965 and 1967:	Do you believe that information about birth control ought to be easily available to any married person who wants it?
June 1971:	Do you think that information about birth control should or should not be made available by the government to all men and women who want it?

Sources : November 1936: Gallup press release (AIPO), January 5, 1965. October 1938 to January 1965: Hazel Gaudet Erskine, "The Polls: The Population Explosion, Birth Control and Sex Education," *Public Opinion Quarterly,* XXX, 3 (Fall 1960), 490 – 95. Fall 1965 and Fall 1967: John F. Kantner, "American Attitudes on Population Policy: Recent Trends," *Studies in Family Planning,* No. 30 (May 1968), p. 6. August 1968: AIPO Poll No. 766, Ropner Public Opinion Research Center, Williamstown, Massachusetts. June 1971. U.S. Commission on Population Growth and the American Future, *Research Papers.*

CHANGES IN ATTITUDES AND PRACTICE IN THE 1960s

During the 1960s, as might have been expected, the principal shifts in opinion took place among Catholics rather than Protestants. (See Tables 3.1 and 3.2.) Protestant approval remained consistently high through the 1960s, at about 80 per cent.

Table 3.1
Attitudes of Catholics Toward Making Birth Control Information Available, National Polls in Selected Years 1936–71
(In per cent)

		Approve	*Disapprove*	*No Opinion or Don't Know*
	1936[a]	43	45	12
December	1959[b]	58	29	13
August	1962[a]	56	38	6
April	1963[a]	53	39	8
January	1965[a]	78	14	8
June	1965[a]	60	28	12
Fall	1965[c]	81	–	–
Fall	1967[c]	83	–	–
August	1968[d]	77	15	8
June	1971[e]	83	12	5

Notes to Chart 3.3 give the exact wording of the questions.

Sources : [a]Hazel Gauder Erskine, "The Polls: The Population Explosion, Birth Control and Sex Education," *Public Opinion Quarterly*, XXX, 3 (Fall 1966), 495.

[b]American Institute of Public Opinion, Poll No. 621, question 39.

[c]John F. Kantner, "American Attitudes on Population Policy: Recent Trends," *Studies in Family Planning*, No. 39 (May 1968), p. 6 (question restricted to availability for married persons).

[d]American Institute of Public Opinion, Poll No. 766, question 18.

[e]National Public Opinion Survey, U.S. Commission on Population Growth and the American Future, question 35.

By May-June 1971, in the poll conducted for the U.S. Commission on Population Growth and the American Future, 87 per cent of the weighted sample agreed that information

Table 3.2
Attitudes of Protestants Toward Making Birth Control Information Available, National Polls in Selected Years 1959 – 71
(In per cent)

		Approve	*Disapprove*	*No Opinion or Don't Know*
December	1959[b]	77	9	13
August	1962[a]	77	16	7
April	1963[a]	80	11	9
January	1965[a]	82	10	8
Fall	1965[c]	86	–	–
Fall	1967[c]	88	–	–
August	1968[d]	76	18	6
June	1971[e]	86	9	4

Notes to Chart 3.3 give the exact wording of the questions.

Sources : [a]Hazel Gauder Erskine, "The Polls: The Population Explosion, Birth Control and Sex Education," *Public Opinion Quarterly*, XXX, 3 (Fall 1966), 495.

[b]American Institute of Public Opinion, Poll No. 621, question 30.

[c]John F. Kantner, "American Attitudes on Population Policy: Recent Trends," *Studies in Family Planning*, No. 39 (May 1968), p. 6 (question restricted to availability for married persons; all non-Catholics included in Protestants).

[d]American Institute of Public Opinion, Poll No. 766, question 18.

[e]National Public Opinion Survey, U.S. Commission on Population Growth and the American Future, question 35.

about birth control should be made available by the government to all men and women who want it – the same percentage as in 1967 favoured having birth control information "easily available to any married person who wants it" (with no reference to the government). (See Chart 3.4.)

During the 1960s Catholic attitudes shifted in two directions, according to Gallup poll data. Between December 1959 and April 1963 (the actual dates the questions were asked), Catholic approval declined by 5 percentage points and Catholic disapproval increased by 10 percentage points, even though the question was asked in the identical manner. This shift suggests that Catholic antagonism toward birth

CHART 3.4
Percentages of Married Couples Who Have Used or Expect To Use Contraception, 1955, 1960 and 1965

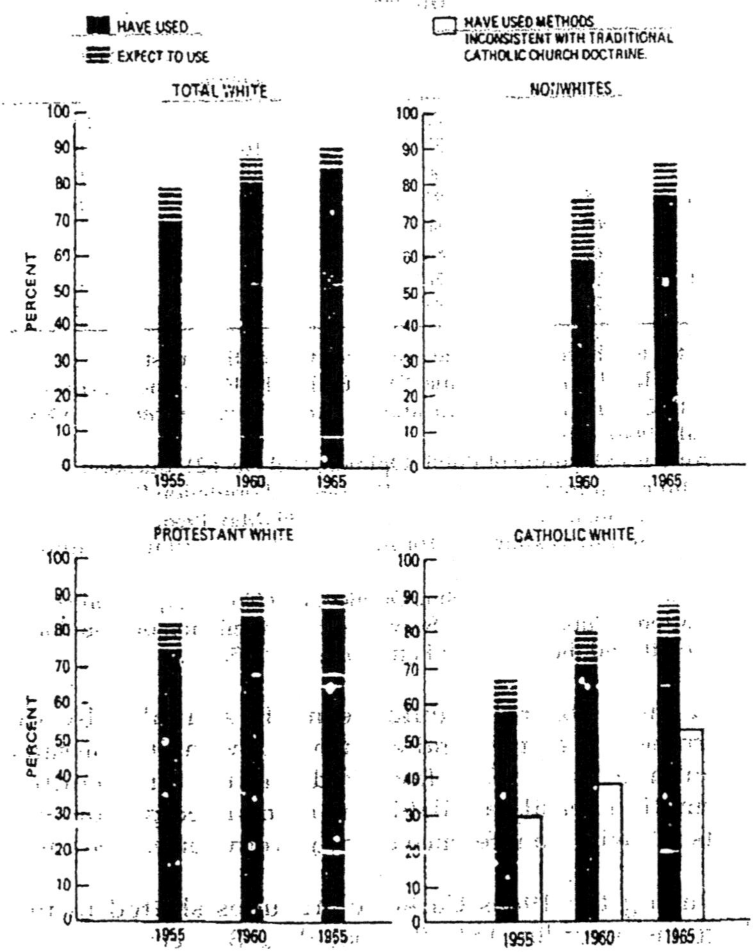

SOURCE: Charles F. Westoff and Norman N. Ryder "Recent Trends in Attitudes Toward Fertility Control and the Practice of Contraception in the United States." FERTILITY AND FAMILY PLANNING A WORLD VIEW, UNIVERSITY OF MICHIGAN, ANN ARBOR, 1939: WESTOFF AND RYDER "UNITED STATES: METHODS OF FERTILITY CONTROL, 1965: 1960 AND 1965." STUDIES IN FAMILY PLANNING. NO. 17. February 1967, p. 5.

control increased during the administration of President Kennedy, who was clearly not a birth control enthusiast. By late November 1964, however, Catholic approval for making birth control available increased by 25 percentage points over the April 1963 figure and disapproval declined by the same amount. Whether these shifts reflected personal habits, events in Washington, indecision in Rome, or a combination, they were permanent and left the church as an institution out of step with many individual Catholics.

With respect to foreign aid and U.S. support either through the United Nations or in response to requests from other governments, the sparse and not fully comparable data suggest a similar and substantial increase in support from 1959 to 1968. The major change again was in Catholic attitudes.

Table 3.3
Attitudes Toward Birth Control and Foreign Aid, National Polls in Selected Years 1959 – 68
(In per cent)

		Approve	*Disapprove*	*No Opinion or Don't Know*
December	1959[b]	54	29	17
April	1963[a]	65	21	14
Fall	1965[c]	58	34	8
Fall	1967[c]	64	30	6
August	1968[d]	72	20	8

Sources : [a]Hazel Gauder Erskine, "The Polls: The Population Explosion, Birth Control and Sex Education," *Public Opinion Quarterly*, XXX, 3 (Fall 1966), 495. Question: It has been suggested that the United Nations organisation supply information on all birth control methods to the people who want this information. Favour or oppose?

[b]American Institute of Public Opinion, Poll No. 621, question 30. Same question as directly above.

[c]John F. Kantner, "American Attitudes on Population Policy: Recent Trends," *Studies in Family Planning*, No. 30 (May 1968), p. 6. Question: Do you think our government should help other countries with their birth control programmes if they ask us:

[d]American Institute of Public Opinion, Poll No. 766, question 18. Question: Are you in favour of the U.S. government helping other nations who ask our aid in their birth control programmes?

Catholic backing increased from 40 per cent in December 1959, when a plurality of Catholics were opposed, to 69 per cent in August 1968 despite the papal condemnation. By 1968 Protestant and Catholic views hardly differed in this area either. (See Tables 3.3 and 3.4.)

Table 3.4
Attitudes of Catholics and Protestants Toward Birth Control and Foreign Aid, National Polls in Selected Years 1959 – 68
(In per cent)

		Approve	*Disapprove*	*No Opinion or Don't Know*
December	1959[b]	40	48	11
April	1963[a]	42	44	14
Fall	1965[c]	55	–	–
Fall	1967[c]	56	–	–
August	1968[d]	69	21	10
		Protestant		
December	1959[b]	58	24	18
April	1963[a]	72	15	13
Fall	1965[c]	59	–	–
Fall	1967[c]	66	–	–
August	1968[d]	71	22	7

Sources : [a]Hazel Gauder Erskine, "The Polls: The Population Explosion, Birth Control and Sex Education," *Public Opinion Quarterly*, XXX, 3 (Fall 1966), 495. Question: It has been suggested that the United Nations organisation supply information on all birth control methods to the people who want this information. Favour or oppose?

[b]American Institute of Public Opinion, Poll No. 621, question 30. Same question as directly above.

[c]John F. Kantner, "American Attitudes on Population Policy: Recent Trends," *Studies in Family Planning*, No. 39 (May 1968), p. 6. All non-Catholic included in Protestant. Question: Do you think our government should help other countries with their birth control programmes if they ask us?

[d]American Institute of Public Opinion, Poll No. 766, question 18. Question: Are you in favour of the U.S. government helping other nations who ask our aid in their birth control programmes?

Even more notable than the shifts in attitude during the 1960s, among men and women of all ages, was the shift in contraceptive behaviour, most notably by younger women. Between 1960 and 1965 the oral contraceptive became "the most popular method of contraception used by American couples." By 1965, although the pill was only five years old, 29 per cent of non-Catholic women (married, living with husbands) and 21 per cent of Catholic women under age 45 had used oral contraceptives. More than half of the women under 30 with some college education had, by 1965, used pills, and nearly 60 per cent of those who had ever used them were still doing so. By 1969 more Catholic women using some form of birth control were using oral contraceptives than the rhythm system, and twice as many were not using rhythm as were using it even after the papal condemnation of all other methods.

Apart from oral contraceptives specifically, the percentage of fecund couples who had used some form of contraception (including the rhythm method) increased from 83 per cent in 1955 to 89 per cent in 1960 to 93 per cent in 1965. Including also those who *expected* to use contraception later the percentages increased from 91 per cent in 1955 to 96 per cent in 1960 to 97 per cent by 1965. "Where two established and institutionalised religious groups support opposing moral norms," it has been observed, "the less demanding norm tends to win the less committed members of both groups." That is what seemed to be happening in contraceptive practice during the 1950s and 1960s.

NON-RESPONSE BY THE GOVERNMENT, 1930 – 59

The response of the U.S. government, to the widespread acceptance of birth control in the United States, to the facts of world population growth, to the studies of the professionals, to the agitation of the activist, and to the continued resistance of the Roman Catholic Church, was essentially a non-response. Within the United States, Margaret Sanger's work and the Supreme Court decision of 1936 had stopped any deliberate federal effort to prohibit private birth control activities. Yet Surgeon-General Parran's permissive policy of 1942 had little effect in promoting state-sponsored birth control activities because resources were limited. State legislation, medical regulations, and municipal agreements hampered operations of clinics. The climate of government disapproval often prevented publicity or accurate records even where birth control services were available. Congress avoided the subject.

Toward population problems overseas beyond the continental United States, particularly those prominent enough to attract any public notice, the government response was even more negative. In Puerto Rico, for example, the federal government had direct responsibility for a crowded, poverty-stricken island where birth rates were double the continental level. In 1936 Ernest Gruening, director of the Division of Territories and Island Possessions of the Department of the Interior, tried to include family planning in the maternal and child health programmes of the Puerto Rican Reconstruction Administration. He sought – and believed he had won – the approval of the Catholic bishop in Puerto Rico for a quiet beginning. But the objections of Cardinal Spellman in New York, relayed privately to Democratic National Committee Chairman James A. Farley in the midst of the presidential election campaign, forced Gruening to sever all official support for birth control. As Gruening later commented, "Who was I to jeopardise F.D.R.'s campaign for reelection? The following November he would carry only 46 out of 48 states."

In spite of the Catholic Church, the Puerto Rican legislature in 1937 legalised birth control, which was then provided through the maternal health clinics until 1946, when the Department of Health downgraded birth control. Meanwhile, the Puerto Ricans were developing their own solution to the problem. Female sterilisation in hospitals following delivery was promoted by private physicians on a fee basis and well-publicised by Catholic pastoral letters (of condemnation). It was relatively cheap, effective and involved only a single "sinful" action. By 1965, when federal funding for family planning resumed, one third of Puerto Rican mothers 20 to 49 years of age had already had "la operacion," two-thirds of them while still in their twenties. By a method that was acceptable to Puerto Rican women and profitable to Puerto Rican physicians, birth control prevailed in Puerto Rico. As in Western Europe and America, however, the process represented a default of timely government action and a deliberate defiance of church doctrine.

The situation in Japan immediately after World War II was not dissimilar. The Supreme Allied Commander in the Pacific General Douglas MacArthur (SCAP) had broad responsibility for demilitarisation and demobilisation of the country. Very soon it was evident that population increase, caused by return to 7 million Japanese to the islands and lower mortality as well as by higher birth rates, would strain employment opportunities and resources. Demographers Warren Thompson and P.K. Whelpton were invited by SCAP to serve as consultants to the Natural Resources Section on demographic factors. Margaret Sanger, however, who tried to visit Japan in 1949, was refused a military permit because of Catholic opposition. At that time, MacArthur issued a statement declaring,

> The Supreme Commander wishes it understood that he is not engaged in any consideration of the problem of Japanese population control. Such matter does not fall within the prescribed scope of the Occupation, and decisions thereon rest entirely with the Japanese themselves.

A SCAP-planned survey of attitudes toward the population problem was promptly cancelled. In 1950 several sentences in a SCAP study, *Japan's Natural Resources*, about balancing population and resources through reduced birth rates were deleted as a result of protests from the American Catholic Women's Club of the Tokyo-Yokohama area, which consisted largely to U.S. Army wives.

Meanwhile, as early as 1946 the Japanese government and press began to study the population problem for themselves. While councils, institutes, foundations, Cabinet committees, and news bureaus were pondering and publicising the issue, the Japanese Diet in 1948 revised the 1940 Eugenics Protection Law to allow induced abortion for eugenic and health reasons. In 1949 and 1952 the law, which also legalised sterilisation and contraception, was further amended to permit abortion for economic reasons and under simplified procedures. Although the importation of supplies for producing contraceptives was allowed, neither SCAP nor the Japanese government provided funds for a national contraceptive programme. Still, the birth rate fell from 34.3 per 1,000 in 1947 down to 17.2 in 1957, a 50 per cent reduction in a single decade. The decline was unprecedented in demographic history. Induced abortion, condemned by demographic, public health, medical, government, civic, and religious leaders as the least desirable birth control technique, was the principal method used. Only later, after 1952, was contraception specifically fostered to reduce the incidence of abortion. Then contraception was depicted as, in Irene Taeuber's words, "a public health activity, a programme to lessen the harm presumably caused by abortions whose performance was presumably permitted to protect health."

In Japan as in Puerto Rico the reluctance of U.S. government policy-makers to endorse or finance contraceptive programmes was undoubtedly a factor in turning people toward a private sector method, profitable to the medical profession, acceptable to the population, and requiring no initial funding, supplies, or government support other than legality. Thus, in both cases the U.S. government's susceptibility to Catholic protests may well have stimulated sterilisation and abortion, although both were less acceptable to Catholic as well as non-Catholic leaders than other means of family planning.

The Japanese case was important not only as another example of U.S. policy default but also because of the widely perceived link between reducing birth rates and speeding economic progress. For example, in 1962 Chikao Honda noted, "It is an important fact to observe that the economic boom in Japan today owes much to the efforts of the people in general to rationalise and modernise their family life on the basis of planned parenthood."

Despite the unwillingness of the U.S. government to acknowledge it, the overseas population problem was hard to avoid. An agricultural mission to China in 1946 recommended reducing population pressure on the land as a necessary alternative to famine. A 1953 Citizens Advisory Committee, composed primarily of educators and economists, urged Mutual Security Administrator Harold Stassen to take "real steps in the direction of conscious promotion of population limitation." Although the report did not use the words "birth control" it warned that the task of economic development would be taken over by the communists if, because of population growth, "the rising expectations of the people have been disappointed."

On Taiwan, the Joint Committee on Rural Reconstruction tried to promote birth control as early as 1950. More than a million copies of a JCRR booklet entitled *The Happy Family*, which advocated family planning by the rhythm method, were distributed. But the brochure was condemned by the Chinese in Taiwan as "a communist plot" to deplete Nationalist armies and as contrary to the teachings of Sun Yat-sen. In 1954, after a demographic study sponsored by the Rockefeller Foundation and Princeton University, the China Family Planning Association was formed and government involvement began. "To avoid misunderstanding by the military," birth control was introduced "as a patriotic measure" in the context of "training in first-aid for women of childbearing ages in military dependents' villages and rural areas to prepare for possible enemy air raids." This unusual approach proved effective.

The U.S. government provided support until 1957 when a Catholic programme officer of the International Cooperation Administration Mission tried to block it. The U.S. mission chief intervened. Upon assurance of no publicity and no

Chinese religious opposition, he overruled the programme officer but renamed the programme "pre-pregnancy health" instead of "reduction of wasteful deaths". Health was always the acknowledged aim of the programme, which was not officially identified as family planning or population control until 1969.

In Ceylon in the late 1950s when government officials approached the U.S. foreign aid mission for help in checking population growth they were referred to the Swedish government, which was just beginning to offer technical assistance in birth control. To mobilise a change in U.S. policy would be too long and arduous a task, the Ceylonese were told, to be worth the small amount of help that could be provided.

The case of India might have been a potent influence on U.S. policy-makers and undoubtedly was an indirect influence on public opinion. The very image of "Mother India" was synonymous with overpopulation and poverty. Yet even though the Indian government was the first to adopt a national family planning policy in the 1950s, the programme was vague and the requirements uncertain. Mahatma Gandhi's opposition to contraceptives, reflected by succeeding ministers of health and Nehru's concentration on industrialisation and capital investment, kept the birth control programme from achieving real priority until the 1960s. Funding for construction of a drug-manufacturing facility that would also have been able to produce contraceptives was cancelled by a wary Draper Committee staff man upon arrival on assignment in India.

On the whole, until 1959 the State Department and foreign aid administrators were not pressed by foreign governments or by internal staff to take any action on the controversial problem. In the field, in places like Taiwan where U.S. aid missions did encourage family planning, those most eager to provide birth control help did so – quietly and indirectly. They went out of their way to avoid high-level review and policy decisions lest the repercussions kill off their own projects. In this way, small beginnings were protected but larger considerations were postponed.

During this period the professionals in population and birth control who were unsure themselves what approach the U.S. government could take overseas, made little effort to convince government officials to take action. Whereas they kept at arm's length from the government, the government itself kept at arm's length from activists like Margaret Sanger. Thus, the considerable private use of birth control in the United States was not automatically translated into approval for public programmes – or indeed even for public discussion. The victories Planned Parenthood won, in New York City, for example, under a Catholic mayor or in Japan where Margaret Sanger was later honoured, were seen by U.S. government officials not as triumphs for a good cause but rather as embarrassments to be avoided. At the government level the institutional voice of the Catholic Church remained many times louder and stronger than the pleas of the ardent activists or the studies of the professionals in the population field.

4

THE DRAPER COMMITTEE SPOTLIGHTS THE ISSUE, 1959

The Draper Committee, formally known as The President's Committee to Study the United States Military Assistance Programme, was not the first advisory body to take note of the population problem but it was the first to spell it out in detail and to recommend specific action. Why did this unlikely panel of high officials – all men, most with some military background, none previously involved in any "birth control cause" – advocate government-supported birth control?

The committee was created to look at a wholly different issue. In August 1958 eight influential senators on the Foreign Relations Committee complained to President Eisenhower that too much emphasis was being placed on military aid and not enough on economic assistance. They called for an immediate presidential review of foreign aid priorities.

U.S. foreign assistance had been born as an emergency relief operation in Europe right after World War II. The Marshall Plan was originally designed to accelerate the economic reconstruction of Europe, but very quickly, under Soviet pressure, it was transformed into a military and economic defense against communism. During the 1950s the worldwide Mutual Security Programme was justified to Congress and the country as an efficient way to subsidise foreign armies instead of sending American soldiers overseas again. At the same time the Point IV programme of technical assistance, initiated by President Truman, provided a small start toward technical assistance and development aid in Asia, Africa and Latin America.

Support for military assistance remained consistently strong in the House of Representatives. In the Senate on the other hand, and among an increasing number of government officials, support was growing for economic aid on a longer-term basis to counter new Soviet tactics of trade, aid and friendship with the developing countries.

Tracy Vorhees, a New York attorney who served with several voluntary groups to promote public support for foreign assistance, suggested to Sherman Adams, then Preisdent Eisenhower's chief aide, that General William H. Draper, Jr., be appointed to head the high-level review.

Draper was a New York investment banker who had served as economic adviser to General Lucius Clay during the German occupation and in a civilian capacity as the U.S. special representative in Europe directing the European Recovery Programme. He was in 1958 Chairman of the Mexican Light and Power Co. Ltd., and thus combined a record in European economic recovery with experience in a developing country.

Compared with other presidential committees or commissions, the 10-member group was noteworthy because it consisted entirely of men who had previously served at high levels of government with considerable military or economic responsibility. There was no attempt to obtain broad representation either of interest groups such as labour, Negroes, universities, or business per se, or of academic experts (except in staff roles). The emphasis was on practical experience in high government posts.

The Draper Committee included the following: Dillon Anderson, attorney, who had recently served as President Eisenhower's special assistant for national security affairs; Joseph M. Dodge, businessman and banker, who had served as financial adviser in Germany and Japan and as director of the Bureau of the Budget; General Alfred M. Gruenther, who had recently served as supreme Allied commander in Europe and was then President of the Red Cross; Marx Leva, attorney, who had been Assistant Secretary of defense and Chairman of a Senate foreign aid review panel; John J. McCloy, attorney and banker, who had formerly been President of the World Bank and U.S. high commissioner for Germany and was then Chairman of the Board of the Chase Manhattan Bank and the Ford Foundation; George McGhee, oil producer, who had served as Assistant Secretary of state and ambassador to Turkey; General Joseph T. McNarney, an air force general who had been commander of U.S. forces in Europe and was then President of Convair; Admiral Arthur W. Radford, who had commanded the Pacific Fleet and served as Chairman of the Joint Chiefs of Staff; and James E. Webb, who had served as Director of the Bureau of the Budget and Under Secretary of State.

Just before Thanksgiving the White House announced formation of the panel under Draper's chairmanship "to undertake a completely independent, objective, and non-partisan analysis of the military assistance aspects of our Mutual Security Programme" and to determine "the relative emphasis which should be given to military and economic programmes, particularly in the less developed areas."

Although Senator J. William Fulbright (D.-Ark.) praised Draper as "a first rate Chairman," several others suggested that the president's committee was "top heavy with military men."

THE POPULATION ISSUE IS RAISED

The question of population had not occurred to anyone as being relevant until the day after the committee was established, when the Chairman received a long wire addressed to him personally. It concluded with the words, "If your committee does not look into the impact and implications of the population explosion, you will be derelict in your duty." The wire was from Hugh Moore.

Draper read the lengthy wire to assembled committee members, who reacted with chuckles. Draper chuckled, too, but he also quietly called in Robert C. Cook, President of the

Population Reference Bureau, to provide the committee members with background materials on the population question.

At approximately the same time – early December 1958 – Draper was nudged from another direction to consider the impact of population growth. President Eisenhower himself raised the issue even though he later repudiated the committee's recommendation. Draper had been invited to a National Security Council meeting on December 3 to discuss the study which the committee would make. In the middle of his briefing the President turned to Draper and commented, "And Bill, don't forget the population problem because that is very serious in some of these countries."

Draper did not forget either the president's words or Hugh Moore's wire. As early as December 29, 1958, the minutes of the committee record that the Chairman "also reviewed the problem caused by the population explosion in the less-developed countries of the non-Communist world." On the same date the committee Secretary was instructed to send to committee members a booklet on population growth (Hugh Moore's *Population Bomb*).

In mid-February, Tyler Wood the economic study coordinator made this note, with obvious lack of enthusiasm:

> The question of the relation of the "population explosion" is brought up frequently in discussions with the Chairman and other members of the committee. It would therefore seem necessary to have a staff paper prepared containing the pertinent facts and certain indicated conclusions which are regarded as relevant to the work of the committee.

Meanwhile, after what one committee member described as "considerable internal discussion and some shadow-boxing with State Department personnel and the White House staff," the committee expanded its review to cover economic aid more comprehensively. Like many such commissions, it wanted a wider scope of reference. More attention to economic aid meant very naturally more attention to the forces stimulating or impeding economic growth. By 1959 it was increasingly difficult to ignore population growth as a factor that in one way or another could strongly influence economic development.

During the first half of the committee's study, which included visits to Japan, Taiwan and Korea, Draper became personally convinced that too-rapid population growth would undermine economic development. Previously, as Under Secretary of the army, Draper had been aware of the postwar population crisis in Japan. He had visited Japan in 1947 and 1948 and discussed population as well as economic problems. Then in 1959 he observed at first hand how, with legalised abortion and considerable publicity, the Japanese people had sharply reduced birth rates and achieved their "economic miracle". The example of Japan influenced Draper as it did Rockefeller and others. Encouraged as he thought by the President, urged on by Hugh Moore and Robert Cook, convinced by the mounting impact of UN statistics, and undoubtedly stimulated by the realisation that others agreed but were fearful of speaking out, Draper grew determined to bring the issue of rapid population growth directly into the light of public policy debate.

He gave the first public expression of this strong concern in his testimony before the Senate Committee on Foreign Relations on May 18, 1959. When Senator George Aiken (R-Vt.) asked pointedly whether all U.S. assistance was not still failing to prevent a decline in per capita income in some developing countries, Draper replied, "The population problem, I'm afraid, is the greatest bar to our whole economic aid programme and to the progress of the world." No one contradicted him.

The other members of the president's committee had not taken a comparable interest in the population issue. There was some feeling that any recommendations on population were beyond the committee's jurisdiction and might even be regarded as intervening in the internal affairs of foreign governments. Others thought that it was difficult enough to build support for foreign aid without antagonising the Catholic Church, and that attention should not be distracted from the committee's major recommendations on foreign aid funding and organisation.

Moreover, the committee members were far closer in background and outlook to the officials they were advising than to either the activists or the professionals in birth control and population. Unlike social reformers they were not in the habit of "rocking the boat" to put their views across; they relied on persuasion, negotiation or, if necessary, command. Most wanted to help, not to embarrass, the administration. Public confrontation on a difficult issue was against their experience and inclination.

Yet Draper was stubborn, and the facts were undeniable. Many of the committee members had considerable experience in economic recovery and development. They were familiar with the sense of "uphill struggle" in their efforts. As McCloy put it, "There were always more mouths the following year than you had planned for the year before." Whatever were the views of the others as to the political wisdom of mentioning population, they could not rebut Draper's arguments. Furthermore, they stood as independent advisers to the President, not as implementers. If such a recommendation did not originate from impartial outside advisers how could it possibly come from administrators in more sensitive operational roles? Draper's clinching argument was: how could the population problem be ignored when President Eisenhower had specifically asked them to consider it?

Nevertheless, two centers of opposition remained. Most important was General Gruenther, a devout Catholic who was unwilling to sign a report that the church might condemn. With considerable difficulty Draper persuaded Gruenther that the subject of population growth could not be ignored. Then Draper worked closely with Gruenther to prepare language that would not be offensive to Catholics. Gruenther took the drafts and conferred privately with Catholic lawyers and experts to ensure their acceptability. The oblique reference to "maternal and child health services" as an immediate way to deal with the population problem testifies to Gruenther's influence on the final statement. After this and similar changes were made the committee hoped that the report would not be strongly criticised by Catholic leaders. Gruenther, after his reluctant agreement, hoped that these recommendations, buried in the larger report, would not receive a great deal of public attention. Both expectations proved wrong – to the committee's chagrin and Gruenther's embarrassment.

Also opposed to any reference to the population dilemma was the committee staff. From the top echelon – Tracy Vorhees, as general counsel, George Lincoln the staff director, and Tyler Wood – right down to at least one of the secretaries who reportedly refused to type a research paper that discussed contraceptives, many of the staff were apprehensive or hostile. Staff opposition, in the days before any agency had staff people directly assigned to population, was typical. Draper's deputies, like Rockefeller's and Moore's before them, saw many good reasons to protect their agencies or organisations from such a sensitive subject.

MAKING A RECOMMENDATION

The various drafts of the report show Draper's increasing personal attention to the subject. The first specific references to population growth in the studies by the staff and consultants were brief and fatalistic. For example, a memorandum dated February 20 on India from Max Millikan stated, "Since population growth can be expected in the neighbourhood of 2 per cent a year . . . output must grow significantly faster if the average individual is to have a sense of progress."

The next version, based on a background memorandum submitted by Robert Adams, Gruenther's modifications and considerable negotiation with committee members and staff, was much more conciliatory. There was no reference to "birth control" or "pre-conditions" of aid. It explained the rapid population growth in developing areas as the result of decreasing mortality caused by public health measures and indicated that to assist the "normal adjustment" toward lower fertility, government birth control programmes had been established "with broad acceptance". An additional paragraph about food shortages was subsequently added. In a move he later regretted, George Lincoln also had a map prepared to illustrate the demographic data. Lincoln was by that time resigned to Draper's decision but still hoped to keep the language brief.

After nearly a dozen drafts, the statement stressed food shortages, public health involvement, assistance only upon the request of another country, and maternal and child welfare. These were the committee's final recommendations:

> *We Recommend:* That, in order to meet more effectively the problems of economic development, the United States (1) assist those countries with which it is cooperating in economic aid programmes, on request, in the formulation of their plans designed to deal with the problem of rapid population growth, (2) increase its assistance to local programmes relating to maternal and child welfare in recognition of the immediate problem created by rapid population growth, and (3) strongly support studies and appropriate research as a part of its own Mutual Security Programme, within the United Nations and elsewhere, leading to the availability of relevant information in a form most useful to individual countries in the formulation of practical programmes to meet the serious challenge posed by rapidly expanding populations.

The most significant point omitted from the committee's recommendation, even though it was developed at considerable length in the staff study, was the call for U.S. government support of "expanded medical research relating to the physiology of human reproduction," and implicitly aimed at development of better birth control methods. That suggestion, although much stressed a few years later, then seemed quite irrelevant to foreign aid efforts and too directly related to the still unmentionable aspects of birth control for Gruenther and the others on the committee to accept.

To publicise the committee's far-reaching economic proposals – which called for an economic assistance agency independent of the Department of State – a press conference was arranged for Draper July 23 in the White House office of Jim Haggerty, Eisenhower's Press Secretary.

Reporters immediately perceived the implications of birth control as a political issue, especially since one of the emerging Democratic contenders for the presidency, John F. Kennedy, was Catholic. Pressed by questioners, Draper first responded that the committee was thinking primarily of "demographic information" but finally conceded that birth control information might be included, depending "on the way the programme is carried out." While Haggerty looked on in silence and his own staff in dismay, Draper held up for the photographers the map showing population growth. Both during the press conference and afterward on the White House porch for television, Draper discoursed at some length on the population problem. He emphasised that assistance would be given only on request and that no specific legislation would be necessary. "We simply wanted to air for public discussion a problem which has for too long been kept under the rug," he pointed out, then and later.

The problem was indeed aired. The photograph of Draper pointing to a map of world population growth and urging action was reproduced around the world. Several U.S. newspapers, including the *Washington Post* and *New York Times*, ran lengthy background articles on the demographic situation. Gruenther was furious that Draper had deliberately emphasised the issue. Monsignor George Higgins Director of the Social Action Department of the National Catholic Welfare Conference expressed the immediate reaction of Catholic officialdom by praising the report generally but calling the population recommendations "extremely disturbing, to say the least." He declared that "The population problem in many parts of the world admittedly is very serious at the present time. But to advocate a programme of artificial birth control as a solution to the problem is not only immoral, it is also a counsel of defeatism and despair."

The Draper Committee report did not cause an immediate explosion. President Eisenhower submitted it to Congress without recommendation, urging only careful study. As Arthur Krock observed in the *New York Times:*

> This recommendation caused a one-day flurry. . . . But the politicians and the people generally paid little heed to the incident. The President made no adverse comment and the sensation was confined to Draper committee members who had hoped the item would not be pinpointed and to the ever-nervous State Department.

CHANGE ON OTHER FRONTS

But in 1959 while the Draper Committee was moving toward new ground those in the population field had not been standing still either. On the activist side the International Planned Parenthood Federation's Sixth International Conference in New Delhi, including some 750 delegates from 27 countries, heard Indian Prime Minister Nehru warn of "a tremendous crisis" if population growth were not checked. A unanimous resolution was dispatched to Dag Hammarskjold the UN Secretary-General, urging that family planning be made an integral part of UN programmes and be considered "a basic human right".

Professional support of a particularly welcome nature came in October when the World Council of Churches approved for circulation a report prepared by the Reverend Richard Fagley strongly justifying all birth control methods used "in Christian conscience". During the year, four major religious groups in the United States endorsed family planning: the United Presbyterian Church, the Union of American Hebrew Congregations, and the American Baptist Convention.

The long-sought backing of public health professionals was won in November 1959 when the American Public Health Association not only endorsed birth control but also recommended that it be made an integral part of health programmes and that scientific research in the whole field be greatly expanded. Dr. Leona Baumgartner, still recalling the impact of the New York City fight of 1958, was influential as President of the APHA in working for compromise language that all could accept.

Even within the government voices were being raised that reinforced the Draper Committee report. A State Department review of world population trends completed in July and released in November warned, "Rapid population growth may prove to be one of the greatest obstacles to economic and social progress and to maintenance of political stability in many of the less developed areas of the world." A study by Stanford Research Institute, commissioned by the Senate Committee on Foreign Relations, pointed out even more bluntly that "in certain parts of the world population control is already a necessity." The institute reported on progress with the new orals and recommended an international research programme to develop and test new contraceptives.

These developments, together with the Draper Committee report which went directly to the President and Congress, could be compared to a critical mass, large enough to generate a strong reaction, too large to be ignored.

5

BIRTH CONTROL AND T'' 1960 ELECTION

Birth control as an issue of public policy emerged from the dim light of crusading, professional, and specialised interest into the full glare of national publicity in the last two months of 1959. As one columnist observed, "Not in our lifetime – never again may be – will the problem go back on the shelf."

CATHOLIC CONFRONTATION

What really attracted national and top-level attention were not the reports and studies of birth control advocates but, as it often was in the past, the criticism of birth control opponents. By November 1959 the Catholic Church could hold its fire no longer. The Catholic bishops of the United States declared in a statement released from Washington, November 25, 1959:

> United States Catholics believe that the promotion of artificial birth control is a morally, humanly, psychologically and politically disasterous approach to the population problem. . . . They will not support any public assistance, either at home or abroad, to promote artificial birth prevention, abortion or sterilisation, whether through direct aid or by means of international organisations.

Where the promoters of birth control had once seen a "conspiracy of silence" the Catholic prelates now discerned a "campaign of propaganda" and denounced "the recently coined terror technique phrase 'population explosion,' " The national effect of the bishops' statement, as Arthur Krock pointed out, was to move "the topic from the areas of private morals and theology into the realm of public discussion of political action . . . a result which organisations and individuals concerned . . . had been unable to achieve in years of dedication."

On the political side, the emerging issue of the 1960 presidential campaign added fuel to the conflagration. For the first time since Al Smith's defeat in 1928 a Catholic candidate, Senator John F. Kennedy of Massachusetts, was seeking the presidency. To the consternation of both parties, the Catholic bishops' warning on birth control precipitated not only the usual Planned Parenthood denunciations but also a provocative political question from Episcopal Bishop James Pike of California: "Was the policy laid down by the Bishops binding on Roman Catholic candidates for office?"

The question was aimed at Kennedy. In an immediate telepnone interview with James Reston of the *New York Times*, Kennedy responded to the substantive question of birth control. It would be a "mean paternalism," the Massachusetts senator replied, and "not in the national interest" for the United States to promote birth control overseas. "It is a decision for the countries concerned to make for themselves," he declared, adding, "I think it would be the greatest psychological mistake for us to appear to advocate limitation of the black or brown or yellow peoples whose population is increasing no faster than in the United States." Upon the overriding political question of the bishops' right to speak for him, Kennedy was equally decisive. He had held these views for some time, he said, and was "not influenced by the Bishops' statement." Moreover, he would certainly not refuse to give other assistance to a country simply because it was carrying out birth control programmes. In other words, Kennedy's answer was "no" – but his reason was not religion or morality. It was reluctance to force birth control upon foreign peoples.

The notion that the U.S. government might coerce other nations to practice birth control was not, of course, the recommendation of the Draper Committee. Coercion was a straw man that all candidates could safely attack while evading the real question of aid on request. When Kennedy was pressed during the campaign about how he might react as President if India or Pakistan asked the United States for help in curbing population growth or if Congress passed legislation providing funds for birth control, his emphasis shifted gradually from a negative assessment of birth control aid to a positive affirmation that he would act solely on the criterion of national interest. For instance, this is what Kennedy told the American Society of Newspaper Editors in April 1960.

> The prospects of any President ever receiving for his signature a bill providing foreign aid funds for birth control are very remote indeed.[*] It is hardly the major issue some have suggested. Nevertheless, I have made it clear that I would neither veto nor sign such a bill on any basis except what I considered to be the public interest, without regard to my private religious views.

Again, in addressing the greater Houston Ministerial Association in September, Kennedy declared, "I do not speak for my church on public matters – and the Church does not speak for me." On birth control as on other issues, "I will make my decision," he asserted, "in accordance with what my conscience tells me to be in the national interest and without regard to outside religious pressure or dictate."

For the other Catholic candidates, late in 1959, the question seemed even more difficult. California Governor Edmund (Pat) Brown was at first "not prepared to answer a question of regulation of births" but quickly shifted to Kennedy's line. So did New York Mayor Robert Wagner, who

---

* Actually, President Johnson signed the first such bill, the *Foreign Assistance Act of 1963* (Public Law 88 – 205) on December 16, 1963, less than a month after Kennedy's assassination.

had remained neutral during the 1958 New York City dispute; but he added sharply, we have "no right to enforce our will on any people. The Roman Catholic position is the view of the Church, period."

Non-Catholics were equally uneasy in their first public comment on an issue never before considered important enough or appropriate for national attention. Like Kennedy, most of the candidates denounced coercion and tried to avoid the real questions. The only positive approval for birth control aid came from Senator Stuart Symington of Missouri, who acclaimed it as a useful way to combat poverty, disease and communism. Vice President Richard Nixon did not comment until April 1960, when he guardedly declared that "if underprivileged countries reach a decision that they want to limit population at a certain point and come to us for assistance, we should give it to them."

EISENHOWER'S VIEWS

But long before April 1960 the question had been somewhat defused by President Eisenhower. Asked at a press conference in December 1959 for his reactions to the Draper recommendations on birth control, Eisenhower declared with his unusual bluntness, "I cannot imagine anything more emphatically a subject that is not a proper political or governmental activity or function or responsibility." Terming it "a religious tenet" in Catholic doctrine, he said that if other governments want "to do something about what is admittedly a very difficult question and an explosive question . . . they will go unquestionably to private groups, not to governments." He concluded, "This government will not, as long as I am here, have a positive political doctrine in its programme that has to do with the problem of birth control. That's not our business." To the dismay of birth control supporters, President Eisenhower had followed the line of the Catholic bishops – that birth control was basically a religious matter and therefore not a legitimate subject for national policy.

Actually, President Eisenhower's comments were determined by political and not substantive considerations. Eisenhower *was* worried about population growth, especially as it might nullify the effects of the foreign aid programme. There is considerable evidence of his concern. As early as the fall of 1958 he surprised officials of the International Cooperation Administration (ICA) by devoting most of a National Security Council meeting on foreign aid to population growth. How can foreign aid succeed if population keeps increasing at the present rate, he wanted to know. Agency officials, particularly James Grant (then special assistant to ICA Director James Smith), pointed out that the technical know-how to make birth control programmes work in countries like India was still lacking, that much more research by government, foundations, and others was necessary to develop better methods before any U.S. government input would be effective. In the meantime, one more controversy added to the existing unpopularity of the foreign aid programme might be the straw that would break the camel's back. At the end of the discussion. Eisenhower commented that he would actually be willing to take on a public battle over the issue if he were convinced that U.S. government aid would make a difference; but he, too, hesitated to add a new note of discord to the programme without greater promise for success.

Draper several years later asked Eisenhower why he had rejected the committee's recommendation. Eisenhower told Draper somewhat apologetically that birth control had become a divisive issue and that he did not want to split the nation more deeply on the eve of a sensitive election.

Early in 1960 ambassador James Riddleberger, then director of the International Cooperation Administration, went to considerable lengths to persuade Eisenhower to allow ICA quietly to support birth control programmes in India and Pakistan. After Eisenhower had turned down a confidential memorandum submitted by Riddleberger arguing the economic importance of reducing birth rates, Riddleberger asked him privately whether he disagreed with the analysis.

Eisenhower replied, "No, Jimmy, I suspect you are right, but I can't do it. If Kennedy is nominated and elected, he could do something about it, but I can't."

Eisenhower wanted to avoid the bitterness of the 1928 Al Smith campaign, but only three years later he wrote in the *Saturday Evening Post:*

> When I was President, I opposed the use of Federal funds to provide birth control information to countries we were aiding because I felt this would violate the deepest religious convictions of large groups of taxpayers. As I now look back, it may be that I carried that conviction too far. I still believe that as a national policy we should not make birth control programmes a condition to our foreign aid, but we should tell receiving nations how population growth threatens them and what can be done about it.

Subsequently in serving as honourary Chairman of Planned Parenthood and in making a number of public statements Eisenhower expressed unusually strong concern about the population explosion and endorsed federal support for family planning. Like a number of other high government officials his backing for such programmes increased as his official capacity to implement them declined.

Eisenhower's comments reflect a characteristic pattern of American political life – "the tacit understanding not to raise issues certain to be disruptive and beyond solution." Philip Converse, analysing the 1960 election in depth, observes among political elites "a remarkable show of consensus in an attempt to stifle religion as an issue in the campaign." That meant also to stifle birth control as an issue, since it aroused dissension between religions. In this sense the early treatment of birth control on the national level provides a good example of the exercise of "non-decision-making power," that considerable power, which Peter Bachrach and Morton Baratz describe, of "creating or reinforcing social and political values and institutional practices that limit the scope of the political process to public consideration of only those issues which are comparatively innocuous."

KENNEDY'S POSITION

If Eisenhower dodged around the issue of birth control for the sake of national unity, Kennedy had equally good reason for not wanting it raised. Scion of a large Irish Catholic family, raised in Massachusetts where birth control was synonomous with the worst Catholic-Protestant feuding and where birth control meant Republican and antibirth control meant Democratic, and reelected to Congress in 1948 during a vitriolic birth control referendum campaign, Kennedy did not have much enthusiasm for the issue or most of its supporters. He once commented that most people think "it is other people's families that provide the population explosion." Although he occasionally referred, in speeches prepared by Sorenson or others, to the population explosion and twice in the television debates with Nixon mentioned India's "population pressures," there is no evidence that Kennedy himself ever took any initiative in promoting birth control policy as an answer to such pressures.

Furthermore, Kennedy's slogan in 1960 was the forceful appeal, "Let's get America moving again." In an achievement-oriented campaign that stressed competition with the Soviet Union, the missile gap, the sputnik scare and, above all, the need for great economic growth, the very idea of population control had a pessimistic, negative ring that was inconsistent with his larger political design. As far as foreign aid was concerned Kennedy's goal was more aid – to promote economic development, to enlarge the size of the pie, not to reduce the number of people to be fed. Like Eisenhower he feared that introducing birth control would jeopardise an already unpopular programme – "you will get neither foreign aid nor birth control."

But in 1959 and 1960, for Kennedy as for Eisenhower, it was not personal inclination or economic orientation that was decisive but rather the more pressing political need to prove to Protestant and Jewish voters that a candidate who was Catholic had loyalties no different from those of any other American. Unfortunately, for Kennedy the bishops' statement dramatised church involvement in public policy along lines that most non-Catholics could not accept. Despite his reasoned response Kennedy was "sharply irritated that so sensitive and divisive an issue had been needlessly dragged into the headlines on the eve of his official campaign." Sophisticated observers like James Reston might argue that the bishops' intervention was proof that the Catholic Church was *not* trying to get Kennedy elected, but to nervous Protestants the bishops seemed to be flexing their political muscles.

Kennedy's aim, like Eisenhower's, was to deflate the birth control issue. But where Protestant Republican Eisenhower tried to remove the political sting by agreeing with the Catholic bishops, Kennedy tried to remove the religious sting by insisting that it was *not* religious but a valid political question to be decided on the basis of the national interest. Eisenhower's was the more traditional approach; the loyal old-line Democratic politicians, anxious to help Kennedy, lined up with Eisenhower to agree that birth control was religious, irrelevant, a distraction. Even Mrs. Roosevelt, an early supporter of birth control, put politics ahead of policy and reversed her previous position. Kennedy's frontal approach, his willingness to discuss what others called "the religious issue" was new, but it was basic to his campaign. He had to demonstrate publicly that there were no "religious issues" that could influence his judgment as President.

THE ROLE OF THE MEDIA

Nevertheless, in spite of the politicians' consensus that birth control should not be on the political agenda the combined impact of the Draper Committee report, the Catholic bishops' denunciation, and the 1960 campaign convinced the press, often the strongest ally of a new movement trying to be heard, that a relevant public policy issue was involved. What Michael Lipsky calls the "Awakening of the communications media" meant that the issue of birth control was finally on the news agenda for coverage, beyond the power of the Catholic Church to silence or boycott.

Newspapers from Boston to San Francisco, from Minneapolis to Miami, suggested, like the *St. Louis Post Dispatch*, that "the question deserves to be seriously considered in other than political terms." Even after the subject dropped from political news on page one it was vigorously debated elsewhere. For example, the *Readers' Guide to Periodical Literature* lists 13 articles under the headings "birth control" and "contraceptives" in the six months preceding the bishops' statements as compared with 36 articles in the three months following. These included not only factual accounts of population growth and a cover story in *Life* but also, significantly for the future, a number of studies in Catholic publications like the liberal, lay-edited *Commonweal* and the Jesuit weekly *America*, in which Catholics began to question their church's role in the birth control controversy. Perhaps Catholics should give up the struggle for prohibitive legislation; perhaps the church should encourage scientific research to make the rhythm method more effective; perhaps a Catholic President could permit public funds to support birth control programmes.

The "publicity explosion" included television. *CBS Reports* daringly featured an hour-long documentary November 11, 1959, on the population problem in India. Beginning somewhat cautiously with an apology for the use of "certain brief phrases pertaining to procreation," moderator Howard K. Smith insisted that "not talking about the problem because it's controversial or uncomfortable is a luxury that we, as leaders of the Free World, cannot afford." The show was rebroadcasted on January 14, 1960 with an additional half-hour of much sharper debate relating to economic development. Some 9 million people saw the first presentation; 9.5 million saw the second, a new record in public exposure and a serious effort to look at the issue from many points of view, not exclusively religious or political.

Even after the first flurry of political excitement had died, birth control and the population problem kept coming up. Apart from any political motivation, for instance, leaders of all faiths felt obliged to clarify their churches' positions.

Geoffrey Fisher, archbishop of Canterbury, declared that "family planning is a positive, Christian duty." Richard Fagley of the World Council of Churches offered a strong moral rationale for birth control in his book *The Population Explosion and Christian Responsibility*. Pope John XXIII, on the other hand, told Catholics not to fear but to welcome all the children God might send them.

Meanwhile, the birth control and population activists, although dismayed by Eisenhower's position, were more active than ever. Restrictive state laws were challenged in the courts not only in Massachusetts and Connecticut but elsewhere as well. The American Civil Liberties Union called them unconstitutional. In May 1960 at a National Conference on the Population Crisis co-sponsored by the Dallas Council on World Affairs and *Newsweek* magazine, John D. Rockefeller 3rd made a plea that was to be repeated many times in the decade ahead:

> The problems of population are so great, so important, so ramified and so immediate that only government, supported and inspired by private initiative, can attack them on the scale required. It is for the citizens to convince their political leaders of the need for imaginative and courageous action – action which may sometimes mean political and economic opposition.

At the same time Hugh Moore began to organise the World Population Emergency Campaign to raise funds from businessmen for family planning overseas and hopefully to transform the International Planned Parenthood Federation from what he called a "debating society" into a powerful force. The campaign was headed by Lammor Copeland, then Vice-President of the DuPont company, and, at Moore's insistence, by William H. Draper, Jr. Draper was being drawn more and more into the birth control field. As Congressman Albert Quie (R. Minn.) has observed, "Recommendations of study groups never have much effect except on those who make them." Certainly one effect of the Draper Committee recommendation – and its rejection by President Eisenhower–

was to stiffen the chairman's own determination to achieve what he had proposed. His first objective, like Moore's was to strengthen the private groups so that they could play the leading role that Eisenhower had suggested for them.

Moreover, in spite of the politicians, questions about birth control policy continued to come up even within the campaign. On October 21, barely two weeks before the election, the three leading Catholic bishops of Puerto Rico issued a pastoral letter instructing Catholics not to vote for the party of popular Governor Munoz Marin because of his support for public schools and birth control.

From Kennedy's point of view the bishops' charge was "the cruelest blow." In spite of disclaimers by leading Catholic prelates in the continental United States, the Puerto Rican bishops defended their stand and a week later threatened excommunication to anyone who voted for Munoz Marin. Such fireworks were not unusual in Puerto Rico where the Catholic Church had been denouncing birth control and liberal government unsuccessfully for decades, but they provoked a violent counterblast from Protestant clergymen to the north. Kennedy, caught between militant Catholicism and militant Protestantism, issued a statement calling it "wholly improper and alien to our domestic system for churchmen of any faith to tell the members of their church for whom to vote or for whom not to vote." Nevertheless, Sorenson reports that "Senator Kennedy knew he had been hurt. 'If enough voters realise that Puerto Rico is American soil,' he remarked to me, 'this election is lost'. "

THE IMPACT OF THE CAMPAIGN

On November 8 Kennedy was elected President by a margin of 118,550 popular votes out of 68,838,979 cast. Survey data indicated that 56 per cent of those who switched from Eisenhower in 1956 to Kennedy in 1960 were Catholic, whereas 81 per cent of those who switched from Stevenson in 1956 to Nixon in 1960 were Protestant. Second only to basic party identification, religious affiliation did apparently influence many voters. The pollster Lou Harris estimated that Kennedy lost 2 million votes in the last two weeks before the election as a result of the crescendo of literature, preaching, and publicity over the Puerto Rican bishops. V.O. Key suggests that nearly 1 million of those who shifted from a Democratic vote in 1956 to a Republican vote in 1960 did so in the week preceding the election.

Except as a factor in this powerful religious equation, birth control was not an election issue. Eisenhower had prevented it from dividing the two parties. In December 1959 only one out of every five people admitted to being "worried" about population increase. Few voters were as single-minded as Margaret Sanger, who declared that she would leave the country if Kennedy were elected. Simple group loyalty and personal impressions undoubtedly carried more weight than policy issues.

A liberal Catholic writer has suggested that if Kennedy had fitted the socioeconomic stereotype of "a typical American Catholic" from a middle-income family, graduate of a Catholic college, and married to a South Boston Irish girl, he could not have been elected. But it may equally be that if Kennedy, even though he was a Harvard-educated ambassador's son, had meekly followed the judgment of the bishops on aid to education and birth control he would not have been elected either. Certainly Kennedy's political strategy of demonstrating to non-Catholic voters how rigidly he separated church and state in policy matters and of urging them to practice an equally rigid separation of church and state in voting matters made it easier for Protestants to support him. More than half of Kennedy's 34 million votes were cast by Protestants.

Birth control as an issue in the 1960 election was more symbolic than substantive, more a test of religious attitudes than of demographic understanding, more significant to intellectual elites than to the masses. Probably, to the extent that birth control had any impact at all on the election, it did sharpen the sense of religious difference and of potential church-state conflict. Certainly it forced Kennedy to declare again and again that the national interest superseded church doctrine.

Clearly, the 1960 campaign and election did influence the development of birth control policy. The immediate effect was perceptible and negative. Right after the bishops' statement and even before Eisenhower's words, officials in the foreign aid programme hastened to assure the press that the controversy was "academic". "Not one penny of foreign aid funds ever has been used for dissemination of birth control information and there are no plans to do so." Because of the campaign, Riddleberger's private effort to persuade Eisenhower in 1960 had no greater success than Draper's public recommendation in 1959. Throughout 1960, administration witnesses emphatically assured congressional committees that birth control would not be included in foreign aid activities. However, not until March 22, 1960, four months later, did ICA dispatch to its overseas missions the text of Eisenhower's statement, without any further comment or guidance as to support for such traditional areas of assistance as census-taking demography or maternal and child health. Characteristically, perhaps, the extended bureaucracy that administered foreign aid was almost as reluctant to implement wholeheartedly the president's prohibition as it later would be to respond to presidential encouragement. Nevertheless, in the short-run politics and the electoral process had set back what might have been the quiet beginnings of birth control assistance.

From a longer perspective, however, the possibilities for government support of birth control advanced. Controversy generated publicity, as we have noted. By mid-December 1959, 75 per cent of the population had heard about the population increase – surprisingly a somewhat higher figure than in 1963 or 1965 (when there was even more publicity but less controversy).

Furthermore, the stand that Kennedy took, although originally negative, could not in the long-run prevent action. Kennedy had insisted so vigorously that he would make his decisions on the basis of national interest and not religion that religion ceased to be a publicly valid reason for avoiding the issue. For the first time a President had openly suggested that the population explosion and birth control were serious questions to be objectively analysed in terms of the national interest.

Since a Catholic candidate could make this distinction between the teachings of the church and the national interest, so could millions of other Catholics. For many, Kennedy's election both symbolised and encouraged the increasingly vigorous and independent role of the lay Catholic man or woman, who often had views of sexual morality that differed from those of the priests. Kennedy himself was not publicly anticlerical (after one struggle over aid to education he remarked privately, "Now I understand why Henry VIII set up his own Church"). However, like his contemporary, Pope John XXIII, Kennedy was not adverse to opening new windows on church or state doctrine.

Finally, too, the election of a Catholic President put strong pressure on those concerned about population growth and birth control to find a way to reconciliation and to marshall their serious arguments about population growth and national interests. Direct confrontation had made gains on the local scene and generated considerable publicity. But to confront or embarrass a Catholic President still further did not seem to be the best way to win government support. May be, as Eisenhower had thought, a Catholic President could take political initiatives that a Protestant could not. After the sound and fury of the campaign, the election of America's first Catholic President provided a new incentive to search for accommodation on a problem that would no longer "go back on the shelf".

6

THE STATE DEPARTMENT : CONSIDERING THE PROBLEM, 1961-62

Relevance, feasibility, priority and urgency – these four qualities must be widely discussed and affirmed before any new government programme is established. First, is the proposed new activity relevant to accepted national objectives? Second, is it feasible – politically, technically, financially? Third, how does it rank in importance with existing programmes? And finally, how urgent is it timewise? The more favourably each of these questions is resolved – whether by the executive branch, by the legislative branch, or ultimately by the public – the more likely is an innovation in U.S. government to be adopted and fully supported.

After the 1960 election the birth control policy debate began to shift from the question of relevance to the question of feasibility. Not only the press but gradually also the government admitted that population growth was directly – and adversely – relevant to economic development. In vain the Vatican and some economists and demographers might call this linkage "simplistic". As a practical formulation, it could no longer be ignored. So with some of the opposition outflanked a new series of questions began to be asked in the 1960s. What can actually be done to check population growth? What kind of policies are politically feasible? What kind of programmes are technically feasible?

Proving the birth control issue relevant required not only data in the form of demographic statistics but also confrontation and controversy, a disruption of the existing consensus to add a new item to the national agenda. Proving that birth control assistance was feasible required something different. Political feasibility meant building the broadest possible support for any measures taken; it required conciliation, negotiation and accommodation. Technical feasibility for a new field meant applying scientific and managerial skills. Both involved a lowering of the emotional tone that characterised birth control as an election issue and a new emphasis on practical possibilities.

An unexpected asset for the population movement that the Kennedy administration itself brought to Washington was an activist orientation toward government, embracing both foreign policy and social issues. Few issues of any kind were considered "not the Government's business". Therefore, despite the president's own hesitation on birth control some of his appointees were ready to accept at face value the campaign comments that population growth and birth control were "legitimate questions of public policy" to be judged calmly in the light of "national interest". Thus, a small group of advocates within the State Department and the Agency for International Development joined the scientists and activists outside of government in promoting a more active policy. If these State and AID insiders seemed at times a small, conspiratorial group, plotting with outsiders against their own bosses, they played an increasingly important role in the policy process, shaping the suggestions and initiatives of the outsiders to conform with the more cautious context of internal executive agency policy-making.

The first step toward a policy on population was taken by George McGhee, a former assistant secretary of state, member of the Draper Committee, and husband of a Planned Parenthood volunteer. Appointed director of the Policy Planning Council of the State Department in January 1961, McGhee learned that a staff study on the foreign policy implications of the world population explosion was already under way. (It had been initiated in 1960, despite Eisenhower's ban, by Evan Wilson, a Foreign Service officer.) McGhee, who had been exceedingly annoyed by Eisenhower's comments, took great interest. The study was reviewed, expanded, printed and circulated as an official Policy Planning Council document.

The report concluded that the ability to control population growth was "the single greatest determinant" of economic development; yet because of religious, political and social attitudes it was "not deemed feasible" for the U.S. government to provide large or publicised assistance. Nevertheless, the U.S. government could encourage research, dissemination of information, greater awareness, and more attention by private organisations and other governments to the population problem.

After an initial negative reaction from Secretary of State Rusk, the final revised version of the report recommended half a dozen "minimum actions" that the department should be taking. These included: a request to the National Institutes of Health to conduct a survey of research then under way in reproductive physiology (toned down from the original request for a specific $10 million per year fertility research programme); appointment of a full-time State Department population officer; encouragement of more population activities in the UN system; reversal of the still-standing Eisenhower ban on foreign aid for birth control; more research by AID on the social and economic factors involved in population growth; and quiet appeals to other government to provide birth control aid.

The actions taken on those Policy Planning Council recommendations set in motion the development of U.S. policy toward world population problems. Both what was done and what was not done following the council report had major and continuing repercussions.

THE RESEARCH CAMPAIGN

The proposal for an expanded research programme at the National Institutes of Health was the major specific recommendation of the Policy Planning Council. It had not originated with the council but rather represented a long-term strategy developed and promoted by those outside government. Originally offered by Bishop Pike on CBS-TV in January 1960, the research strategy involved a crash programme administered and financed by the National Institutes of Health to improve all techniques of birth control including the rhythm method.

Planned Parenthood officials had long believed that a large-scale research effort could "hold the key both to substantial progress in dealing with the population problem – and to a lasting solution of the bitter religious dispute about contraception." The research approach minimised Catholic opposition by stressing agreement on the principle of "responsible parenthood" or a legitimate "regulation of offspring" and not disagreement over specific methods. Despite the negative tone of *Casti Connubii* in 1931, Pius XI had endorsed the rhythm system in 1951 and specifically expressed hope that science could develop a more secure basis for its use. Bishop Pike's proposal, framed as a response to that hope, was applauded by liberal Catholic scholars like Father John O'Brien at Notre Dame.

An expanded research programme also minimised the differences within the birth control movement between activists and scientists, demographers and physicians. Everyone recognised the need for new and better birth control methods. Planned Parenthood and the Population Council had jointly sponsored a conference at West Point in 1959 to identify promising areas for research in reproductive physiology. Although some wanted to go farther and faster, while others were dubious about a "crash programme," no one within the population field was opposed to more research.

At the same time the 1950s had been a tremendous and popular expansion of health research through the National Institutes of Health. Mary Lasker, President of the Albert and Mary Lasker Foundation and also a Planned Parenthood supporter, led the crusade to find a cure for cancer and to upgrade mental health activities at NIH. Her success encouraged the birth control activists to promote a similar campaign.

When McGhee undertook his policy review he conferred with Draper and Canfield. They urged the enlarged research programme as a good starting point and the Policy Planning Council agreed. But Secretary of State Rusk did not approve their recommendation. First Rusk wanted to know exactly how the $10 million figure was arrived at. Then he implied that the population problem was far more complex than McGhee imagined. From his own experience as assistant secretary of State for Far Eastern affairs and later as President of the Rockefeller Foundation Rusk felt he understood the problem better than his advisers did.

In general, Rusk was reluctant for the State Department as he had been for the Rockefeller Foundation to push other nations – or agencies – forward in this field. The United States should wait for the developing nations to make their own requests. The State Department and AID should also not get too far ahead of U.S. domestic policies. In his judgment, knowledge and competent people were more important than money.

Nevertheless Rusk, like Eisenhower before him, could not wholly veto courses of action that his subordinates wanted to pursue. By late August 1971, when Rusk rejected even the watered-down proposal for a survey of research already under way, McGhee's aides had already approached NIH informally. Dr. David Price, Deputy Director of NIH, was asked to help defend the $10 million target figure which had been partly educated guesswork and partly an extrapolation from the costs of developing the Salk vaccine. Price was sympathetic. Without waiting for the formal request from Secretary Rusk – which never came – Dr. Errett Albritton, who had prepared a comparable summary in 1960, was assigned to compile an up-to-date report on actual and potential levels of research in human fertility.

The initial version of the Albritton report listed U.S. research on fertility amounting to $ 5.7 million, of which NIH was funding $ 1.7 million, but concluded as follows: "Research and research support in the area of birth and population control are only a fraction of what they should be when measured by the urgency of the medical and public health problems."

Furthermore, the report, which had been prepared with the assistance of an outside advisory panel including representatives from Planned Parenthood, the Population Reference Bureau, and the Population Council, recommended annual NIH funding of nearly $17 million (plus $ 4 million in capital costs for eight population research institutes at various university and medical centers.)

The higher echelons of the Department of Health, Education and Welfare (HEW) were alarmed by such obvious advocacy. HEW Secretary Abraham Ribicoff was planning to run for the Senate from Connecticut. The report circulated widely through HEW but was not released to the public.

News leaks about the "suppressed report" appeared in November 1961 and with greater detail in April 1962. The stories were ferreted out by David Broder, whom one official called "more help than Planned Parenthood". Rusk was then asked at a press conference whether HEW was holding up a State Department request for increased research in "population control methods". Calling the matter "a tempest in a teapot," Rusk stressed that population policy was "preeminently a question for each country to decide for itself, and as a practical matter something which each family must decide for itself." Avoiding the real question he nonetheless took a small policy step forward, saying,

> For us to be indifferent to population factors would be, I think, reckless on our part and we do take very seriously the population trends, the impact of population growth upon development plans and we shall continue to follow that problem.

In September 1962 Dr. Luther Terry, surgeon-general of the Public Health Service and Price, taking full responsibility on themselves, announced that the report would not be released "because it might be misunderstood". Within 24 hours, Congressman John Moss, Chairman of the House Subcommittee on Foreign Operations and Government Information, announced that there would be an investigation; Pierre Salinger, White House press secretary, declared that President Kennedy was not involved; and the Secretary of HEW Anthony Celebrezze, who was to be embarrassed more than once by rumours of his antibirth control stand, ordered the report updated and released by the year's end. Through this deliberate maneouver two birth control sympathisers put themselves in an unfavourable light in order to force their unsympathetic boss to overrule them and release a report which he, not they, would have preferred to shelve.

One of the first, though by no means the last, instances of combined internal-external-press-congressional pressures on top officials, the effort had mixed results. The revised report was released in December 1962 as a compilation of ongoing research. Father John C. Knott, Director of the Family Life Bureau of the National Catholic Welfare Conference, praised it as an excellent, objective summary of basic research.

> The fact that such information could be used for what we, as Catholics, would consider immoral purposes should not prevent us from supporting those seeking the truth. Rather we as Catholics should positively encourage all efforts which have as a goal unlocking nature's secrets.

But all the recommendations for additional research, crash programmes, or higher funding were deleted. The final version flatly stated the exact opposite of what the Policy Planning Council had initially recommended:

> A research programme to find new techniques which would be less expensive, or aesthetically, religiously, or culturally more acceptable or less prone to failure by reason of 'human error' is not an objective toward which NIH has a planned effort.

Dr. Thomas Kennedy, assistant to the director of NIH, explained that the original recommendations had been eliminated because they were "not germane" and represented "special interests" rather than "the normal scientific channels. The incident was a sharp reminder that the birth control activists were taking a risk whenever they forced the birth control issue up to the top level. They could still be slapped down as "special interests," not fully admitted to the scientific community. Yet if they did not take the risk they were likely to be left out or suppressed anyway.

Thus, McGhee's proposal for research, which Rusk never formally authorised and which subordinates at both the State Department and NIH promoted beyond their explicit authority, resulted by early 1963 in little more than a compilation of ongoing research, considerable tension between NIH and the activists, and a strengthened desire at HEW to avoid the issue.

A POPULATION OFFICER FOR THE DEPARTMENT

Secretary Rusk approved McGhee's specific suggestion that a full-time officer be assigned to the Under Secretary for economic affairs, then George Ball, "to maintain a continuing review of the foreign policy implications of the world population problem and to take such actions as are called for in the national interest." At the annual World Bank meeting in September 1961 Ball asserted more publicly than any other high official had to date that prevailing rates of population growth were a burden on economic development. Our goal, his speech concluded eloquently, is "a world in which every birth in accompanied by a birthright."

Ball agreed that Rusk's decision should be implemented at once. Robert A. Barnett, a Foreign Service officer, then counsellor in Brussels, was invited to become the department's first full-time population adviser. Barnett, whose background was economics and Chinese affairs, was considered a better choice for such a sensitive post than any unpredictable outside demographer. In December 1961

Barnett joined the small undercover group in the State Department who were beginning to promote a positive U.S. government policy toward the population problem. The group included Robert Schaetzel, a Foreign Service officer on Ball's staff, William Nunley, also on Ball's staff, Leighton Van Nort, a demographic analyst in the research office, Blanche Bernstein in International Organisation Affairs, Henry Owen of the Policy Planning Council, and Richard Gardner, Deputy Assistant Secretary for international organisation affairs.

"Talk about the problem all you can but don't put anything in writing," Barnett was advised when he took over the new job. He obeyed the first instruction – talking so constantly about population in fact that some people began to avoid him in the elevators. But he soon perceived that conversations did not make policy. Gradually he developed his own strategy. It included, first, open discussion, to make sure that population was recognised as an appropriate issue in the context of economic development; second, active liaison with the private groups involved; third, tentative manoeuvers to get his own superiors on record whenever possible, more and more publicly and at higher and higher levels, in favour of positive policies; and finally development, in the process, of a cautious definition of what the U.S. government was actually prepared to do.

A small breach had already been made in the official wall of silence when Ambassador T.P. Plimpton, deputy U.S. representative at the United Nations, spoke at a Planned Parenthood meeting in October 1961 but in a personal, not an official, capacity. In December 1961 William Nunley, on Ball's staff, went a step further. At a National Conference on International Economic and Social Development he revealed publicly for the first time,

> We are thinking about population problems, talking about them, attempting to get other people to think and talk about these problems – to stimulate individuals, organisations, and governments to add to the total store of knowledge on this subject.

Robert Barnett's first achievement was clearance, all the way through the White House, of a new form letter, an explicit embodiment of the "openness" approach, repudiating what Barnett privately called the Eisenhower administration's "do-nothing and know-nothing" attitude. In reviewing all the old mail on the subject, Barnett had discovered less than five specific requests for assistance, but hundreds of complaints about the government's "no-policy policy". Many of these were prompted by a full-page advertisement entitled "20¢ a day to live on," sponsored by the Hugh Moore Fund in August 1961 and signed by such notables as Eleanor Roosevelt, Elmo Roper, Ellsworth Bunker, Will Clayton and David Lilienthal.

In essence, this is what Barnett's revised form letter said:

> The United States during 1961 began to give attention to population problems as they are related to economic and social development. We are seeking to encourage scientific research and discussions by foundations, private organisations, and individuals, and to keep abreast of the results of such research and discussion. . . .
>
> We believe that the greatest contribution which the United States can make at this stage to the solution of the joint and important problems of population growth and economic development is to stimulate the acquisition of adequate and accurate knowledge. The United States is not prepared to advocate, much less to impose, any specific decisions or policies regarding population controls which other countries might, in due course, consider necessary.

The formulation in the letter was important. Taking for granted the fact that population was relevant to economic growth, the letter explored what kind of government activity might actually be feasible. It shifted the focus of attention from "artificial birth control" (which was not politically feasible) to "acquisition of adequate and accurate knowledge" (which was becoming politically feasible). A good example of how policy may be made by answering the mail, the substance of the letter might well have been front page news if the Secretary of State had included it in a speech, but as a routine form letter signed by a lower-level bureaucrat it was used in Washington and relayed overseas without attracting attention or criticism.

With equal lack of publicity, liaison between State Department officials and private organisations grew apace. Barnett conferred widely – with William H. Draper, Jr., and Cass Canfield, with Robert Cook of the Population Reference Bureau, with Fred Jaffe of Planned Parenthood, with Oscar Harkavy of the Ford Foundation, and with John D. Rockefeller 3rd. Barnett spoke to an off-the-record meeting at the Council on Foreign Relations in May 1962, warning that policy advances would be slow, quiet and undramatic but adding that requests for assistance, especially information and training, would be considered.

Canfield and Draper made the Washington rounds a number of times, promoting various proposals. They recommended to Barnett, McGhee, Rusk and Walt W. Rostow at the Policy Planning Council and to McGeorge Bundy at the White House that the President follow Dr. John Rock's suggestion and appoint a commission of experts in the social and biological sciences to study the problem. They called on Dr. James Shannon the Director of NIH to plead for more research on fertility.

The highest-level interaction was a meeting between Secretary Rusk and the heads of some 30 large foundations in November 1962 in New York. Draper and Canfield had proposed that Rusk speak privately to a gathering of foundation executives about how government and the foundations might collaborate in dealing with population problems. Rusk agreed to speak if Rockefeller would arrange the meeting. Rockefeller, who was much more sensitive than Canfield and Draper about twisting official arms, arranged the meeting. Such was the delicacy of the issue that Canfield, then President of Planned Parenthood, was asked not to attend.

Rusk's comments were disappointing to the activists. He did not urge the foundations to give high priority to population, though he said that government needed the stimulus of private ideas and research. He attributed the "explosion" of interest in population partly to the government shift toward longer-term foreign aid planning but he emphasised the need for the U.S. government to wait until other countries developed their own policies and requested aid. There were no simple, uniform solutions, he insisted, suggesting that rash experiment and subsequent disappointment could set back further progress for 20 or 30 years. The government cannot and should not crusade, he warned.

It was a very low-key approach, but the fact that the secretary came at all may have carried weight. The Ford and Rockefeller Foundations were already reassessing their small contributions to population work and were on their way toward the major programme commitments that were announced in 1963. Other foundations also began to take an interest. Ironically, Rusk may have been more successful in spurring private groups to activity than they ever were in spurring him.

REVERSING THE FOREIGN AID BAN

The Policy Planning Council report included two specific recommendations for the foreign aid programme:

First, that AID should "no longer consider itself restricted in the giving of information by its public health and other technicians, on request, on the various aspects of human reproduction"; and second, that AID take steps, including necessary preliminary studies, toward "bringing about social and economic changes which will assist countries in meeting a recognised population problem." Rusk approved the first, fairly straightforward proposal but did not press for any implementation. The second, rather vague proposal he did not approve.

Within the foreign aid agency, the most conspicuous obstacle was the airgram ICATO XA758 of March 20, 1960, which contained simply the text of Eisenhower's press conference statement. Henry Labouisse, Kennedy's first foreign aid administrator, agreed with McGhee that the Eisenhower message was no longer operative. But the real problem was how to communicate this shift in policy without developing a whole new policy or raising an issue that would embarrass the President. Labouisse once jokingly suggested that the missions simply be advised with reference to airgram ICATO XA758 that Eisenhower was no longer President.

A further obstacle was the massive 1961 review that eventually transformed the International Cooperation Administration into the Agency for International Development. During most of 1961 Labouisse was very much involved in planning and obtaining congressional support for the reorganisation. Therefore although Labouisse was sympathetic he did not pay much attention to McGhee's report and he let McGhee know that he wanted no messages on the subject sent to the field. As a result only a handful of people in Washington knew that Eisenhower's blanket prohibition was no longer meant to apply.

The reorganisation of the foreign aid programme did not enhance the immediate prospects for action. The Kennedy administration was committed to systematic economic development that stressed comprehensive country planning with long-term development loans rather than short-term technical assistance projects of the Point IV type. In the reorganised agency the four regional bureaus (Latin America, Africa, the Near East and South Asia and East Asia) had more influence than the expert staff office (which was not even established on a comparable level until 1962). This shift sharply reduced AID assistance in the health field and put priority on government-directed income and job-producing investments. In the long-run, as Rusk observed, the change focussed attention on the economic impact of population growth but in the short-run it downgraded the medical personnel who might have assisted in specific family planning projects.

At the same time the staff of the foreign aid agency through its many permutations lacked the continuity and experience of State Department officers. As Senator Gruening observed of AID administrators, "Most of them have suffered the face of Henry VIII's wives – they haven't lasted very long." After the reorganisation Labouisse was succeeded in November 1961 by Fowler Hamilton, a law partner of George Ball, as the first administrator of the Agency for International Development. Hamilton was succeeded in December 1962 by David Bell, an economist and former Director of the Bureau of the Budget. It was late 1961 or 1962 before many of the second-level personnel came into the agency, with its new administration and three directors in three years.

At the root of many of the bureaucratic problems in the foreign aid agency was of course, the fact that the programme had an uncertain base of support in the country and in Congress. AID officials had to face twice as many congressional committees for annual funding as did their State Department colleagues. They were therefore inclined to be twice as cautious about issues like birth control. This caution could only have been reinforced by Secretary Rusk's explicit warning when Fowler Hamilton took office that AID employees should avoid "errors" that could be "seized on by enemies" to diminish public support.

Thus, the activists in the State Department like McGhee, Barnett, Schaetzel, Gardner and Van Nort were constantly frustrated during the early 1960s in their efforts to push AID ahead. When McGhee suggested in June 1961 new legislation to provide a secure base for action, AID officials immediately demurred. McGhee concluded in annoyance, "You have the authority but you don't intend to act."

Throughout the early 1960s Schaetzel and Barnett kept prodding AID to brief mission directors on population problems, to stimulate direct requests for aid from Taiwan and Korea where government-approved programmes were already under way, to appoint full-time staff, to prepare a manual on outside organisations that could guide nations seeking help, to gather demographic data and relevant literature, and to promote population research. Yet without decisive backing from above, the Young Turks in the State Department could only propose and persuade. The power to initiate – or in 1961 and 1962, not to initiate – assistance programmes remained with AID, despite its many internal handicaps.

In the summer of 1962, after Rusk's first public comment, Harry Krould, who became the new Director of the AID health programme and did favour birth control, obtained clearance through AID and the White House for a classified AID manual order that called demographic factors "of strategic importance". AID missions could therefore play two "significant roles"; one was to help with census-taking and demographic analysis – as had been done for nearly two decades; the other was to recommend on request other sources of information and help in dealing with population problems – including the United Nations, other governments, and "private foundations such as the Population Council, Inc., Planned Parenthood, and the Ford Foundation."

Immediately the National Catholic Welfare Conference objected, through a Catholic senator, to any official U.S. endorsement of a contraceptive programme for population control. This connotation was conveyed merely by mentioning the words "Planned Parenthood". Fowler Hamilton insisted on the responsibility of the agency to help nations that were looking for relevant data and tried to make a distinction between information and advocacy. Nevertheless, the prompt Catholic protest did not reassure AID officials.

Early in the fall of 1962 Dr. Leona Baumgartner, Commissioner of Health for the City of New York, joined the agency as assistant administrator for Human Resources and Social Development (HRSD, later renamed Technical Cooperation and Research, TCR). Her first AID contact with the population problem was, like Barnett's, answering the mail. Dr. Baumgartner had a long-standing interest in birth control, tempered somewhat by nine years in the political atmosphere of New York City, and a high reputation in health circles, having just served as President of the American Public

Health Association. With Krould's encouragement she soon became a focal point for AID activities in population and was formally given that role in November 1962, when she accompanied Rusk to the meeting of foundations in New York. Her first act was to withdraw the contested manual order and promise further guidance shortly. But despite Rusk's approval she was not immediately successful in persuading either Frank Coffin the acting administrator or later David Bell to send a clarifying message out to the overseas posts.

Parallel to, but relatively independent of McGhee's Barnett's and Baumgartner's activities. Teodoro Moscoso, the assistant secretary in charge of the Alliance for Progress, also began in late 1961 to stimulate interest in population problems in the Latin American region. Having worked with Planned Parenthood in Puerto Rico, Moscoso had no great fear of the Catholic Church. In the summer of 1962 he asked Dr. Edgar Berman, a health consultant, to look into the population situation. Moscoso was convinced that without birth control Latin American economic and social progress would be impossible. As a result, operating through the nearly autonomous Alliance for Progress, Berman also began to investigate what might be done despite the supposed monolithic opposition of the Catholic Church in Latin America.

Thus, in AID as in the State Department, but nearly a year later, the first important forward steps were the selection of personnel, who were partly assigned to the problem but partly operated on their own initiative. All distinctly able, ambitious, energetic, and somewhat competitive personalities, they constituted not so much a team as a group of friendly rivals, each trying to advance the same cause in a slightly different way through the tangle of what Nunley had first called "a jungle that is largely unexplored".

7

THE UNITED NATIONS PRECIPITATES A DECISION, 1962

Of all the Policy Planning Council's recommendations, none came to more significant fruition than the brief reference to the United Nations. The Secretary of state approved without hesitation McGhee's proposal that the United States "give maximum support consistent with avoiding undue publicity to work in the population field in the UN." With this endorsement and for other reasons, both institutional and personal, the United Nations became the forum for the first significant shift in U.S. government policy.

As an institution the United Nations moved at its own pace and set its own agenda. Unlike any private organisation it could force governments to stand up and be counted on issues. In 1960 and 1961 the government of Sweden attempted to place and in 1962 finally succeeded in placing on the agenda of the General Assembly a resolution entitled "Population Growth and Economic Development". Richard Gardner and Robert Barnett obtained clearance not only from the Secretary of state but also from the White House for the United States to support the resolution.

The crucial paragraph endorsed this view:

> . . . the view of the Population Commission that the United Nations should encourage and assist the Governments, especially of the less developed countries, in obtaining basic data and carrying out essential studies of the demographic aspects, as well as other aspects, of

> their economic and social development problems, and that the United Nations give technical assistance, as requested by governments, for national projects and programmes dealing with the problems of population.

The State Department's initial support was based on the argument that no new authority was involved. The United Nations already possessed the power to provide technical assistance in any area requested – an argument used many times in the next decade to justify both support and non-support of various measures. The White House accepted the argument, as eager as the rest of the U.S. government to let the United Nations lead.

The personal ingredient was provided by Richard N. Gardner, Harlan Cleveland's Deputy Assistant Secretary for international organisation affairs. Gardner, as a junior member of President Kennedy's Task Force on Foreign Assistance, had suggested in January 1961 that Kennedy's technical advisers should take the President at his word and review the population problem in the light of national interest. But he was overruled by Ball, Cleveland, Rostow, and the others who only replied, "Don't you know the President is Catholic?" Just as some members of the Draper Committee had hestitated to embarrass Eisenhower by raising the issue, so Kennedy's advisers tried to shield him from it.

Gardner persisted. He volunteered to handle the Swedish resolution when it finally came before the United Nations in December 1962. Well-supplied with data plus the form letter and scraps of other approved statements, Gardner wanted to stress quality as well as quantity and the need for discussion and a wider dissemination of knowledge. Julia Henderson, then Director of the UN Bureau of Social Affairs, provided further help and encouragement in New York.

A gracefully executed "scissors and paste job," Gardner's speech gave the whole issue new stature and significance. At the core of the statement he transformed the cautious, negatively phrased form letter into a positive affirmation of the "great need for additional knowledge on population matters." For example, where the form letter stated that "the United States will not place obstacles in the way of other governments which . . . seek solutions to their population problems," Gardner declared, "The United States believes that obstacles should not be placed in the way of other governments." Whereas the form letter categorised UN research as "this valuable work that can cast significant light on the complex interrelationships," Gardner asserted, "It is the hope of the United States that these valuable efforts will be substantially expanded."

At the last minute Gardner dispatched his draft by teletype from New York to Washington for clearance Harlan Cleveland and Robert Barnett took the speech to Rusk. The Secretary read it through from beginning to end. "It doesn't present any problems to me," Rusk said. "Let's go ahead." With the further approval of Ralph Dungan in the White House, Gardner proceeded.

The most controversial portion of the resolution was, as expected, the language authorising technical assistance for national projects and programmes. Originally Gardner had authority to vote in favour of the whole resolution. But before the vote specifically to delete that paragraph and those words, a spokesman from the National Catholic Welfare Conference came to Gardner and pointedly asked, "Are you going to support the paragraph about technical assistance?" In a manner that seemed very threatening, the Catholic visitor suggested that, if so, Catholics in the United States would withdraw their support from the United Nations and mobilise in opposition. It was the traditional Catholic threat of boycott. Gardner felt himself on rather thin ice with no clear line of support from above. Fearing that Catholic opposition could make the whole effort backfire, Gardner compromised. The United States supported the resolution in its entirety when it was finally approved by a vote of 69 to 0 (with 27 abstentions). But the United States abstained in committee when that entire operative paragraph was barely retained by a vote of 32 to 30 (with 35 abstentions). The United States also abstained on a much more critical vote in the General

Assembly when the reference to technical assistance was deleted by a separate vote of 34 to 34 (with 32 abstentions). As it was an important question, a two-thirds majority was required. U.S. abstention on both votes was explained officially on the grounds that the United Nations already had full authority to provide technical assistance and that the paragraph "is therefore superfluous". Thus, the United States abstained publicly on the key votes for the very reason that had earlier been used internally to justify support for the resolution.

Gardner argues that:

> Abstention on the controversial section – and its consequent defeat – was the price that had to be paid for achieving a broad consensus among the membership. It was also the price the United States and some other members had to pay for this first big step forward on population, given the uncertain state of domestic opinion.

After the debate Gardner and his colleagues in the State Department waited apprehensively for criticism. None came, except a cable from a Planned Parenthood fan protesting U.S. abstention. Although it was the first General Assembly debate on population and the first official U.S. government statement, the press played it down. The *New York Times* was on strike at the time. Wire service reports indicated only that the United States had abstained on several votes but supported the resolution.

Nevertheless, Gardner's initiative was important, not because he said anything new or startling, not because the UN resolution really conferred any additional authority, and not because the episode attracted wide attention at the time but rather because of the way it was used and interpreted afterward. Dr. Baumgartner in AID had not been consulted or even advised in advance of cardner's move, but she was one of the first to see that here was a public banner under which AID policy could advance, even if high AID officials refused to clear AID cables. She persuaded Gardner that the speech and resolution should be reprinted as a pamphlet entitled

"Population Growth: A World Problem" and subtitled "Statement of U.S. Policy." Under that imprimatur and financed by AID, the speech was dispatched to U.S. embassies and AID missions around the world. After three years, the ghost of Eisenhower' ban was finally exorcised from the State Department.

Furthermore, when no opposition developed other than a handful of Catholic editorials, Gardner and Baumgartner pressed further. In a not uncommon bureaucratic pattern, what had originally been depicted as a minimal decision was reinterpreted after the fact as a maximal one. By May 1963 Gardner was describing the UN action as "a turning point" in world recognition of the population problem.

Throughout 1963 and 1964 Gardner used every occasion to confirm the importance and the official nature of the policy shift. President Kennedy personally had approved his statement, he said. No one contradicted him. Although at the top level McGhee, Labouisse and Rusk had agreed among themselves as early as 1961 that Eisenhower's policy was no longer in effect, their private agreement made much less difference than a Deputy Assistant Secretary's speech to an empty hall, because they deliberately refrained from communicating their decision and Gardner deliberately tried to communicate his.

In the long-run, the speech, the resolution, and the UN vote acquired significance because Gardner and birth control advocates believed that they were significant and spoke and acted vigorously upon that assumption. Two years of study and preparation, two years of behind-the-scenes work may have been necessary and helpful for government policy reorientation and to reassure nervous officials (although polls suggest that Catholic opposition to domestic birth control programmes increased during this period of lesser publicity. But it was Gardner's speech at the United Nations and above all the later publicising of it as a great leap forward that seemed to pull both government and public opinion toward a new policy consensus much more effectively than did the quiet off-the-record discussions that had occupied the previous two years.

8

THE PRESIDENT AND CONGRESS ENDORSE RESEARCH, 1963

The momentum that had been building up within the government, authorised by Rusk's decisions of August 1961 and precipitated by the UN debate in December 1962, did not develop in a vacuum. The environment outside the State Department was changing also. From the private organisations came a deluge of publicity and agitation. In addition to the making of repeated trips to Washington by notables like Draper and Canfield, Planned Parenthood for example circulated a "Statement of Conviction about Overpopulation." With signatures of 179 distinguished national and international figures from 19 nations, it was printed as an advertisement and presented to UN Secretary General Dag Hammerskjold in late November 1960. On the local level, state restrictions on birth control were contested, as in Connecticut, and state welfare policies were protested, as in Illinois.

Hugh Moore's World Population Emergency Campaign staged a lively symposium in May 1961 at which Catholics were openly criticised for their resistance to birth control. Marriner Eccles, former Chairman of the Federal Reserve Board, called world population growth "more explosive than the atomic or hydrogen bomb." In an editorial entitled "The World Population Explosion" the *New York Times* agreed. Planned Parenthood files include nearly 50 editorials dated 1961 from all over the country urging government consideration of the population problem.

The International Union for the Scientific Study of Population, on the other hand, reacted against activist alarmism. Demographers derided the "emotional" phrase "population explosion". Dudley Kirk was quoted as saying, "The term is unfortunate and would not be used at a scientific meeting such as this. We are a scientific society and not a social movement." Nevertheless, both the term and the idea were coming into common usage.

More conciliatory than Hugh Moore's meetings and advertisements was the November 1961 speech of John D. Rockefeller 3rd's in Rome to the UN Food and Agriculture Organisation. He repeated his call for government involvement but urged study before action. Rockefeller wondered "whether the issue of birth control – only one of the facets of the population question – has not in some countries pushed the entire question beyond public discussion." Tact was the new tactic.

On the professional side, the Population Council increased its budget from $1 million in 1959 to more than $ 5.5 million in 1963. Between November 1962 and April 1963 the council sponsored three overseas advisory missions – to Korea, Tunisia and Turkey – and in 1964 established a new Division for Technical Assistance, reflecting the growing interest of other governments in population. The first experiments with the new intrauterine contraceptive device also provided "a basis for optimism" that a major breakthrough in contraceptive technology was at hand.

Three important publications in 1961 and 1962 also stressed compromise and conciliation. An article by the Catholic physician John Rock, who had organised field trials for the first oral contraceptives at his infertility clinic, appeared in the July 1961 issue of *Good Housekeeping* under the politically appealing title, "We Can End the Battle Over Birth Control." Senator Fulbright privately called Rock's article "the most sensible statement I have seen." In October 1961 in an article in *Look*, Father John O'Brien of Notre Dame University also suggested, "Let's Take Birth Control Out of Politics." The doctor and the priest both emphasised the wide areas of agreement between Catholic doctrine and other religions; both called for more dialogue on the issues and more scientific research on human reproduction.

From many sides and professions, the population problem was beginning to be redefined. *Does Overpopulation Mean Poverty?* was the suggestive title of a bright red pamphlet by Joseph Marion Jones, with an introduction by World Bank President Eugene Black. The brochure was issued in 1962 by the Center for International Economic Growth but was promoted, sponsored, financed and distributed by the population organisations, with help from Mary Lasker.

Important voices from overseas also raised the birth control question and prompted further U.S. editorial comment. General Ayub Khan, President of Pakistan, during his July 1961 visit bluntly told Americans to stop squabbling and spur their scientists to develop a cheap, simple pill. His appeals influenced Vice President Johnson considerably. India's Prime Minister Jawaharlal Nehru also referred to the problem. Yet the only government prepared to offer help was Sweden, which announced in 1962 that birth control would be a major part of its expanding foreign aid programme.

While Protestant and Jewish institutions became increasingly positive about the virtues of "responsible parenthood," the Catholic Church found itself under far greater pressures not only from the birth control movement but also from its own communicants. Pope John XXIII reaffirmed traditional Catholic doctrine on birth control in the encyclical *Mater et Magister* of July 15, 1961, but few were completely convinced that it was the last word. A new spirit was in the air. The once-radical proposal that Catholics should stop opposing the practice of birth control by others was gradually being supplanted by the far more revolutionary recognition that many Catholics did not themselves agree with the teachings of their church. By the end of 1962 the first rumours were circulating that Pope John had started to consult very seriously with physicians and demographers as well as bishops and theologians. The slightest hint of doubt in the Vatican powerfully accelerated doubts elsewhere.

But in the United States the pressures that were building up for a change in policy on birth control were aimed at the White House far more than the Vatican. After 1962 the prize to be sought in Washington was no longer just a private meeting with the Secretary of State or a speech by a representative at the United Nations but rather the public support of the President and the legislative backing of Congress. In terms of a power struggle, by 1963 the population activists had finally built a scientific and religious coalition strong enough to undermine the organised opposition and large enough to demand attention. In terms of intellectual progress, the 1962-63 *Report* of the Population Council announced:

> During . . . 1962 and 1963, a turning point was passed in general public awareness of the problems of population growth. . . . The views of scientists became the views of the people, at least of enough people to influence national decisions in enough nations to make an impact on the world. . . . Concern with population problems and action on their solution now have come into the public domain.

In more realistic terms the pro and con division of U.S. public opinion had not shifted toward birth control. On the contrary, the opposition of the Catholic man in the street may have increased. But government policy-makers, *New York Times* editorial readers, and opinion leaders of various kinds had become much more accustomed to thinking and talking about population. Similarly the leaders of the Catholic opposition were more acutely aware that they could no longer speak with firm assurances of lay Catholic or Vatican support. The change in thinking in the early 1960s was more a subtle change on the part of opinion makers than a massive transformation of national attitudes.

PRESIDENT KENNEDY SPEAKS

For the first Catholic President of the United States, birth control lacked the political priority that he attached to parochial school aid and the international priority that he attached to an effective foreign assistance programme. As a matter of principle Kennedy would not give blanket endorsement to Catholic Church doctrine and privately criticised the Catholic bishops. But as a matter of politics Kennedy and his aides still feared that birth control was dynamite. "Endorsing birth control was like endorsing the A.D.A., you lost fifty votes for every one you gained." As a matter of policy, Kennedy and his contemporaries clearly preferred to think in more positive and invigorating terms. What Kennedy once called the "mean paternalism" of birth control was both intellectually unconvincing and emotionally unappealing to him as a shortcut to economic success. Or, as Lee Rainwater put it in his analysis of common pronatilist attitudes, "the good person in a good world has a large family."

Kennedy's top policy aides shared much of his optimism about economic development and his skepticism about birth control as a panacea. Furthermore, McGeorge Bundy, Theodore Sorenson, David Bell, Robert Kennedy, and other associates did not want to embarrass the President by raising the question where it was not strictly necessary. Ralph Dungan, whom Schiesinger described as "a thoughtful Catholic of the John XXIII school," served as informal liaison with the Catholic Church and gradually became the keeper of the White House gate on birth control. Dungan recognised and sympathised with the liberal stirrings in the Catholic Church but he was more anxious for Kennedy to remain within the limits of Catholic consensus than to use the prestige of the White House to advance the frontiers of birth control.

Nevertheless, President Kennedy's desire for a strong and substantial foreign aid programme made it almost impossible to ignore population. His very first Foreign Aid Message pointed out,

> The magnitude of the problem is staggering. In Latin America, for example, population growth is already threatening of outpace economic growth.

But Kennedy deliberately refused to link economic development and birth control as the State Department was trying to do. In a 1961 press conference he observed,

> Population control is a matter which goes very much to the life of a country. It is a personal decision and a national decision which those nations must make. The problem is not altogether an economic one. We help countries which carry out different policies in this regard and it is a judgment in my opinion, which they should make.

Kennedy gave the same answer again in 1962 when asked for his reaction to the Jones pamphlet.

In the summer of 1962 President Kennedy asked Draper, whose views on birth control were then well known, to undertake a confidential mission to Brazil to assess the political and economic status of President Goulard's government. Draper found the situation in Brazil very serious. Robert Kennedy arranged for him to make a personal report to the President. After reporting fully and answering questions on the main purpose of the mission, Draper asked, "Do you have ten or fifteen minutes, Mr. President, to hear about the population problem which is especially serious in Northeast Brazil?" Kennedy replied with interest, "Yes indeed." So Draper described conditions in that area – where per capita income was not much higher than in India and where annual population growth rates of over 3 per cent exceeded the annual increase in food and jobs. Kennedy listened attentively and raised several questions.

After Draper's presentation, the President asked, "Why doesn't the Ford Foundation concentrate all of its resources on the population problem around the world?"

Draper replied that the Ford Foundation had done more than any other organisation, and that he too had asked John McCloy, then Chairman of the Board, why the foundation did not do more. McCloy's reply was that there were a lot of other problems to work on, too. A few minutes later, as Draper was leaving, Kennedy commented again at the door, "I just don't see why the Ford Foundation doesn't concentrate on this issue."

The Ford Foundation was indeed expanding its commitments in population, partly because of Rusk's encouragement and partly because of the active campaign Draper and several trustees and staff members had been waging. But the foundation's leaders shared Rusk's fears that there were too few trained people in the field and too great a danger that "highly visible failures" might prejudice future efforts. Kennedy wanted the Ford Foundation to lead but the Ford Foundation's general policy in the early 1960s was that while it would support research and training it would not support action programmes or public information (or propaganda) except where the government had first adopted a favourable policy. Until then, Ford Foundation programmes in the United States were discreetly directed at the very leaders who were waiting for the foundations to lead.

By the spring of 1963, however, other initiatives from government and private advocates forced the issue to national attention. First, on April 18, Dr. John Rock's book *The Time Has Come. A Catholic Doctor's Proposals to End the Battle Over Birth Control* appeared. The subtitle carried the message. From the clinical professor emeritus of obstetrics and gynecology at Harvard came a plea for tolerance by American Catholics and non-Catholics alike. It was also a plea for research by the American government, and a plea for approval by the Vatican of the new oral contraceptives as a natural, physiological (not artificial) method of birth control. Richard Cardinal Cushing of Boston disagreed with Rock's argument about the pill but took the unusual step of commenting, "In this book there is much that is good."

The very next day, with a timing that was coincidental but a common theme that was not, the National Academy of Sciences released a panel study entitled *The Growth of World Population*. Sponsored and personally supported by Dr. George Kistiakowsky, former science adviser to President Eisenhower, the report grew from his own frustrated recognition that the scientific community outside of government had to move first before the scientists inside government would be allowed to act. Every time

Kistiakowsky had tried to urge Eisenhower to do something about population or to stimulate the National Science Foundation he had met great reluctance. Those he conferred with in the Kennedy administration during 1962 and 1963 – from the State Department and AID to the White House – strongly encouraged his effort – but warned that if he mentioned their names they would have to deny everything.

Dr. William McElroy, Chairman of the Biology Department of Johns Hopkins University, prepared the report including, at Kistiakowsky's insistence, a very specific section on biomedical research. The report did not mince any scholarly words. "Either the birth rate of the world must come down or the death rate must go back up." Since high birth rates impeded economic development and since lower birth rates could be hastened with better, more acceptable contraceptives, the report called for increased government and private support of biomedical, demographic and social research and training. It was a wholehearted endorsement by the prestigious scientific community for the research approach to government population policy.

Two days later Richard Nixon, then a private citizen, added his voice, calling for a "critical reappraisal" of foreign aid and birth control. This "immensely controversial subject can no longer be swept under the carpet," he maintained. "The United States cannot justify spending billions of dollars for economic assistance for the purpose of raising living standards and discover year after year that population growth outruns growth of the economy.

Planned Parenthood staff and others, including Barnett in the State Department, deliberately encouraged reporters to raise the population issue at the next presidential press conference. Barnett and Baumgartner drafted a sympathetic response for Kennedy. In response to a direct question about the NAS and Rock proposals, Kennedy hedged somewhat, then finally said:

> If your question is, can we do more, should we know more about the whole reproduction cycle, and should this

> information be made more available to the world so that everyone can make their own judgment, I would think it would be a matter which we could certainly support. . . . Whether we are going to support Dr. Rock's proposal, which is somewhat different, is another question.

With these words President Kennedy gingerly opened the door halfway. He said just enough to legitimise and encourage what was already being said and done but not quite enough to support any significant new programmes. He gave legitimacy to the research approach but he still did not touch upon the economic issue.

President Kennedy's last statement on population, on June 5, 1963, came closer than any other to acknowledging the Malthusian implications of population growth. Addressing the World Food Congress in Washington, D.C., he declared:

> Population increases have become a serious concern. . . . The Population growth rate is too often the highest, where hunger is already the most prevalent.

Within the next few months two other former political rivals of President Kennedy added their support for birth control. Adlai Stevenson, then Ambassador to the United Nations, spoke to Planned Parenthood in October 1963 about the urgency of the population problem. In a *Saturday Evening Post* article. General Eisenhower candidly admitted he had been wrong in barring government programmes and that regardless of religious differences the population problem was too important to be ignored. Other private organisations like the American Assembly endorsed and expanded on the need for more research and for technical assistance, as requested, overseas.

The momentum for support of birth control was clearly building up. Even Kennedy's limited approval of more research and greater access to it was widely hailed by scientists and activists alike. The spring meeting of Planned Parenthood, a symposium on "Man's Future," provided the scenario for coming action. Dr. John Rock urged a massive

"Manhattan Project" in medical research to find acceptable means of fertility control. Draper praised Kennedy's "wise leadership" and affirmed that "this is a big milestone passed". Then, with what one observer calls "his ratchet-like tendency" to check any backsliding by immediately moving on to the next step, Draper urged Congress to take up the issue. Draper suggested that if the National Institutes of Health did not have any mandate to conduct applied research–as NIH Director Shannon still implied – then Congress should provide a "direct authorisation" for a massive, coordinated research and development effort. He further proposed that the money the Clay Committee had just recommended cutting from foreign aid programmes be applied instead to educate the world about the population problem.

That was the first direct public appeal to Congress for specific action. Until then, most of the population activists, including Draper, had tiptoed around Congress trying not to stir up opposition and hoping for progress within the less-exposed atmosphere of the executive agencies. But after April 1963 the endorsement of a Catholic President provided protection for more overt moves elsewhere.

Draper was extremely impatient with what he called the "skittishness" of lower-level federal employees who "exaggerated the seriousness" of Catholic opposition. He had talked with Dr. Shannon several times but always came away with the feeling that NIH did not consider contraceptive development its responsibility. He was not satisfied with the usual NIH response that no good applications for research on fertility were ever turned down. He thought NIH should be deliberately stimulating more proposals. He had talked with Secretary of State Rusk and other State and AID officials but he did not agree with the State and AID position that other nations had to move first. He thought the U.S. government could exercise leadership.

In short, at a time when officials in both agencies were still thinking in terms of how to respond to outside initiatives, Draper was advocating a directed research programme in

NIH and an action programme in AID. Fully convinced to the relevance and feasibility of such a course, he was already pressing for higher priority, more resources and faster timing. Not surprisingly, some officials began to dread his visits. So Draper went directly to Congress.

CONGRESS ACTS

Actually, Congress had not ignored the population problem. Senator J. William Fulbright, (D.-Ark.), Chairman of the Foreign Relations Committee, told foreign aid officials in India in 1958 that they certainly should be doing something about population growth even if they did not report it to Congress. Questions came up with increasing frequency at congressional hearings. By 1961 when the Kennedy administration requested $ 4.3 billion for foreign aid and defended the request by pointing to vast underdeveloped and impoverished populations, Fulbright began to raise even more pointed questions. He asked Under Secretary of State George Ball whether "more direct action" might not be required to reduce population growth. He privately suggested to the horrified Secretary of the Treasury Douglas Dillon that the population question should be discussed with Latin American nations at the 1961 Montevideo Conference. This frustrating exchange with Wymberley Coerr, acting Assistant Secretary for Latin America in 1961, explains Fulbright's mounting impatience:

> Fulbright: You say that economic growth of these countries is slower than population growth. Could I conclude that you are concerned about population growth? You think, perhaps, something ought to be done about it?
>
> Coerr: I would rather not pronounce on the population growth.
>
> Fulbright: You would not?
>
> Coerr: I would rather not make any recommendation about the population growth itself.

Fulbright: Why not? It is not secret.

Coerr: No, it certainly is no secret . . .

Fulbright: A large part of this has been brought about by your programme because you are working on health conditions in these countries.

Coerr: That is right, improving their health.

Fulbright: You talk about health. Why don't you talk about population control? Why is that forbidden to you?

Coerr: I think you are right, sir, probably it should not be forbidden to me. I just recognise it as a politically sensitive subject.

Fulbright: I know it is. . . . This is one of the things, among others, that causes me a sense of complete helplessness or hopelessness.

But the largest cuts in the increasingly embattled foreign aid programme in 1961, 1962 and 1963 were made in the House of Representatives, not in the Senate. The House Committee on Foreign Affairs included at least three members, Clement Zablocki (D.-Wisc.), Edna Kelly (D.-N.Y.), and James Fulton (R.-Pa.), whose support was needed for the foreign aid bill as a whole but who were openly opposed to birth control. As Fulton put it in 1960:

> I think that a U.S. foreign aid programme of economic and military assistance has nothing whatever to do with the population of a country, and especially when birth control cuts across religious views that are strongly held . . . We in the United States should stay out of sex problems of foreign countries.

A not uncommon view, perhaps, was that of Congressman Barratt O'Hara (D.-Ill), who projected the official views of the Catholic Church upon the whole country:

> I think the great majority of our Americans, regardless of religion, would be against birth control. There is something in the thought of birth control that just isn't American, and yet population pressure is a serious problem.

The administration was clearly more alarmed by the possibility of a Catholic revolt against foreign aid in the House than by Fulbright's sense of "helplessness or hopelessness," especially since the Arkansas senator had almost no Catholic constituents. Rusk continued to deny that the population problem was merely numbers, emphasising instead that good health, training and technology would make the same numbers of people an asset rather than a liability.

In the spring of 1963 Draper went to see Senator Fulbright, whom he had known from Marshall Plan days. He suggested that Fulbright simply include language in the bill to convince "skittish" bureaucrats that Congress did want action.

On July 20, 1963, the Senate Foreign Relations Committee, without opposition, added an amendment offered by Senator Fulbright specifically authorising "research into the problems of controlling population growth" and "technical assistance to cooperating countries in carrying out programmes of population control." This "explicit authority" was provided, the committee report pointed out, because of the "profound impact of population growth on economic development."

In the Agency for International Development Dr. Baumgartner thought the amendment was "fine". Nevertheless the official AID position (described in a memorandum to the White House on November 25 while Baumgartner was out of the country) remained "neutral". "The language would convey no authority not now in the legislation. House conferees are likely to oppose the provision. The executive branch has been, and we believe should remain neutral."

In conference with the House of Representatives Zablocki, as expected, raised objections and the reference to "technical assistance" was dropped. In its final form, the amendment read: "Funds made available to carry out this section may be used to conduct research into the problems of population growth." As Fulbright later told Baumgartner the text "should not be read legalistically, but . . . should be interpreted as a broad mandate to the administration."

The foreign aid authorisation, with Fulbright's amendment, was signed into law by President Johnson December 16, 1963. What Kennedy had once considered "remote" had occurred, partly as a result of his own actions, partly as a result of his administration's apparent inaction.

Three weeks after Fulbright quietly offered his amendment, two other senators, Joseph S. Clark (D.-Pa.) and Ernest S. Greuning (D.-Alaska), introduced a formal resolution (S. Con. Res. 56) to increase NIH research and to encourage a Presidential Commission on Population. In the first postwar speech on the Senate floor about population, Clark emphasised Dr. Rock's reasoning and appealed to the National Institutes of Health to "spare but $ 2 or $ 3 million a year for fertility research out of a budget of close to $ 900 million." "I am confident," Clark concluded, "that we in Congress can play our part in the solution of one of the most difficult problems today confronting the human race."

Senator Fulbright's action applied what were basically the policy-setting and administrative oversight powers of the Congress directly to legislation under his own committee's jurisdiction. As committee Chairman he required neither outside publicity nor public pressure to get the amendment adopted. Nor was there any statutory need for congressional action at all. Fulbright and AID officials both agreed that AID already possessed full legal power to do everything in the amendment and more besides, but there was a hortatory purpose to be served by specific congressional endorsement in such a sensitive area. Then, as later, AID's refusal to suppo[r]t the amendment confirmed Fulbright's conviction tha[t] additional pressure was necessary.

The action of Senators Clark and Gruening, on the other hand, was a call for debate rather than for immediate legislation. Even though it was referred to the Committee on Labour and Public Welfare of which Clark was a senior member, the resolution was not expected to pass in the form introduced. It was primarily a vehicle for hearings and discussion, the first step in making a case for legislation or appropriations. It was an example of Congress, acting in its very broad educational role, trying to air important issues even when no clear solutions were yet in sight. Both of these congressional initiatives were made politically possible by Kennedy's support, prompted specifically by Draper's suggestions but undertaken only because of the long-standing concern of each of the senators involved. Both went beyond any previous executive agency action.

Although the assassination of President Kennedy, the inauguration of the new Johnson administration, and the election campaign of 1964 pushed the issue of birth control out of political sight until 1965, the initiatives taken in 1963 remained on the record. Kennedy had acquiesced in the need for more research. Congress had gone still further in asserting the relevance, feasibility and increasing importance of a more active U.S. government role. In the foreign aid field the responsibility for implementing such a programme clearly rested on AID.

9

AID REACTS, 1963-64

Within AID had anyone suggested in January 1963 that by the end of the year President Kennedy would have endorsed more population research and Congress would have passed new legislation directing AID to move ahead, most officials would have been incredulous. Although Baumgartner did succeed in circulating Gardner's speech, all the other signs were negative. She could not get clearance within AID for the instructions needed by the overseas missions. Moreover in late 1962 Barnett became Deputy Assistant Secretary of State for Far Eastern affairs, under Averell Harriman, leaving no one in the State Department with full-time responsibility for population until 1966.

Even in his new post Barnett tried to press AID officials to be as forthright in their congressional testimony as Gardner had been at the United Nations. In a memorandum signed by Harriman. Barnett cited the "apparent timidity" of AID missions and concluded with the warning:

> General William Draper is but one of those saying privately that unless the Administration takes account of the population problem in planning its programmes of economic assistance, the time will soon come when the Congress will consider prolongation of our aid activities to be irrational.

Bell did not appreciate this State Department intervention. Three days later, on March 11, the Regional Assistant Secretaries of State met and decided, on Bell's insistence, that future strategy, tactics and timing on population issues should be left to him, possibly in consultation with the White House. Bell would decide when and whether to use Gardner's still-unpublicised statement or to issue a further clarification. For three and a half months drafts and revisions of proposed testimony for Congress circulated through AID until the issue finally became academic because half a dozen State Department and AID witnesses, including Rusk, had already answered a variety of questions in a variety of different ways.

ARTICULATING AID POLICY

It was not until late April, after Dr. Rock's book, after the National Academy of Sciences report, and, above all, after President Kennedy's statement, that Baumgartner finally succeeded in sending to the field the explanatory airgram that had been promised in December. Referring to the new "focus of public attention" on population, the AID airgram affirmed that AID was now interested in the subject of population but indicated that any real assistance would have to come from other sources. Specifically, the message identified Baumgartner's office as the focal point for population in AID-Washington; listed U.S. support for various UN activities including a proposed $ 500,000 contribution which was later made to the World Health Organisation for research on human reproduction; expressed willingness to consider requests to support "research activities" or to build "research institutions" for social science, demography, and census work; and asked that Washington be notified of requests for help. On the other hand, after quoting President Kennedy on "socio-biological aspects" the airgram pointed out that since AID had "no specialised professional competence in this area" requests would be referred to private institutions, and in the U.S. government to the Public Health Service and Children's Bureau.

President Kennedy's statement and the lack of public opposition encouraged the State Department to advance. Gardner obtained first departmental and then White House clearance for an amplifying policy statement to be made at an American Assembly meeting on population on May 4. There he announced more specifically that the United States would support international cooperation in demography, medical research on reproduction, and the establishment of general health services (which could provide the necessary infrastructure for family planning). The impact of Kennedy's statement was also reflected in the difference between Secretary Rusk's equivocating response to the House Committee on Foreign Affairs on April 5 and his strong affirmation to the Senate Committee on June 11 that Gardner's latest words were "officially spoken on behalf of the Department." In fact, he assured Fulbright that if countries "asked for assistance in terms of information, in terms of technical assistance, in terms of building up their medical centers, their population research centers, and things of that sort, yes, I think we would."

AID also became bolder. During the 12 months following, two more airgrams were dispatched to all AID missions overseas. AIDTO Circular A-44 (August 10,1963) was a follow-up to the UN Secretary-general's demographic questionnaire. AID-Washington asked whether the host country was able to respond to the inquiry: whether demographic assistance had been requested; and, if not, why not, or if so, with what results. A second airgram, AIDTO Circular XA-1149 (April 17, 1964), included a list of books, articles, and other educational materials on population that AID could supply on request. Together they represented a small start toward an information programme.

In mid-April 1963 Baumgartner's office was reorganised and expanded somewhat. Dr. Philip Lee was recruited to replace Dr. Eugene Campbell, a birth control opponent who had directed AID health programmes. The affable Philip Lee got along better with David Bell than did dynamic, talkative Leona Baumgartner, but he did not push as hard. Later Dr. Edward O'Rourke and Dr. Bruce Jessup also joined Human Resources and Social Development and in December 1963 the noted demographer Irene Taeuber became a regular consultant. Although Draper's suggestions that full-time population officers be appointed "in every country where population is expanding at an excessive rate" was not taken very seriously by Lee or Baumgartner – nor were funds available – a Population Reference and Research Branch was officially established within HRSD in June 1964.

Events overseas also were pushing AID toward a bolder posture. The First Asian Population Conference was held in late 1963 in New Delhi under the auspices of the Economic Commission for Asia and the Far East. The conference, which was by, for, and about governments, concluded with a government appeal to all UN agencies to provide technical assistance on request for research and action "in all aspects of population problems." At the Asian conference, for the first time Communist hostility to birth control was somewhat muted. Baumgartner was an active participant. She reassured the Catholic Philippines that "natural" methods of birth control were also included. The Asian governments (five of which already had programmes) were well ahead of the rest of the world in the specifics of birth control work. "The Asian Population Conference," Baumgartner pointed out, "marks the great divide between deliberation and the dedication to decision, plan and programme."

In Washington, too, a lesser divide seemed to have been passed after Kennedy's statement in 1963. At Bell's suggestion Baumgartner and Gardner began to touch congressional bases. Senators Fulbright and Humphrey urged AID to move ahead "quietly". Congressman Otto Passman, generally considered the scourge of AID, expressed his private approval for both research and technical assistance, since population growth might otherwise "eat up everything we had poured into the foreign aid programme." Even Congressman Zablocki indicated that he would not object to family planning research and study as long as it was not overemphasised. All the congressional reactions turned out to be much more favourable than expected.

Yet when Baumgartner tried to send a further summary of developments and another policy statement to the field in 1964, no one, from Stevenson, Bell and Rusk to Dungan and Bundy in the White House seemed to feel that it was necessary. The subject had already been talked to death, they thought. It was "a dead issue," a boring question already settled, she was told.

Indeed, after nearly three years of off-the-record consultation, trial-balloon public statements, and conciliatory dialogues about "our pluralistic society," an acceptable formulation of public policy had been reached. As Leona Baumgartner put it in a 1964 speech at the Johns Hopkins University:

> First of all, what we do and say must be based on a concern for human well-being and on facts uncovered by studies of the relations of population growth to economic and social development as well as on results of biomedical research programmes now under way. . . .
>
> Second. . . . There is no one solution. . . . A balanced programme to raise the plans of economic, social and family relationships is needed both at home and abroad.
>
> Third, it is recognised that the decisions as to population policies and their implementation in other countries are to be made by individual countries and families in accord with their own needs and values. . . . The U.S. government feels it desirable that all health facilities supported by public funds shall provide such freedom of choice, so that persons of all faiths are given equal opportunities to exercise their choice without offense to their consciences. . . .
>
> And, finally, in accord with our government's support of the United Nations, its regional commissions, and specialised agenices, as well as the tradition of governmental co-operation with private groups and friendly governments, we stand ready to work cooperatively with such groups.

Protected in such humanitarian generalities, AID population policy did not indeed present much of a target for political attack or even a subject for discussion. For the moment the great bogey of coercion was thoroughly dissolved. At the same time there were no specific AID projects to criticise. Moreover, AID and State Department officials had already made a considerable concession to Catholic opinion. Vastly relieved as they had been to find that Catholics would not really oppose research and information programmes, the policy-makers on their part had leaned over backward to assure Catholic spokesmen that the U.S. government would not become directly involved in the cotraceptive business. Contraceptives had been on the prohibited list for commodity assistance since 1948. Senators Fulbright and Humphrey had both indicated, when pressed, that the only AID actions that might be embarrassing to Congress were large shipments of "already manufactured" contraceptives. Gardner conceded therefore in his May 4 speech, with Baumgartner's agreement, that the implementation of family planning programmes remained an area where major disagreements "exist or will continue to exist for the foreseeable future." He concluded, "The provision of materials for this purpose can best be done by those governments whose citizens are not divided on this question, by private foundations and by business firms."

This prohibition was, like many AID restrictions, erected into an even higher barrier within the agency than the senators had intended. For instance, when Barnett urged AID in May 1964 to provide an investment guarantee to a U.S. firm for construction of a contraceptive manufacturing facility in India at the Indian government's request, Bell and his Deputy William Gaud both drew back. "It is not clear to me," Gaud wrote, "why the government of India has to use our rupees rather than its own to support its population planning activities." In 1964, he and Bell did not want anything to do with contraceptives.

But the peculiar anomaly of a talked-to-death policy combined with no programme at all was beginning to be recognised. Baumgartner, Lee and Jessup knew they had first to convince the economists who dominated AID that population programmes would make some difference. They began during 1964, in contracts with universities and research groups and a series of policy meetings, to build up the economic arguments and to specify exactly what help AID could provide. Slowly, carefully and quietly they began to consider how the new AID policy could be translated into feasible projects.

DEVELOPING A LATIN AMERICAN PROGRAMME

While Baumgartner and her colleagues struggled over the relationship between an articulated policy and a feasible programme, elsewhere in AID another population programme was proceeding unexpectedly fast without regard for any policy statements. In the Alliance for Progress, Moscoso had asked Dr. Edgar Berman in 1962 to take a look at the Latin American population problem. Berman was not a bureaucrat. He insisted on serving independently in a consultant capacity. He wanted direct access to Moscoso, to Dungan in the White House, and to friends on the Hill. Baumgartner was apprehensive about a second population effort but Dungan as well as Moscoso wanted Berman to make a start, even if no meaningful results could be achieved for some time. So in the region where opposition to birth control seemed strongest Berman moved forward where angels feared to tread.

First he made contacts in the United States. The Latin American Science Board of the National Academy of Sciences agreed to serve in an advisory capacity for AID. Meetings with the Milbank Memorial Fund, Population Council, Population Reference Bureau, and Planned Parenthood showed Berman what a small but enthusiastic start had been made by the private organisations. With Dungan's help Berman sought out Catholic leaders. He conferred with Monsignor James Gremillion and others at the Catholic Relief Services; he discovered that Dr. Benedict Duffy wanted to start a research center on the rhythm method at Georgetown University (which the Ford Foundation later financed while Duffy joined Berman's AID staff); and he learned that Notre Dame had a Latin American family study project. Berman was surprised to find out that some of these U.S. Catholic groups wanted his help as badly as he wanted theirs – and that some of the population organisations were much more reluctant than Catholics to accept AID support.

After a number of meetings with most of the private and government agencies involved, in January 1964 a Population Office was formally established in the Alliance for Progress – the first in the agency. Then Berman turned to Latin America. In the first six months of 1964 he visited seven Latin American countries, trying to see heads of state, finance ministers, planning commissions, medical leaders, and then the highest representatives of the Catholic Church. To his further surprise, most of the Latin Americans were eager to talk to him about population, but even more eager to find out from him what their own colleagues had said. The issues that Berman discussed with them – the economic, social and health hazards of rapid population growth – most of them had never discussed with one another.

After the indication of interest, Moscoso and Berman obtained the quiet approval of the Senate Foreign Relations Committee for two grants in fiscal year 1964. They represented the first Washington funded, U.S.-dollar support for population work by AID. These grants went to CELADE in Chile, a UN-sponsored demographic training center ($100,000) and to the Pan American Health Organisation for a feasibility study on research training programmes ($ 40,000).

This activity was not unnoticed in the House of Representatives. Zablocki complained to Assistant Secretary Thomas Mann (who replaced Moscoso in 1963) that "nowhere in this legislation has AID been given authority to promote control of population growth by scientific devices." Mann assured him that AID only supported "talk" and "private concerns that are largely engaged in an educational problem [sic]." Ten days after the congressman's criticism, Mann's deputy William Rogers addressed a Puerto Rican meeting of the International Planned Parenthood Federation, which AID had helped to finance. Representatives, mostly governmental, attended from every country in Latin America.

Barely a month later Berman and his assistant Lee Bullitt (wife of an Assistant Secretary of the treasury and as little intimidated by the AID bureaucracy as Berman) dispatched a five-page airgram to all the Latin American missions. Unusually forthright and positive, the airgram quoted President Kennedy and asserted:

> AID is prepared to assist host governments as fully and effectively as possible in the areas of (a) information, (b) training, (c) research, and (d) Institution-building. . . . We now have the opportunity to convert the broad principles of AID policy into meaningful programmes for Latin America.

The missions were instructed to "consider the population programme as a priority area." Citing a number of specific proposals as "the product of intensive examination" by the prestigious National Academy of Sciences advisory group, the AID missions were further requested:

1. "to designate a high official to be responsible for population programmes" in each mission;
2. to inform host governments that AID considers it "appropriate" further to develop population programmes; and
3. to report promptly to AID-Washington "any indications of interest by host governments or activities by public or private organisations."

Unlike Baumgartner, Berman did not clear his airgrams with Bell, Gaud, or four other bureaus. Less than a week after Bell had declined to discuss with Rusk or send to the field a much less forceful statement that Leona Baumgartner had been working on for months, AIDTO Circular La-158 (May 11, 1964) entitled "Action Programme – Population" was dispatched to Latin America.

Even Draper and Canfield, who were beginning to be regarded in Washington as population fanatics, expressed astonishment at Berman's activities. Canfield predicted that he would soon be fired. In fact, Berman (with Moscoso's and Mann's encouragement) broke all the precepts of stated AID policy. First, he took on an area where everyone assumed that population control was contrary to national culture, conscience, and habit. Second, he took the initiative himself in finding individuals and organisations who would use help rather than waiting for requests to come to him. Third, he emphasised the private sector and international agencies and paid little attention to the presence or absence of an official government population policy. Finally, he did what very few other AID and State Department officials have done even yet; he sought out the very highest-ranking officials who would see him and brought the issue directly and candidly to their attention. With great charm and a gallant air, he carried off what many thought impossible.

Berman had a separate population unit in January 1964 five months before the HRSD unit. He had a larger population budget in fiscal years 1964 and 1965 than the rest of the agency combined, and he insisted on having a population officer in every Latin American mission nearly a full year before the other missions were asked to appoint them. Although many ambassadors and U.S. missions in Latin America did very little to implement Berman's appeal, a clear start had been made.

Admittedly, the Alliance for Progress enjoyed a privileged place in the State Department and AID and a much more generous appropriation. Admittedly, too, Edgar Berman had less official standing than Leona Baumgartner, an assistant administrator with worldwide responsibility. He was less likely to call his own free-wheeling activities the position of the U.S. government. Therefore, he could say more. But the two critical variables in the population programme seem to have been the strong support from the top – Moscoso, Mann, Rogers, Jack Vaughn, Lincol Gordon – and Berman's own enterprise. After the support from above disappeared and Berman, Duffy, and their immediate successor, George Coleman, left, the programme declined appreciably. But in the mid-1960s when the issue was still controversial the Latin American region had led the agency in suggesting that population be considered "a priority area" in U.S. foreign aid.

Thus by late 1964 the U.S. government had moved a considerable distance from President Eisenhower's assertion that birth control was "not our business". The Kennedy administration came into office publicly committed to the view that population was a legitimate policy issue even though most of the top officials were privately determined not to raise it. Below the top level, however, a handful of activists were convinced that population growth was important, so important that the government had to find a way to do something about it.

The first steps were assigning personnel and semiopenly discussing the issue. Well-supplied with advice and encouragement from private groups, fortified by the first signs of a religious accommodation, and pressured by the United Nations and foreign governments, the U.S. government advocates moved cautiously ahead to define the problem and identify programme possibilities. Sometimes they exceeded their authority and found themselves rebuffed. Sometimes they rebuffed the increasingly insistent activists outside government who were willing to take much greater risks to achieve a decisive result. But generally the policy shift proceeded without major setback. Within three years the State Department and then AID were officially on record, first, that population policy was relevant to economic development, and second, that a population programme concentrating on research and information was politically feasible and technically useful.

10

PRESIDENT JOHNSON SPEAKS OUT, 1965

The year 1965 was in the words of one journalist "the year in which the politicians, at home and abroad, awoke to the population explosion." As before, the progress publicly recorded was, on the one hand, a continuation of accelerating behind the scenes activity and, on the other, a reflection of new people in key positions and new problems rising to national attention. As before, the arguments of relevance were repeated, refined and reenforced but the major policy debates of the middle 1960s centered on questions of feasibility and priority. To what extent was it feasible to provide help beyond information and research? And then, to what extent did birth control deserve priority over other programmes in order to achieve the basic objectives of the Johnson administration?

Immediately after the 1964 election activists both inside and outside of government were ready and waiting to raise the issues to the highest levels of government. On November 9 Draper announced that former Presidents Eisenhower and Truman would serve as Honorary Chairmen of Planned Parenthood. Each had agreed separately to Draper's invitation – on condition that the other also accept. Thus, both were enlisted in the cause they had once deplored. Thomas Mann, then Assistant Secretary of State and U.S. coordinator for the Alliance for Progress, became the highest U.S. official yet to address a Planned Parenthood gathering. Contrary to the official line that still emphasised government requests and avoided all reference to Planned Parenthood. Mann candidly admitted that the alliance was already working with private organisations here and in Latin America.

Shortly after the election both William H. Draper, Jr. and John D. Rockefeller 3rd, sought appointments with President Johnson. To their disappointment the President did not want to see them. After several attempts AID officials were emphatically advised not to send any more birth control advocates to the White House.

In mid-November Rockefeller was invited instead for lunch with Secretary Rusk and other officials at the State Department. Rockefeller strongly urged creation of a presidential commission to study the whole population problem. Rusk and most of the others were equally strongly opposed. They were afraid that any such commission, acting under White House sponsorship, might provoke a premature and unnecessary confrontation with the Catholic Church that could only embarrass the President. Out of the impasse came an alternative suggestion: that the President include some reference to population in the State of the Union Message. Rusk agreed to try to arrange it.

The same suggestions reached the White House through several other channels. Rockefeller also spoke to McGeorge Bundy, then Johnson's top White House adviser on foreign policy. Bundy was equally negative about the commission but agreed that the President might make same public statement about the problem. Cass Canfield was in touch with several personal friends of President and Mrs. Johnson, including Horace Busby in the White House, about the possibility of a statement. Hugh Moore ran an advertisement in Texas papers to catch the President's eye after he had been talked out of his first plan to organise a birth control march on the White House. Leona Baumgartner was in touch with Donald Hornig, President Johnson's science adviser, who was also developing a possible policy statement for Johnson.

Most important, Secretary Rusk as he had promised sent a memorandum directly to the President in late November noting that:

> .... President Kennedy made the subject of population a matter proper for urgent and responsible public consideration, and did so without having to lend explicit support to particular programmes – except research. By moving a little further along this line, it is possible, I believe, for our government to avoid becoming a target for attack, and still encourage responsible research and programme activity on many fronts, both governmental and private.

He advised against a commission but recommended that Johnson express concern in the State of the Union Message. Rusk also suggested that the President assign someone on the White House staff responsibility for population matters, that he "direct the NIH to explore" ways to respond "to the increasing demand for more knowledge about human fertility," and that he "direct other agencies to expand research, training, and health services related to the population problem." Rusk's memorandum to the President of December 1, 1964, was reminiscent of McGhee's 1961 suggestions that Rusk had rejected but even more specifically designed to activate domestic agencies.

The various imputs converged on the desk of Richard Goodwin, Johnson's speech writer. The outcome was a single sentence in the State of the Union Message, delivered January 4, 1965:

> I will seek new ways to use our knowledge to help deal with the explosion in world population and the growing scarcity in world resources.

Only 25 words out of several thousand, yet in those words President Johnson gave greater encouragement to the birth control movement than any of his predecessors had done. Although reflecting the traditional concept of overpopulation and static resources rather than the newer formulation of economic growth and development, the President's statement set a new and deliberate priority upon the issue. The sentence was an open invitation to federal agencies to move forward more freely. It was undoubtedly the most-quoted sentence in the message.

Despite Johnson's desire to remain somewhat aloof from the birth control activists and to spring his own surprises upon them, he fully accepted the economic and health arguments for birth control and questioned only how fast and how far he could move without provoking resistance, either from Catholics or later from black militants. He did not want to alarm the pope, just to prod him gently and steadily in the direction of change. He also wanted to be sure that everything was checked out first with the Catholic Church. "You can do a lot if you observe the amenities," he would insist.

During 1965 President Johnson volunteered four specific references to the population problem. They represented a "calculated escalation" designed partly to test the public reaction but increasingly to encourage federal government officials to act. At the twentieth-anniversary celebration of the United Nations in San Francisco (June 25, 1965), Johnson urged:

> Let us in all our lands – including this land – face forthrightly the mutiplying problems of our multiplying populations and seek the answers to this most profound challenge to the future of all the world. Let us act on the fact that less than five dollars invested in population control is worth a hundred dollars invested in economic growth.

When John Gardner was being sworn in as Secretary of Health, Education and Welfare, Johnson declared:

> This Administration is seeking new ideas and it is certainly not going to discourage any new solutions to the problems of population growth and distribution.

Upon the opening of the Second World Population Conference in Belgrade, August 30, 1965, President Johnson sent a special message to United Nations Secretary-General U

Thant, which Ben Duffy wrote and routed through the State Department in record time:

> . . . it is my fervent hope that your great assemblage of population experts will contribute significantly to the knowledge necessary to solve this transcendent problem. Second only to the search for peace, it is humanity's greatest challenge.

Of these four statements – which were widely acclaimed and circulated by the population activists – only the San Francisco comment aroused any criticism. The purely economic formulation that assigned a quantitative value to population control 20 times higher than to other economic development programmes annoyed Latin Americans, who suspected that Johnson only wanted to reduce foreign aid; it annoyed some health professionals who saw their own values ignored; it annoyed many Catholics, like Ralph Dungan, then Ambassador to Chile, who feared that what communists called the "Johnson genocide" approach to economic development would put economic efficiency above common humanity; and it annoyed economists of different theoretical schools who doubted that any precise formulations of economic benefit could be derived entirely from measures of demographic change. The reactions were an example of the pitfalls that lurked along any but the broadest, most unspecific pathways of population policy.

Johnson's first population statements were directed toward the foreign problem. But within the United States birth control was becoming increasingly relevant to domestic goals. Willard Wirtz, Secretary of Labour, and Stewart Udali, Secretary of the Interior, whose department provided health care to impoverished American Indians and the Pacific territorial islands, were the first cabinet members to endorse birth control in trial balloon statements preceding Johnson's comment. They saw it as a domestic economic benefit.

At the heart of Johnson's Great Society programme was the war on poverty, formally initiated by Congress in 1964 and directed by Sargent Shriver, President Kennedy's brother-in-law. Just as during the Kennedy administration a stronger government commitment to the strategy of economic development overseas inevitably focussed more attention on the population factor, so the commitment of the Johnson administration to a U.S. war on poverty focused attention on the big families and the lack of adequate birth control facilities characteristic of the American poor. Television scenes of large impoverished families became in effect the best advertisement for Planned Parenthood. Shriver agreed that a "local option" policy would permit communities to support birth control if they wished. The first birth control project in Corpus Christi, Texas, was actually underway before Johnson's State of the Union Message.

By late 1965 more than a dozen projects – developed largely by Planned Parenthood affiliates – were under way in which the Office of Economic Opportunity was financing medical personnel, clinics, and even contraceptive supplies for indigent women. Although Shriver and particularly his wife Eunice Kennedy Shriver insisted on restrictions against public propaganda, against sterilisations, against unmarried women, and even on dollar limits on contraceptives – all of which were strongly opposed by Planned Parenthood and some officials in HEW – his programme was in fact publicly subsidising birth control services at a time when other agencies were still talking about research and information. A policy that Kennedy might not have relished made genuine good sense to Congress and to President Johnson. In fact, Johnson once commented to a group of visitors at the White House, "Why should a woman with money be able to control her family size while a poor woman has got nowhere to go? We're going to quite that." As far as foreign aid was concerned Johnson was equally down to earth – if there were not enough doctors to provide family services in a country like India, the sensible approach for the United States was to help them out by sending jeeps.

Johnson's wholehearted support for family planning services to underdeveloped nations overseas and to poor families at home pushed the research strategy of the early

1960s into the background. Planned Parenthood had at first greeted the State of the Union Message with a plea for a new $100 million research effort, but attention quickly shifted toward federal support of service programmes. A significant goal-directed research programme at the National Institutes of Health was still opposed by Dr. Shannon, the NIH Director, and by Congressman Fogarty (D.-R.I.), a Catholic, who was Chairman of the Labour-HEW Appropriations Subcommittee and NIH's most generous advocate.

Other benefits of birth control were highlighted in the spring of 1965 by several major developments that had been long in the making. In May, the National Academy of Sciences issued a second report on *The Growth of U.S. Population* that called family planning "a basic human right". Even more significant, in June 1965 the Supreme Court finally ruled on an issue Planned Parenthood had been litigating for nearly 10 years. By a 7 to 2 vote the Court overturned the "uncommonly silly" Connecticut law that prohibited the use of contraceptives and proclaimed a new marital "right to privacy".

The timing of President Johnson's 1965 statements also coincided with a quantum jump in birth control technology – from condoms, diaphragms and douches to the pill and intrauterine device (IUD). Even the *Saturday Evening Post*, the voice of small-town America, approvingly called these two new methods "implements of . . . one of the most dramatic socio-medical revolutions the world has ever known." Certainly until medical science had devised means of fertility control that could work in the city slums and the illiterate rural areas of the underdeveloped world no large-scale government programme was possible. By 1965 the pill was proving itself a remarkably popular and effective method in the United States, regularly used by about 4 million women. Also by 1965 intrauterine devices had been widely tested overseas. Following the successful second International Conference on Intra-Uterine Contraception, sponsored by the Population Council in October 1964, IUDs were just about to be incorporated in the new nationwide programmes of

Taiwan, Korea, Hong Kong, Singapore, India and Pakistan. President Johnson's political endorsement of birth control came just as medical and popular endorsement of the new techniques opened the way for the very programmes that could use substantial government support. To put it another way, the research of U.S. scientists had made technically feasible what President Johnson in 1965 declared to be both politically feasible and nationally important.

AID MOVES – SLOWLY

what was the effect in AID of a presidential commitment obviously intended for the foreign aid field? How much difference did four presidential statements make in 1965 for a policy that was ambiguously articulated and a programme that was just beginning to move?

In retrospect the President's words seem to have made a tremendous difference. Virtually all official AID accounts of population programmes from 1965 through 1968 cite Johnson's statement as the beginning of the AID population programme. Earlier expenditures were not even recorded. The State of the Union Message was followed two months later by a new AID airgram announcing that technical assistance (although not contraceptives) would be available for family planning and, by the first funding, just over $2 million, for population. After January 1965 AID officials began making public speeches in the United States about AID support for population.

But actually there is considerable evidence that within AID the President's statement did not turn night into day or alter policy radically at all. In fact, all of the actions taken in the next six months had been decided upon in principle in December 1964 and were not substantially changed as a result of Johnson's initiative. The reconstructed accounts, the repetition of Johnson's statements, the protection afforded by the President's support eventually clouded the fact that AID policy was in the short run much less influenced by the President's words than by its own internal momentum – and its own internal constraints.

Informal requests for help had by late 1964 come to AID from the governments of India, Pakistan, South Korea, Turkey and the United Arab Republic. Further guidelines were due to be sent to the field. In December 1964 two executive staff meetings were held on population policy. The immediate need, Leona Baumgartner felt, was to persuade AID economists to look beyond five-year projections, to recognise the new birth control technology, and to overcome their repugnance toward some of the publicity tactics of the birth control activists. A memorandum prepared by Bruce Jessup with help from Dr. Leslie Corsa of the University of Michigan argued for U.S. government support of research, training, and technical assistance, including grants to expand maternal and child health services, loans for jeeps and other transport for family planning workers, a release of local currencies held by the United States, and more attention to demographic factors throughout the economic planning process. Most convincing to Assistant Administrator Hollis Chenery at the December meeting and to other critical AID economists, who tended to look on population as an independent variable not subject to deliberate alteration, was a very simple graph based on Pakistani statistics that showed how per capita income would be affected by 1970 both with and without a comprehensive family planning programme.

At the AID executive staff meeting held on December 1, 1964, a definite decision was made to go beyond the information policy defined by Gardner and the research policy authorised in the 1963 Fulbright amendment:

> It is proposed that the full complement of assistance tools available to AID be brought to bear on the population problem. This would involve: . . . provision of commodity inputs (with the exception of contraceptives); . . . authorising releases of counterpart and PL-480 Loans and Grants . . . provision of technical assistance . . . it is clear that private resources in the U.S. cannot alone cope with the demand . . . . We therefore propose to provide on request, technical assistance for less developed country

family planning programmes. To the extent possible, such assistance will be given in the context of maternal and child health projects.

That decision, proceeding to Rusk in draft form for approval, then back to Baumgartner's office and the programme office for drafting, led directly to the airgram that subsequent history attributed to President Johnson's intervention. The first draft of the airgram, by Philip Lee, was written before Johnson spoke (December 29, 1964); the next draft, by Robert Smith in the programme office, included the President's sentence in the third paragraph (January 1, 1965). During most of January the airgram was cleared through all the AID bureaus. Characteristically, Berman wanted to go faster to make grants to Planned Parenthood openly; the Near East-South Asia Bureau with the biggest populations as well as the biggest government programmes was most negative, questioning the need for either special population officers or additional resources. The AID information officer complained that there was not much specific news in the message, but David Bell wanted to keep the airgram deliberately low-key. Various Catholic advisers quietly reviewed and approved it.

Horace Busby in the White House complained that the AID draft included too much "strained review of U.S. policy positions" which contributed "nothing except a false and unneeded image of continuity." As with Richard Gardner's United Nations speech in 1961 the first internal formulations sought to play down the extent of the policy shift. Only later was the policy significance upgraded and even exaggerated. It was Busby who put President Johnson's statement first. AID officials agreed with some of Busby's editing that made the first page "more dramatic" but they insisted on including their review of policy positions. Except for the opening statement by President Johnson the final text reflected prior AID policy decided upon and drafted within AID.

Therefore, despite President Johnson's support and White House clearance, AIDTO Circular-Airgram 280 sounded cautious and negative. Although the message actually authorised AID missions to support a broader range of

activities than before, it conveyed less sense of priority and urgency than Edgar Berman's Latin American directive of May 1964. Basically, the guidelines asked that each AID mission assign one officer to become familiar with population dynamics and related programmes (not a high official, as in the 1964 Latin American message); and indicated that:

> ... Requests for technical assistance will be considered as in any other field, on a case by case basis. We are prepared to . . . consider requests for commodity assistance . . . such as vehicles and education equipment . . . also . . . requests to assist in local currency financing.

But for each positive statement there seemed to be at least two negatives or qualifications, for example,

> Requests for assistance in this field, as in others, will continue to be considered only if made or approved by appropriate host government authorities. Such assistance would, in any case, be merely additive to the host country's own efforts and assistance from other sources . . . .
>
> AID will not consider requests for contraceptive devices or equipment for manufacture of contraceptives. Experience has made it clear that the cost of these latter items is not a stumbling block in countries that are developing effective programmes.
>
> . . . Finally, AID does not advocate any particular method of family regulation . . . . Freedom of choice should be available.

Nowhere did the airgram identify population as a "priority programme." Nowhere did it suggest, as the 1964 Latin American message did, that the time had come "to convert the broad principles of AID policy into meaningful programmes."

Clearly, Johnson's – and Rusk's – recognition that the time was politically right was not fully shared in AID. David Bell told his staff he would rather be criticised for going too slowly than for going too fast. He was most insistent that the

programme be an inconspicuous, relatively minor part of AID's activity. Bell's decision to proceed was minimal; it was not, like President Johnson's, an attempt to influence or lead others; it was rather what Bell himself called "catching up with the L.A. programme." It reflected not only Bell's reluctance to jeopardise any of the rest of the AID programme but also his continuing doubt that birth control could be an effective part of economic development or that the United States could promote it without a political backlash from developing countries.

Following the airgram, by the end of fiscal 1965 some 15 different grants totalling $ 2,134,000 (of which $1,197,000 was in the Latin American Bureau) were made and publicly acknowledged, a funding level that had been agreed upon in December before the President's statement. The largest went to the Universities of California (Berkeley), Notre Dame, Johns Hopkins and North Carolina to provide a variety of long-term professional training and consultative services. Some of these extended programmes that the Population Council and the Ford Foundation had originally supported. Agreements that had been made in the past with government agencies like the Census Bureau and National Center for Health Statistics were now more explicitly oriented toward the problems of population change.

The newest elements of the programme in 1965 were, on the Latin American side, support for private organisations such as the Latin American Center for Studies of Population and Family (CELAP) headed by a controversial Jesuit priest in Chile; the Colombian Institute for Social Development (ICODES) to prepare audio-visual materials; the International Planned Parenthood Federation (Western Hemisphere Region) for family planning conferences and education; the American Assembly of Columbia University for a population conference of Latin America leaders in Cali, Colombia; and the Population Council for various research and analysis projects. From Baumgartner's office there were innovations in the support of a Children's Bureau (HEW) training programme for foreign midwives and of a Johns Hopkins orientation course for AID personnel.

What difference did President Johnson's statement really make if the basic policy shift had been decided upon in December and the specific programme and budgetary actions were already under way?

First, the President had changed the whole atmosphere and environment in which the issue would be handled. Originally a daring step quietly taken by a nervous agency, support for population was after January a legitimate government policy supported by the President.

Second, although the language of the airgram and the grants did not fully reflect this new atmosphere of approval, the very fact that the airgram was sent was significant. Many plans, projections and airgrams had been prepared by the Population branch in the past and would be prepared for several years to come without necessarily being dispatched or implemented. Had President Johnson not spoken, the December decisions would probably not have become the March-June actions. Had plans not already been under way for a presidential statement, the December decisions might not have been made.

The effect of the President's interest was, moreover, cumulative. When the first reference was followed by three more statements in 1965, when the Gruening hearings both publicised and pushed the President ahead, all the AID initiatives were reinforced. The momentum was forward. Although in the next few years many opportunities in AID were lost through inertia or non-action, few were deliberately vetoed as they had been before.

Certainly for the agency as a whole the President's support was a powerful moral stimulus. In late 1964 Leona Baumgartner had concluded that "what we need is less talk and more action." After President Johnson's statement in January 1965, just as after President Kennedy's statement in April 1963, it was easier for AID both to talk and to act. In many cases talk began to lead more directly toward action. The gist of the March 3 airgram, for instance, was made immediately available to the public in a question-and-answer format. Dr. Lee repeated the language in a March speech at

Michigan State University. Each of the regional bureaus in Washington followed the Latin American example by assigning someone to handle population. The Far East and the Near East-South Asia Bureaus dispatched additional messages of encouragement to their overseas mission. In Taiwan and Korea where local currency had already been used to support family planning, this practice was at last publicly acknowledged and encouraged by Washington.

OBSTACLES WITHIN AID

President Johnson affirmed in terms that no federal official could dispute that the population problem was relevant to government policies and that government programmes to deal with it were politically feasible. But, as many Presidents have noted, even the President's orders do not always get carried out. It was quite obvious in 1965, for example, that very few AID officials really believed, as Johnson had said, that "less than five dollars invested in population control is worth a hundred dollars invested in economic growth."

From the top of the agency right down to the lowest levels the priority of the issue was evaluated and the possibilities for action were weighed by existing institutional and personal standards rather than by the President's words. Thus, David Bell told the House Foreign Affairs Committee,

> The population field, as distinct from the food field, is not a field in which AID has any major activities. While I expect our activities will gradually grow, I foresee no big change in the immediate future.

Despite President Johnson's interest in jeeps for India, most of the vehicles were negotiated as part of a complex AID loan agreement and not actually available until mid-1969.

Symbolic of the agency's "Yes-I-will; no-I-won't" attitude toward birth control was the refusal to provide any kind of funding for contraceptives. It was the first and most obvious target for activist criticism. "Pretty timid," was the verdict of the *New York Times*. "This plan to provide propaganda in ways without supplying the means is an obvious attempt to appease foreign and domestic critics of birth control." In part, of course, this was true. Catholic opposition centered around contraceptives, since these were the "artificial methods" specifically condemned by Rome. Bell called contraceptives "the reddest red flag of all". Liberal Catholic support for the March airgram depended, Dr. Duffy emphasised, on four points: no coercion, freedom of choice, only responding to requests and no contraceptives. The principle of family planning was permissible, but the contraceptives were not.

To some extent AID's ban on contraceptives – particularly after 1965 – reflected still another ambiguity in AID policy. How was it logically possible to affirm in one sentence that "freedom of choice" as to method "should be available" and in almost the next sentence that "the cost of contraceptives is not a stumbling block?" These statements were actually made in the year 1965 when nearly 5 million U.S. women were regularly taking oral contraceptives at a monthly cost of $1 to $ 2 and when any casual newspaper reader knew that "the pill" was an important element in the agonising reappraisal by the Catholic Church.

These apparent contradictions were reconciled by the assumption most of the population professionals made in 1965 regardless of U.S. or Puerto Rican experience, that the pill at any price was unsuitable for the developing countries. If, as they believed, the little plastic IUD, which could be produced cheaply anywhere, was the new solution to the world's population problem, then it was true that the cost of contraceptives was not an important stumbling block to an effective national programme.

The controversy of pill versus IUD, as it developed in the AID programme, can be seen in some ways as a continuation of the old activist-scientist rivalries. The activists, usually associated with the various Planned Parenthood associations, had to supply whatever methods their patients demanded or else close their clinics. Increasingly Planned Parenthood clinics in the U.S. and overseas relied on the pill because that was what the women seemed to prefer.

The professionals, however, following the public health strategy for birth control developed in the 1940s and 1950s, looked at the experience of successful public health programmes like smallpox eradication and malaria control and concluded that a one-time, no-variation method not requiring daily cooperation of the patient and which could be administered on an assembly-line basis by an extended public health bureaucracy would be best. The IUD seemed to fit that pattern. Just as many physicians of the 1920s and 1930s found it difficult to embrace a medical solution to a non-pathological problem, so many public health administrators and statisticians of the 1960s found it difficult to support the concept of a genuine patient's choice of contraceptive method. The medical norm that the doctor knows best was translated in government policy terms into the concept that for the developing countries the programme administrator knows which contraceptive is best.

The principle of free choice was duly repeated in AID policy statements to protect the rhythm system even though funding prohibitions made it impossible to apply the principle to any AID-assisted programmes until 1968. The final irony was that the method most readily acceptable to individual Catholics, after the rhythm method, was the oral contraceptive which, because of cost, was most effectively barred by the 1965 guidelines. For Catholics as for non-Catholics, protecting institutional doctrines was given a higher political priority than protecting the free choice of individuals. In 1965, however, these conflicts over method were barely visible below the surface of an AID policy that was still trying to define what technical assistance in population really was and how the United States could provide it.

Top AID and State Department officials were also inhibited in 1965 by the view that the United States, which had a high postwar birth rate and no government family-planning programmes of its own, should not try to impose a policy on other nations. In one sense, it was the old "coercion" and "psychological mistake" argument that Kennedy had once used, but with new stress on the notion that the U.S. government should not subsidise overseas what it was reluctant to provide for citizens at home.

There was renewed pressure upon the Department of Health, Education and Welfare after 1965 to support family planning services. The antipoverty programme continued to set the pace with family planning projects developed by Lizabeth Bamberger Schorr and then Dr. Gary London. But gradually in HEW the replacement of Secretary Celebrezze by John Gardner, the public statements of Katherine Oettinger, Director of the Children's Bureau, and early in 1966 the release of guidelines for domestic family planning programmes by Secretary Gardner helped to bring domestic and foreign aid policies into better alignment.

AID was also handicapped institutionally by its difficulties either in recruiting high-calibre medical or demographic personnel on a permanent basis or in removing less competent people from the agency. AID was widely known as a "dumping ground for the least enterprising and the least capable Public Health Service officers." Unable to develop a satisfactory relationship with the Public Health Service, which was itself involved in a permanent feud over medical programmes with the Children's Bureau, and continually susceptible to the theft of its best people by the foundations, AID was hardly in a position to provide the professional advice and consultation that it seemed to be offering instead of contraceptives. Efforts to borrow or fund experts from other U.S. government agencies worked reasonably well in a non-controversial field like census taking but did not work at all in family planning where no one wanted to be out in front.

Efforts to finance the specialised agencies of the United Nations in a technical assistance role ran aground on the reluctance of the World Health Organisation either to take the lead itself or to allow UNICEF (the UN Children's Emergency Fund) or the Food and Agriculture Organisation to enter a field of medical competence. AID was therefore compelled to turn to the private organisations including a few universities willing to undertake overseas projects, the Ford Foundation, and Population Council, and even the International Planned Parenthood Federation (which in 1965 was still not mentioned by name in any public statements) to provide the know-how that was needed for government programmes.

From an administrative point of view population work was further handicapped by its location in the agency. The Population Reference and Research Branch of the Office of Technical Cooperation and Research (TCR) possessed little leverage and a very small budget. "Action programmes" had to be funded by the geographic bureaus or country missions; in the mid-1960s, these could only be advised of persuaded, never commanded.

For the agency as a whole a complex funding pattern that required loans for all commodities, U.S. purchases and shipping wherever possible, local currency expenditures for non-foreign exchange costs, and innumerable time-consuming programme reviews that made it almost as difficult to supply commodities as it was to hire people. To these routine bureaucratic difficulties were added the extra challenges of a politically sensitive subject and a declining economic assistance appropriation.

The final impediment to action in 1965 and 1966 was personnel. At the very point when Johnson offered his presidential blessing and encouragement to the programme, most of the individuals associated with it left the agency.

Their replacements came gradually from other activities and learned slowly how to work in AID. With concern increasing over world food shortages, Dr. Baumgartner's successor was Albert Moseman, an agricultural specialist from the Rockefeller Foundation. Dr. Malcolm Merrill from the Health Department of the State of California replaced Lee and recruited Dr. Reimert Ravenholt, an epidemiologist who took Jessup's job in February 1966. George Coleman, an information specialist, replaced both Drs. Berman and Duffy in the Latin American Population Office in the spring of 1966. Just as the new men were beginning to find their way about in 1966, David Bell left AID for the Ford Foundation to be succeeded by his former deputy, William Gaud. Although many of the new people were eager to push ahead in population work, the time lag was considerable. As in 1961 and 1962 there was no clear focus of experienced leadership for AID population programmes for nearly two years.

How great a loss this was may be measured by the final recommendations that Baumgartner made on leaving the agency – recommendations that clearly called for a reordering of priorities within the agency that only continuous determined leadership could provide. In a memorandum for Bell dated August 11, 1965, she urged more attention to ambassadors and mission directors whose "personal interest and knowledge" makes more difference than the actual population problem of the country; more qualified and high-level staff in the field and in Washington more vehicles and support for medical personnel in rural, areas; more analysis of economic and social aspects; and above all "a flexible attitude . . . without endless review in Washington and the field." "Ideally," she observed, "the Missions probably ought to earmark funds for population programmes. . . . [Freedom] from many of AID's usual bureaucratic practices is important if we want to move programmes along. We now are likely to be criticised for not doing enough."

In a final comment to David Bell in November 1965 she reiterated:

> AID's ability to be useful to the LDCs [less-developed countries] in family planning operations will be directly related to the imagination, flexibility and realism with which problems are attacked. I have a real concern over handling affairs in a routine way – waiting for "a project" to be completely outlined before some immediately useful activities are undertaken, second guessing all along the line without further information, being afraid to work with Population Council, Ford, etc., having programme officers massage proposals endlessly, being maladroit in working for or handling requests, having inadequate AID staff. These are some of the worst pitfalls.

Unfortunately, she was accurate in her prediction but unsuccessful in her persuasion. All the obstacles she mentioned continued to plague the programme. To the extent that they *were* surmounted, that funds *were* earmarked, that more adequate personnel *were* assigned, and that AID *did* finally develop a more flexible programme, it was done over the objections of many of the agency and bureau chiefs. The first initiatives came from outside the agency, from the activists, and from Congress, with increasingly effective internal support from a forthright and determined programme director.

In sum, the president's words made some difference. In the short-run the difference was minimal; in the long-run it was far greater. The willingness of a chief executive at last to involve his own prestige and influence by talking about population did reinforce the population activists in AID. The President's words did help to bring the issue out from the bureaucratic bowels of a nervous and insecure agency into the open where programming could be measured against policy, where political pressures could be measured against economic benefits, and where, in continuing sequence, the level and timing of the population programme could be measured against the level and timing of comparable programmes. But until the President – or Congress – was willing to provide more than just verbal support, this impact could all too easily be diluted simply through the normal procedures, personal predispositions, and personnel changes of a complex operating organisation.

11

ECOLOGY, EQUALITY AND ETHICS

Between 1969 and 1972, while the Agency for International Development and other organisations were adjusting their operating programmes toward a new technology and bureaucracy, the public policy debate on population also took on new dimensions. Before 1969 U.S. government support of birth control was justified primarily by its economic impact and to a lesser degree by the impact on individual health. Individuals and nations both, it was thought, could accelerate their economic transition to affluence if they would also accelerate their demographic transition to lower fertility.

In 1969, however, the issues of environmental protection and women's rights burst into public attention even more abruptly than had the population explosion. Ecologists, biologists, feminists, and students demanded zero population growth, more contraceptives and abortion. For these ardent new advocates, both professional and activist, birth control was more than just an economic asset, a way to get rich faster. It was a natural and social imperative to stave off ecological disaster and guarantee equal rights to women and the younger generation. At first these ideologies had little impact on government population programmes but gradually they provided strong reinforcement for existing programmes and increased urgency for new ones.

ENVIRONMENT AND ECOLOGY

The environmental argument was hardly new. It dated back at least to the conservation movement at the turn of the century and such continued warnings as Fairfield Osborn's 1948 book *Our Plundered Planet*. For decades conservationists and scientists both had lamented diminishing resources but, like that of Malthusian economists, their doom-saying was always rebutted by new discoveries, new technology. In the later 1960s, however, such warnings took on new relevance. Increasing and well publicised pollution – in water, air, and land, by oil spills, electric power failures, traffic jams – gave the issue special urgency. Evidence came through all the senses that even though resources might be expanded the very expansion would damage other parts of the environment.

Dr. Durward Allen, a wildlife ecologist, put population and conservation together with a powerful new twist in March 1969. Addressing the National American Wildlife and Natural Resources Conference he bluntly observed that at the American standard of living the entire world could support only half a billion people. Not only was economic development on the American model impossible for the rest of the world, he warned, but also increasing environmental pollution was the price America would have to pay for its own "growth obsession". Population control was necessary, not for economic progress but for ecological survival. "The problems of human welfare," Allen insisted "are biological, behavioural and economic – in that order."

For the population movement, which was still debating the merits of family planning services versus motivation and calculating cost-benefit ratios, the advent of ecology coincided with President Nixon's message and the triumphant moon-landing. Like Johnson's comment in July 1965, the July 1969 message had a ratchet-like effect on public debate. No sooner did the President promise family planning services for all Americans and priority for population research than the policy debate moved on to more radical formulations. Even the spectacular Apollo flight, hailed in the message, instead of bolstering confidence in science portrayed instead on worldwide television a hostile and uninviting universe. The whole country could see what the pessimistic population-controllers had predicted. There were no alternatives in outer space to "our precious little planet, this blue-green cradle of life."

While the President stressed better planning and help for the indigent, the new breed of advocates began to criticise the behaviour of the affluent. Dr. Jean Mayer of Harvard took direct aim at the notion that rich countries or rich families could afford to keep on growing. Even with no population growth at all, he pointed out, the developed nations used more non-renewable resources and produced more pollution than the developing ones.

Speaking with the prestige of the scientific community the National Academy of Sciences issued a report in 1969 on *Resources and Man* in which it observed,

> Although it is true that man has repeatedly succeeded in increasing both the space he occupies and its carrying capacity, and that he will continue to do so, it is also clear that both the occupiable space and its carrying capacity have finite limits which he can approach only at great peril.

Minimising the power of science to produce new technological miracles, the scientists urged as their first policy recommendation,

> . . . that efforts to limit population increase in the nation and the world be intensified by whatever means are practicable, working toward a goal of zero rate of growth by the end of the century. . . . Ultimately this implies that the community and society as a whole, and not only the parents, must have a say about the number of children a couple may have.

The academy's report was publicised in two days of congressional hearings chaired by Henry Reuss (D. Wisc.) during which several witnesses criticised President Nixon's message for not specifically recommending a two-child family, a stabilised population and legalised abortion.

To the studies of the ecologists and biologists in the late 1960s were added the unexpectedly vociferous voices of an active younger generation. During the 1950s and 1960s Planned Parenthood and the other population organisations represented mainly an older generation. Past child bearing themselves, they looked with some suspicion at the coming youthful cohorts whose very numbers made population growth inevitable. In 1968 Hugh Moore again helped to light the new fuse and arouse the new generation by subsidising nationwide distribution of Paul Ehrlich's book *The Population Bomb*, which was an immediate success on college campuses. Moore also persuaded one of his protégé organisations, the Association for Voluntary Sterilisation, to cooperate with the National Conference on Conservation in October 1969 for what was billed as the first joint meeting of conservation and birth control groups. At the session the AVS became the first of the population groups to adopt a resolution favouring the two-child family. Also at that session Paul Ehrlich, a professor of biology at Stanford University, who had had a vasectomy himself, was a featured speaker. Shorty thereafter he became President of a small organisation founded by a Connecticut lawyer with the provocative title "Zero Population Growth".

Under Ehrlich's charismatic leadership Zero Population Growth (ZPG) grew from a technical demographic term to a popular slogan to a national organisation that by the spring of 1970 rated a cover story in *Life*. Earth Day, April 22, 1970, marked a new highwater mark of student and teenage concern over the deteriorating environment. It was followed by a National Congress on Optimum Population and Environment (COPE) in Chicago in June 1970 that tried with mixed success to explore the broad policy issues that might unite birth controllers and conservationists, youths, blacks and women. Compared with controversial ideas like stopping economic growth, support for voluntary birth control was taken almost for granted. Even militant black pronatalists, who often equated birth control with genocide, refocussed their protests against the new possibility that environmental protection for the future might jeopardise their opportunities for the present.

The reaction of the professionals in the population field, to the environmental approach was at first ambivalent. Paul Ehrlich's *Population Bomb*, like Hugh Moore's bomb 20 years earlier, was considered too polemical, not sufficiently objective. Ehrlich was described somewhat sarcastically in a Planned Parenthood publication as the "new high priest of ecocatastrophe". The pollution problem, like the earlier food problem, had complex causes of which population growth was not the major one, family planners argued. Crisis rhetoric was dangerous because it could weaken the commitment to long-term programmes. As Frank Notestein put it at the 1970 session of the Population Association of America, "In political terms, relating pollution to population may have done harm to a serious attack on both pollution and on population growth."

The demographers answer to ZPG, a term that suddenly dropped out of technical use, was NRR – Net Reproduction Rates. A net reproduction rate of one meant that each mother would have one daughter and thus each generation would exactly replace itself. A 1968 analysis by Tomas Frejka of the Population Council, however, demonstrated that even if a net reproduction rate of one were established in the United States immediately, a zero rate of natural growth, with births equalling deaths, would not be achieved for 70 years, after an overall population increase of nearly 40 per cent.

The intricacies of net reproduction rates, however, had far less public impact than did ZPG, which by January 1971 had nearly 30,000 members, increasing by 1,000 each month. Far from discouraging the younger generation, the call to ZPG on a polluted planet seemed entirely congenial to the baby-boom generation that had felt the pressures of overpopulation since it first entered kindergarten. Whether from conviction, or economic pressures, or social change, the younger generation already seemed to appreciate the lessons of demography better than did its parents. U.S. birth rates, which in the late 1960s had risen much less than demographers predicted, dropped in 1971 to 17.3, the lowest level since 1820, even as the number of potential parents rose. The Washington Center for Metropolitan Study in a well-publicised report called the phenomenon a "baby bust" instead of a "baby boom". Young people were staying single longer, having children later or not at all.

Even the older generation was demonstrating new concern about population growth in the United States as well as overseas. In the fall of 1965 and 1967, 54 per cent of the population considered U.S. population growth a serious problem. By 1971, 65 per cent considered it serious. Despite rebuttals by some experts, 57 per cent agreed in 1971 that population growth was "causing the country to use up its natural resources too fast." It was agreed by 48 per cent that "population growth is the main reason for air and water pollution." That "population growth is producing a lot of social unrest and dissatisfaction" was agreed to by 64 per cent. Not surprisingly, therefore, 56 per cent of those polled in the spring of 1971 thought that the government should "try to slow down population growth in the United States." Interest, if not yet support, was clearly developing for a broad range of population and environmental measures that might challenge not only motherhood but also the economic, political and sexual *status quo* in America.

ETHICS, EQUALITY AND ABORTION

The economic justification for birth control emphasised enlightened self-interest as the stimulus that would in time bring families and nations to lower fertility. The ecological justification almost demanded individual birth control for the good of society. Garrett Hardin in a provocative article entitled "The Tragedy of the Commons" put the case for government control of reproduction on the common need to protect a limited environment from exploitation by a few. To the older generation – the activists and the professionals, the doctors and demographers – as to most Americans – such arguments remained impractical, even repugnant. Individual rights were more important than social restructing. Economic growth to benefit all was a more attractive goal than the redistribution of finite resources. Among the general public, even though in 1971 57 per cent thought people should "limit the size of their families even though they can afford a larger number of children," nevertheless 68 per cent opposed even the largely symbolic pressure of antinatalist tax laws.

Within the population field the logic that rebutted, at least temporarily, the ethics of coercion was developed in large part by Charles Westoff, professor of sociology at Princeton, from the data of National Fertility Surveys and used enthusiastically by family planning activists to support ongoing programmes. Coercion was not needed, Westoff argued, because surveys showed that some 20 per cent of American births were unwanted and therefore could be prevented by purely voluntary means such as better contraceptives and better clinics. Even talking about compulsory birth control is "unnecessary and dangerous," Harriet Pilpel, counsel to Planned Parenthood, argued when most states still placed innumerable and unnecessary restrictions on voluntary family planning.

Easier access to better birth control methods, including repeal of outmoded restrictions, offered a logical and seemingly acceptable alternative to coercion. That tactic coincided with the developing strategies of another movement. Women's liberationists also demanded greater freedom and an end to all measures that forced women into second-class status. In the field of reproduction, a woman's right to choose included not only pills and IUDs but also abortion – legal, safe and inexpensive. The "right of marital privacy" proclaimed in the 1965 Supreme Court decision on birth control was translated by a militant feminist movement and sympathetic physicians into the right of women to control their own bodies, the right to avoid "compulsory pregnancy" by legal, medically protected abortion. The international publicity in 1969 and 1970 over the safety of oral contraceptives added fuel to feminist fires. Why, the women wanted to know, should they be guinea pigs for unsafe drugs? Why not more research for better male contraceptives?

On the issue of abortion, the environmentalists, the younger generation, the militant women, the family planners, and most of the doctors and demographers could agree. To fulfil Margaret Sanger's demand that women control their own bodies, to reduce the pressures of rapid population growth, to rebut arguments for coercion by ensuring that no unwanted babies be brought into the world, to increase the safety margin of other contraceptives by providing a backstop when they failed, and above all, to lower the mortality and distress from continuing illegal abortions that took place in any case – the logical solution was legal abortion. Abortion as a surgical procedure had already become technically feasible and safer than childbirth decades earlier. In the late 1960s the new technique of vaccum aspiration made abortion possible on an outpatient basis, as a clinical service not very different from inserting an IUD.

While the Catholic Church was absorbed, first waiting for the pope's decision on contraception in *Humanae Vitae* and, after July 1968, arguing about it, the women, the doctors, and the lawyers began to work on abortion laws. With strong professional legal reassurance through the model liberalised abortion law drafted by the American Law Institute, 4 state legislatures amended existing statutes in 1966 and 1967 (Mississippi, California, Colorado and North Carolina). By mid-1971, 17 states had removed legal restrictions to some degree, 3 by judicial interpretation of existing statutes. Even more significant, in 1970 New York, Alaska and Hawaii enacted bolder laws allowing abortion on request without a health justification. In April 1970 Senator Packwood introduced federal legislation to make abortion available on request regardless of state law. In abortion policy the transition from stress on professional, medical, or legal judgment to greater individual choice seemed to have taken barely five years.

Suddenly Catholic leaders perceived that their internal debate over a cause already lost had given the abortion advocates a powerful head start. Within the Catholic Church abortion in 1969 occupied approximately the same place as birth control in 1959. Militants organised Right to life groups which, beginning in 1970, effectively blocked further liberalisation of the Maryland law and threatened new restrictions in New York. The issue that abortion advocates defined as a woman's right to privacy and a doctor's right to professional judgment, the Catholic opposition defined as murder. Opponents spoke of abortion "on demand," instead of "by request". As a decade earlier in the birth control struggle, political leaders caught between militant proabortionists and organised religious opposition faced an unhappy choice. When, in 1971 the Defence Department relaxed restrictions on abortion in military installations the White House was deluged with letters of protest. President Nixon responded that laws regulating abortion were a state matter not to be overruled by the Defence Department. But he went still further to give his own personal comment. Abortion was "an unacceptable form of population control," he said. "Unrestricted abortion policies, or abortion on demand, I cannot square with my personal belief in the sanctity of human life – including the life of the yet unborn." Again in May 1972 when Right to Life groups were trying to repeal New York's liberal abortion law the President wrote directly to Cardinal Cooke applauding as "truly a noble endeavour . . . your decision to act in the public forum as defenders of the right to life of the unborn."

Unlike President Eisenhower who had suppressed his personal views to avoid a religious confrontation, President Nixon intervened directly to make his personal views known even on a question of state jurisdiction. Although the New York State Assembly and Senate passed the repeal bill, Governor Nelson Rockefeller vetoed it – as he had earlier pledged to do – with a strong statement.

> I can see no justification now for . . . condemning hundreds of thousands of women to the dark ages once again. . . . Every woman has the right to make her own choice. . . .
>
> I do not believe it right for one group to impose its vision of morality on an entire society. Neither is it just or practical for the state to attempt to dictate the innermost personal beliefs and conduct of its citizens.

But it was clear that Catholic opposition, stressing the rights of the unborn, would not only contest any further liberalisation of abortion laws but also would seek whenever possible to reinstate restrictive laws or conditions.

Actually, public support for unrestricted abortion was nowhere near the level of public support for birth control even a decade earlier. Throughout the 1960s, as Judith Blake has documented, a majority of men and women approved of abortion only for health reasons, that is, only where the mother's health might be jeopardised or where the child might be deformed. Throughout the 1960s a majority of men and women disapproved of abortion for economic or social reasons, that is, where the family could not afford or simply did not wish to have another child. Despite the active role of women's liberation groups, among the public at large, males, the well-educated, and non-Catholics were most favourable to abortion reform.

But between 1969 and 1971 a substantial change took place both in the formulation of the issue and in the public and political response. While advocates, especially female, stressed freedom of choice and legislators struggled with the various alternatives such as length of pregnancy, place for termination, and residency, the moral question was supplanted by a jurisdictional one. As reflected precisely in public opinion polls, the issue in the 1969 was, "Would you favour, approve or legalise abortion under various circumstances?" To that formulation, a majority throughout the 1960s answered "No. Not unless the mother's life or health are endangered." The issue in 1971 and 1972 was, "Do you think that the decision to have an abortion in the early months of pregnancy should be made solely by the couple – or the woman – and her doctor?" To that version, in May 1971, 50 per cent of the total population and 39 per cent of the Catholic population said "Yes". In January 1972, 57 per cent of the total population and 54 per cent of the Catholic population said "Yes". In other words, at the policy level abortion could be permitted – even by those who did not approve of it – as a lesser evil than government interference in private behaviour. By redirecting attention from the pros and cons of abortion itself to the level at which the decision should and in fact would be made, advocates of abortion hoped ultimately to win the substance of their argument.

Thus, political support for abortion, which five years earlier seemed impossible, developed not only as a tactic in an economic or even a health strategy but also as part of a struggle for equal rights. As Catholic opposition became more vocal, abortion advocates sought to substitute the jurisdictional question of "who should decide" for the moral question of approval or disapproval. In an atmosphere of greater concern over population and environment, abortion seemed to be gaining both relevance and urgency through the agitation of women's liberationists and the arguments of the professionals – on health, safety and pragmatic grounds. Publicised more by opponents than by advocates, abortion reform in the 1970s, like birth control in 1960, was becoming an issue of public policy that could not easily be ignored or controlled by political leaders, whatever their views.

THE COMMISSION ON POPULATION GROWTH AND THE AMERICAN FUTURE

Ecology, equality, ethics and abortion had not yet burst into public attention in the spring of 1969 when President Nixon and his advisers decided that family planning and population growth were sufficiently important to warrant study by a Population Commission but not sufficiently controversial to embarrass the White House. Legislation to establish a national, not merely a presidential, commission was drafted through Moynihan's office and introduced without hesitation by Republican and Democratic members of the appropriate committees. Promptly approved in the Senate, the measure was amended in committee in the House of Representatives at the suggestion of Rodney Shaw, an enterprising Methodist minister. Besides population trends and government programmes, Congress directed the commission to inquire into:

The impact of population growth on the environmental pollution, and on the depletion of natural resources; and

The various means appropriate to the ethical values and principles of this society by which our nation can achieve a population level suited for its environmental national resources and other needs.

The House of Representatives delayed action, partly because of a personal rivalry between retiring Speaker John McCormack and Morris Udall, a population advocate, and partly because of the Speaker's traditional Boston Catholic dislike for the whole issue. But in March 1970, eight months after the president's message, the bill became law. John D. Rockefeller 3rd was named by President Nixon as Chairman and by June 1970 the 24-member body was ready to start work.

The Rockefeller Population Commission, compared to the Draper Committee of 1959, was much more professional and academic in its membership, much more representative of the whole country, including men and women, young and old, public figures and private citizens. The population professionals included Bernard Berelson, President of the Population Council; Joseph D. Beasley, M.D., founder of the Louisiana family planning programme and Chairman of Planned Parenthood; Otis Dudley Duncan, Professor of Sociology at the University of Michigan and a noted demographer; Margaret Bright, Professor of Behavioural sciences at the Johns Hopkins University; and David Bell, Executive Vice-President of the Ford Foundation. Two economists, D. Gale Johnson and John R. Meyer, Professors of Economics at Chicago and Yale Universities, respectively, were included, as were a businessman R.V. Hansberger, Chairman and President of the Boise Cascade Corporation, and a banker, George D. Woods, director and consultant, the First Boston Corporation (and former President of the World Bank). Howard D. Samuel, Vice-President of the Amalgamated Clothing Workers of America, represented labour. Dr. Paul B. Cornely, M.D., former President of the

American Public Health Association and Professor at Howard University; Lawrence Davis, an Arkansas college President; and Arnita Young Boswell, a University of Chicago professor, represented blacks. Christian N. Ramsay, Jr., M.D., a young physician, James Rummonds, a law student, and Stephen Salyer, an undergraduate, were the youngest members. Marilyn Brant Chandler and Joan F. Flint were housewives, although exceptionally able, active, and well-connected ones; Grace Olivarez was a Mexican-American lawyer.

Six members of Congress served on the commission but the four remaining at the end were Senators Robert Packwood (R.-Ore.), Alan Cranston (D.-Cal.) and Congressman John Erlenborn (R.-Ill.) and James Scheuer (D.-N.Y.). Although three members were Catholic there was, deliberately, no specific representation of any religious denomination. Nor were there any biologists or ecologists. A major concern of the White House was to avoid people who might take uncompromising positions on any issue. The most conspicuous activists were the only members not chosen by the White House – Senators Tydings (later replaced by Cranston) and Packwood and Congressman Scheuer (Who replaced Blatnik). Although their influence within the commission was minimal, except for the more conscrvative Congressman Erlenborn, one or another of the congressional members had in fact proposed or supported all the major or controversial recommendations – although in different, less acceptable form – before they were reviewed, argued, modified, accepted, and to a further degree legitimised by the commission.

The commission started slowly, reviewing the whole field, commissioning outside research, avoiding publicity. However, the Chairman and administration spokesmen emphasised that the commission studies were not intended to delay other actions. The Tydings-Scheuer-Bush Family Planning Services and Population Research bill, introduced in May 1969, passed the Senate in June 1970. At Senate hearings in December 1969 chaired by Senator Thomas Eagleton (D.-Mo.) the only serious opposition came from the Department of Health, Education and Welfare which at the last minute proposed a different bill with less money that would keep services and research separate.

In the House of Representatives, however, by the summer of 1970 hostile Catholic witnesses were attacking the bill as a back door route to federally subsidised abortion. Sympathetic Catholic spokesmen had to reassure Speaker McCormack that no such thing was intended. The final version, a three-year bill authorising $ 382 million for services and research, passed the House of Representatives by a vote of 298 to 32. It included the sentence, "None of the funds appropriated under this title shall be used in programmes where abortion is a method of family planning." Nevertheless it was a major victory for Planned Parenthood. Family planning was no longer controversial even if members of Congress, caught between birth control and the right to life, wanted as little as possible to do with abortion. Dr. Louis Hellman, who had helped to precipitate the 1959 birth control confrontation in New York City, became the new Deputy Assistant Secretary for family planning and population.

Three months after passage of the first comprehensive bill providing separate federal support for family planning and population research, the Population Commission issued its interim report. Widely acclaimed for translating demographic expertise into language clear to the general public, the report moved a step beyond family planning to ask, "What kind of national population policy is desirable now for the long-run?" The single most salient point was made by a graph that showed how much faster U.S. population would grow if the three-child family – not the two-child family – remained the norm. Within 100 years, a difference of one child per family would mean the difference between 950 million or 350 million Americans.

For six months following the interim report the commission heard testimony around the country. Some members were impatient at the first year's pace. Senator Cranston introduced a sense of Congress resolution with eventually some 50 co-sponsors to declare zero population growth as a national goal. After a series of hearings and finally in December 1971 after winning the endorsement of the commission the resolution was postponed when a flood of Catholic telegrams labelled it proabortion. It was a warning that the Catholic opposition was alert and on the offensive.

From December 1971 to March 1972 in a new environment of plummeting U.S. birthrates and mounting controversy over the role of women, youth and abortion, the commission tackled the final recommendations and language of the report. The commission was divided into three major viewpoints:

1. The unwanted child view, put forth most cogently by Charles Westoff the executive director, Berelson, and Beasley, that emphasised the need to help individuals control reproduction through better birth control methods and services.
2. The social justice view, urged by Cornely, Olivarez and Boswell, that gave first priority to equalising the rights of women and racial minorities and minimised the importance of other population factors, and
3. The crisis or ecological view, presented strongly by Rummonds, Duncan and Packwood, that called for basic changes in economic and other value systems to restore a sharply deteriorating environment.

All three positions were reflected in various parts of the report. Of the 22 major recommendations, 9 dealt with improved education, information, services and techniques for individual fertility control, reflecting primarily the voluntarist, wanted-child approach; 5 dealt with population distribution and statistics calling for more federal, state, and local planning, better data, and an end to discrimination in housing; 4 sought higher status or better care for women, children, and racial minorities; 2 proposed limits and studies on immigration; and 1 recommended governmental changes including a Department of Community Development, a National Institute of Population Sciences within NIH, and an Office of Population Growth and Distribution in the White

House to consider the further need for national population policies.

Most of the commission members were reluctant to endorse any overall population policy that would be inconsistent with the general stress on avoiding coercion and enlarging individual freedoms. The phrase "zero population growth" was avoided; answers were given in "qualitative not quantitative terms". Nevertheless, common sense concern over population growth rather than an ironclad logical proof of the link between individual choice and social goals dictated the commission's overall conclusion:

> Recognising that our population cannot grow indefinitely and appreciating the advantages of moving now toward the stabilisation of population, the Commission recommends that the nation welcome and plan for a stabilised population.

There were no specific recommendations for economic, tax, or environmental policies although these had been included to some extent in the outside research. In part this gap reflected the untimely death of Ritchie Reed, who had directed the economic research; in part it reflected the Commission's own reluctance to spell out the implications and options of non-growth. The economic message of the report was simply, "We have looked for and we have not found any convincing economic argument for continued national population growth."

The two specific points on which major political controversy loomed were abortion and contraceptives for teenagers. Yet despite dissents on varying grounds the report declared that "no woman should be forced to bear a child" and recommended that the New York law, most liberal in the country, be the model for other state laws. Moreover, federal, state, local and insurance funds should be available, the commission recommended, to finance abortion services. The commission also urged that contraceptives services and sex education be fully available to minors and that legal impediments to such services be eliminated by the states.

The report was released in three parts in March and April 1972 with publicity and Catholic opposition centering on the abortion issue. For several weeks President Nixon remained silent. Then on May 5 he commented, singling out for attention two points.

> . . . I consider abortion an unacceptable form of population control. In my judgment, unrestricted abortion policies would demean human life. I also want to make it clear that I do not support the unrestricted distribution of family planning services to minors. Such measures would do nothing to preserve and strengthen close family relationships. . . . I believe in the right of married couples to make these judgments for themselves.

Like President Eisenhower on the eve of a critical election, President Nixon rejected the most controversial findings of the group he had appointed. But unlike Eisenhower he deliberately stimulated "an emerging debate of great significance." Whether and which political figures will benefit from the debate is not clear but, if history is any guide, for the thousands of women seeking abortion and the millions of minors using contraceptives a national debate on the issues seems more likely to promote than retard the commission's objectives.

In a literate society like the United States with active communications media the very selection and definition of issues through the policy-making process becomes itself a means to the resolution of the problem. More particularly in a field like population, unlike, for example, space exploration, the ultimate success or failure of the policy will depend in the final instance not on the government programme but on the individual response. As Samuel Huntington concludes:

> The continuing debate and discussion over the adequacy of the programmes, however, and the conflict over what did constitute desirable criteria tended to insure that at least the minimum programmes would be innovated in

time and maintained sufficiently. Prophecies of disaster when credited by the right people are self-non-fulfilling.

For American population policy in the field of reproduction the right people are not the President and his advisors, but rather the millions of young women and men who will reproduce in this and future generations. During the late 1960s and early 1970s they were already deciding for more contraceptives, legal abortion and lower fertility. Within the United States the history of birth control policy may well be a series of self-non-fulfilling prophecies in which the informed public response to the crisis obviates the need for a more drastic policy.

12

POPULATION AND DEVELOPMENT IN THE UNITED NATIONS

No account of U.S. policy toward world population growth would be complete without recognition of the increasingly important role played by the UN system. On the one hand, the initiatives of Rockefeller, Notestein, Gardner Baumgartner, Draper, Claxton, Ravenholt, and other Americans, the policy directions of the State Department, and eventually, the resources of AID strongly influenced and accelerated UN programmes. On the other hand, the development of a major UN role in the population field will increasingly affect the nature of AID programmes. How the population mandates and activities of the UN system were formally established has been told by others. The purpose of this chapter is to identify some of the crucial initiatives and to compare very briefly the process of institution-building in the UN system between 1965 and 1972 with that which took place in AID during the same period. Necessarily and regrettably, very little attention is given to specific programmes of the specialised agencies like the World Health Organisation (WHO), UNESCO, the International Labour Organisation (ILO), the Food and Agriculture Organisation (FAO), or to regional programmes of the UN Economic Commissions and demographic centers, or to the World Bank, each of which would in itself represent a separate case of institution-building. The focus of this overview is on the UN itself, operating primarily from its New York headquarters, and on the inception and growth of the

Population Fund as a coordinating unit for international population programmes.

In the UN, population policy-making can be traced through the same arguments of relevance, feasibility, priority and argency that marked U.S. policy-making. Although the UN process remained throughout the 1960s about two years behind U.S. moves, significant parallels exist in the events and some of the institutional changes that characterised the growth of both programmes. The first full-fledged General Assembly debate in 1962, like the first U.S. public discussion following the Draper Committee report in 1959, revolved around the question of relevance: was population control relevant to economic development and should it therefore be included as an integral part of systematic technical assistance programmes? In both cases, the official answer was "No" as President Eisenhower rejected his committee's proposals and the General Assembly in 1962 deleted the words "technical assistance" from the proposed resolution. But the interest and publicity aroused by these discussions led in both cases to a growing recognition by policy-makers that the problem was indeed relevant and that some public action might well be feasible.

The legitimising of the issue represented in U.S. politics by President Johnson's statement of January 1965 occurred in the UN in December 1966 when Secretary-General U Thant first accepted a Declaration on Population from twelve world leaders. At the same time the General Assembly approved a resolution linking population and economic development, thereby putting the stamp of relevance and political feasibility on some form of technical assistance in population.

From 1967 to 1970 in the UN, as in AID from 1965 to 1968, priority on the programme level lagged behind the announced feasibility on the policy level. Recruiting staff and meeting national needs under the constraints of a tight central budget and in attempted coordination with stronger, independently funded bodies proved difficult. In both cases, a somewhat separate unit was then designated to mobilise a larger effort. The transfer of the Secretary-General's Trust Fund to the UN

Development Programme in 1969 for worldwide administration corresponded roughly with the establishment of the AID Population Service in the War on Hunger in 1967.

Higher priority for both programmes came largely from new and generous funding mechanisms promoted by non-bureaucratic outsiders and activists who controlled the purse strings—that is, for AID by the U.S. Congress and for the UN by contributing governments—and rather reluctantly accepted by high administrative officials. Thus, the first substantial AID funding—$ 35 million—came from earmarked Title X funds in 1968 over Gaud's objections, whereas the first major UN commitments for population work—about $32 million—were made through the Fund for Population Activities (UNFPA) in 1971 against a background of UN rivalries.

For both programmes, the urgency or timing factor has depended primarily upon external events such as crop failures, shortfalls in meeting development targets, environmental concerns, and in the UN system the necessity, stimulated by governments, of planning for the World Population Conference and Year in 1974. A key element in the timing of the UN programme has also undoubtedly been the timing of U.S. efforts. Each advance in U.S. policy or resources was followed, after a period of U.S. reorientation and consolidation, by U.S. pressures on the UN for similar advances. These pressures were applied in the official positions that the U.S. took on policy resolutions and funding commitments as well as through the non-official influence of population activists like Rockefeller and Draper.

The Scandinavian governments, especially Sweden, were often ahead of the U.S. in promoting UN population programmes. Not only by precipitating the first General Assembly debate in 1962 and making an initial contribution to the Population Fund in 1967, but also more recently during the May 1972 sessions of the Economic and Social Council (ECOSOC) by calling for a Global Strategy on Population Sweden set the pace. But without support from the U.S., Swedish initiatives could not prevail against the combined hostility or indifference of Catholic and communist governments.

From the first General Assembly debate in 1962 it was clear that in the UN there were consistently two opponents to Malthusian thinking, rather than one. Not only did the Catholic countries oppose birth control – on similar grounds as American Catholics – but also the communist countries contested the Malthusian formulation, even as refined by Coale and Hoover, that rapid population growth could retard economic development. For Marxists, population control was a capitalist strategem to postpone the real solutions – a reorganisation of society and redistribution of wealth. Therefore, the relevance of population policy throughout the UN could not be as strongly identified in economic terms as it was in the U.S. UN population policy also had to include, in the words of the 1966 General Assembly Resolution, "consideration of economic, social, cultural, psychological and health factors in their proper perspective."

Human rights were repeatedly stressed in the mid-1960s as a justification for population programmes. The World Leaders' statement, a broad declaration of support which was circulated by John D. Rockefeller 3rd and signed by thirty heads of state by December 1967, emphasised that "the opportunity to decide the number and spacing of children is a basic human right." U Thant first received and officially welcomed the statement with twelve signatures on Human Rights Day, December 1966, commenting "We must accord the right of parents to determine the number of their children a place of importance at this moment in man's history." The economic implications in the Declaration were muted: "We believe that the population problem must be recognised as a principal element in long-range national planning if governments are to achieve their economic goals. . . ." Yet even so, compared with three leaders of Catholic countries, only one Communist leader, Tito of Yugoslavia, signed. In language considered "non-controversial," the 1968 International Conference on Human Rights at Teheran reaffirmed for couples the "basic human right to decide freely and responsibly on the number and spacing of their children." Within the UN Secretariat, Julia Henderson, Director of the Office of Technical Cooperation and an early birth control supporter, was influential in helping to define the need for birth control in social and cultural terms rather than exclusively economic ones.

For enunciating policy and drafting resolutions, human rights provided an eloquent and acceptable framework. But for allocating funds and initiating programmes, human rights and social concerns were much less persuasive. In the UN, even more than in the U.S., both the relevance and the feasibility of family planning programmes as a social benefit were weakened by lack of wholehearted support from the professional health organisations. Just as the U.S. Department of Health, Education and Welfare (HEW) did not have a family planning policy until more than a year after President Johnson's statement and continued until 1969 to oppose any specific authorisation of funds for family planning, so also WHO was slow in assigning priority to family planning work. At the 1966 session of the World Health Assembly, Director General M.G. Candau argued that overly vigorous promotion of family planning would divert funds from malaria and cholera control and that public health services had to precede family planning programmes. Rejecting a U.S.-sponsored resolution, the World Health Assembly restricted WHO's role to giving "technical advice upon request, in the development of activities in family planning, as part of an organised health service, without impairing its normal preventive and curative functions." Although the 1966 resolution represented a considerable advance over a 1965 resolution which had specifically precluded WHO even from advising operational activities, family planning in WHO, as in several U.S. health programmes, was long considered a "special interest" rather than a "normal function" of health programmes. WHO was not authorised to help "integrate family planning within basic health services" until 1968 and, despite the efforts of the U.S., Scandinavian, and some Asian governments, did not actively seek funds to do so until 1971.

TECHNICAL ASSISTANCE FOR FAMILY PLANNING

As long as the health professionals denied that birth control was relevant to health and the communists denied that it was relevant to economic development, the UN system could not easily move beyond demographic research and training into full-fledged technical assistance for national family planning programmes. The birth control advocates had to work through the existing, mainly demographic institutions of the UN secretariat to try to build a case against Catholic and Communist opposition in the intergovernmental bodies. Through the mid-1960s the Population Commission, and its staff in the Population Branch, later Division, continued to provide the major internal impetus. The General Assembly resolution of 1962 had deleted the words "technical assistance" but on French initiative called for a Demographic Inquiry from the Secretary-General to governments on the relationships between population growth and economic development. Analysis of the replies and preparation for the 1965 World Population Conference kept population issues alive within the UN structure.

Yet in spite of Communist objections, as economic development became a major UN objective, population growth was increasingly and publicly linked to it. Statements by U.S. and UN leaders in 1965 and 1966 signalled the policy shift. At the 1965 summer session of ECOSOC, after President Johnson's first statement, Secretary-General U Thant called special attention to the "preoccupying" problem of population. Despite the efforts of the first UN Development Decade, he observed, the gap between per capita incomes in the rich and poor nations was widening. At the same session ECOSOC for the first time specifically authorised technical assistance for family planning. Although the World Population Conference of August 1965 barely mentioned the words birth control, much of the discussion emphasised the relevance of demography to development. The widely distributed non-technical summary of the Conference was entitled *World Population: Challenge to Development*.

In 1966 the Population Commission was enlarged from 18 to 27 members to accommodate more of the developing nations. The new members from Asia, Africa and Latin America were more interested in finding out what the real impact of population growth on development might be than in rehashing theoretical Malthusian or Marxist arguments. Again in 1967, with even greater emphasis and strong U.S. support, the Commission approved expanded research, training, and assistance to governments on request for action programmes in population.

For the UN as for AID, the critical world food shortages of 1966 and 1967 hastened a policy change that was already emerging from the preliminary evaluations of the first Development Decade. B.R Sen, Director-General of FAO, blamed high rates of population growth for declining per capita food production. Through FAO's Indicative World Plan, projecting future food needs and production, he sought to document for agriculture what the Coale-Hoover thesis proved for other areas of economic development. In this climate of international concern, just as the routine re-enactment of the Food for Peace Act by the U.S. Congress in 1966 became a vehicle for additional amendments on population, so also the routine adoption by the General Assembly of the biennial resolution approving the expanded two and five year work programmes of the Population Division became in 1966 a clear mandate to expand UN population activities. The 1966 General Assembly resolution referred specifically to the Secretary-General's concern, the World Population Conference, and "the growing food shortage in the developing countries which is due in many cases to a decline in the production of food-stuffs relative to population growth"; it called on the entire UN system "to assist when requested in further developing and strengthening national facilities for training, research, information and advisory services in the field of population."

The real thrust of the resolution was to focus further attention on the Population Division within the Department of Economic and Social Affairs. Milos Macura, an energetic

Yugoslav, had been appointed director of the enlarged Population Division in 1966. But as in AID the new title and personnel did not immediately mean extra money for technical assistance. Thus, Macura, instead of continuing the traditional demographic studies for which the division was known, found most of his time occupied trying to develop a technical assistance programme in a new and controversial field with restricted resources from a position of limited bureaucratic leverage. Although the United Nations post was more prestigious than AID's Population Branch, the two units faced similar problems in 1966. Like Ravenholt, Macura soon became discouraged by the prospects before him. In December 1967 he observed:

> I am less optimistic than I was eight months ago about the pace of developments because we will be faced soon not with lack of money but of personnel. Before the momentum comes, staff should be trained, the organisation should be prepared, people should be more thoroughly informed.

Funding and personnel were both serious obstacles for the UN population effort in the late 1960s because many governments refused to pay assessments for the Congo peace-keeping operation. The UN resources allocated to population in 1966 and 1967 were $1.6 and $1.7 million respectively, compared with $1.2 million in 1955, a decade earlier. For the United Nations, as for AID, at the very moment that birth control was becoming politically acceptable as a tactic in the organisations' larger strategies those larger strategies lost some of their own political acceptability. Tight budgets made it impossible to start any new programme without external pressures or resources. During the period 1966 - 69 Macura struggled to line up the resources and develop the strategy for an expanded UN population programme.

On the resource side, Draper tried to play the same role for the United Nations that he had played for AID and the International Planned Parenthood Federation. He had concluded in 1966 that three men held the key to world action in population – President Johnson, Pope Paul VI, and U Thant. President Johnson was already moving; Pope Paul's study commission was reviewing the subject; and in mid-1966 Draper approached U Thant. The Secretary-General was fully sympathetic. At his invitation an important luncheon was held June 14, 1967. When, at the last minute, U Thant was detained, the meeting was chaired by Under Secretary Philippe de Seynes. It included Draper, Rockefeller, Richard Gardner, senior officials of the International Planned Parenthood Federation and the Population Council, Julia Henderson, and Milos Macura. The real issue, it was agreed, was no longer research, statistics, or even training but rather how to put together and finance under UN auspices a major technical assistance programme that could encourage and coordinate the resources of the entire UN system to help national population and family planning needs.

The first solution – agreed upon in principle, outlined, and announced by the Secretary-General within a month – was to establish a trust fund, comparable to those used by WHO to promote international health campaigns, and open to voluntary contributions from governments and private sources. U Thant acted boldly and promptly without waiting for further mandates. The fund was intended to support not only the five-year programme of activities approved in the December 1966 General Assembly Resolution but also "experimental field projects". Macura estimated the cost between 1967 and 1971 as only $5.5 million, of which $ 4 million would provide increased staff resources at UN headquarters, in the regional economic commissions and elsewhere overseas.

The Secretary-General's fund, initially called the United Nations Fund for Population, was never the massive international programme of technical assistance envisaged by Draper and Gardner. Rather it was "seed money" that, as Julia Headerson pointed out, could build the UN infrastructure for "careful planning and imaginative programming" that would enable the United Nations to help government family planning programmes. In other words, to answer the recurring question that also troubled AID in 1967, of how generous funding could sensibly be used to support population programmes when no one knew what needed to be done, the United Nations proposed to train staff and build up technical competence. Since UN aid funds that could actually be turned over to governments for their own use were considerably less than U.S. AID funds, the natural tendency of UN officials, even more than of AID officials, was to give priority to training.

With the announcement of the Trust Fund by U Thant and the contribution of $ 500,000 from the United States, the UN seemed ready to move forward. Two obstacles – both essentially the product of bureaucratic constraints within the UN system – held the Population Division back between 1967 and 1969. One was the long time-lag required by UN procedures for recruiting staff. The first Population Programme Officers, whose mission was to help governments prepare projects for UN or United Nations Development Programme (UNDP) funding, did not complete their training and go to their posts until February 1969. That was nearly two years after the time proposed in the original aide-memoire, which had emphasised that–

> elaboration of detailed regional programmes and the working out of regional and country projects, should be carried out in 1967 and 1968. This is the most critical element of the whole programme, on which future expansion of the United Nations activities in the field of population will largely depend.

That two-year delay in hiring and training what were essentially middle level demographic programme officers seriously undermined support for the Population Division's programme.

The other major roadblock was coordination, especially between the UN and the specialised agencies. Most of the UN bodies were divided along professional and disciplinary lines; their headquarters and regional offices were, for political reasons, located in many different countries. The function of coordination was undertaken by UN headquarters and exercised through an interagency working group which in 1968 became a subcommittee of the Administrative Committee on Co-ordination. But, as an outside consultant's report pointed out, "much time is spent on what might be called negative coordination, of a jurisdictional character. There is, however, a need for 'positive coordination' by which the resources of all relevant disciplines can be rapidly and harmoniously brought to bear at the planning, programming, operational and evaluation stage in population activities."

Relations between the United Nations and the World Health Organisation were particularly difficult. "The restrictive mandates" of the World Health Organisation barred WHO from providing assistance to family planning services, where, as in Pakistan, they were not integrated within the health services. Interdisciplinary assistance projects, which were an increasingly important part of Ford Foundation, Population Council, and AID programmes, were supposed to be a major UN contribution, but they were increasingly handicapped by independent initiatives from WHO, UNESCO, and the Population Division, by duplication of experts, or by "very lengthy negotiations between agencies" that took place "before assistance is given which requires cooperation between disciplines." Governments wanting help were impatient. As one recipient observed:

> Multilateral agencies. . . have very little funds, very little experience and very little expertise. . . I think it is unfair for a country that is embarking on a programme also to have to subject itself to getting assistance from an agency that is learning to administer assistance.

In short, the coordination of equals proved difficult. No one agency could seriously influence the policies or funding levels of the others. Lacking an ample funding mechanism like the earmarked AID population money, Macura and the Population Division had no leverage either with UN agencies or with governments seeking aid. Awkward jurisdictional disputes often surfaced during the interagency missions dispatched to governments, such as to India in 1965, to Africa, to Pakistan, and to Colombia in 1968, and to India again in 1969. These missions constituted a major UN activity. Their purpose was to evaluate existing programmes and lay the groundwork for comprehensive UN technical assistance in the future. Their voluminous reports usually pointed to a broad range of needs or programme deficiencies in every field which the developing countries could not easily repair – certainly not without more sustained programming assistance and more resources.

Apart from the UN missions and the Population Programme officers, however, the Population Division interpreted the Trust Fund mainly as a means for augmenting the demographic research and training programmes of the secretariat rather than an operational arm for technical assistance from the entire UN system. Paradoxically, although the need for resources seemed limitless, contributions to the Fund and expenditures from it lagged. Of the $1.1 million contributed mainly by the United States, the United Kingdom, and the Scandinavian countries during 1967 and 1968, very little was allocated until 1969.

During 1968 it became increasingly clear that the limited functions of the fund, the negative coordination of the UN system, and the training and advisory emphasis could not generate the level of technical assistance requests or resources anticipated. Not only individuals like Draper and Rockefeller but also donor governments like the United States and Sweden grew restive. Furthermore, by July 1968, the successful earmarking and then obligation of $ 35 million by AID strengthened the arguments of activists like Draper that much more money was needed and could be well spent. Declining birth rates in Korea and Taiwan strengthened the influence of the professionals, like the Population Council, who for the first time could point to a pay-off in these programmes.

Draper's strategy had always been to persuade Paul Hoffman that birth control was an integral part of economic development and should be supported as such. Hoffman was in many ways the father of intergovernmental development assistance, first through the Marshall Plan for Europe and then through various UN funds and activities which eventually became the United Nations Development Programme. Draper, a close friend, had helped to recruit him for both jobs and kept reminding him that population growth in many areas was thwarting economic gains. At first skeptical about birth control, by the late 1960s Hoffman was ready to agree that rapid population did retard economic development, that national family planning programmes could help reduce fertility, and that the issue was no longer to controversial as to undermine the fragile base of development assistance. In December 1967, at a panel discussion Draper arranged, Hoffman declared:

> We have had conferences and conferences, all perhaps very useful . . . But the time now is for action. As far as the United Nations Development Programme is concerned, we act only on the request of governments. But we are very willing to give quick consideration to any request from any government for an action programme in the population field.

Only the UNDP had a worldwide network of resident representatives with experience in framing, processing and monitoring technical assistance projects. Hoffman, at Draper's suggestion, agreed to ask the resident representatives what kind of population requests might be made if funds were available. In April 1968, almost a year after the first meeting, another luncheon took place including Draper, Hoffman and U Thant. To Hoffman's complaint that it was not lack of money but lack of requests for aid that deterred UNDP, Draper responded:

> The situation is very similar to what has transpired in AID in our own government programme. During the past two fiscal years, less than one-quarter of one per cent was obligated for family planning. . . . These small

> programmes resulted from the fact that family planning is comparatively new as a source of projects, just as it is with the UN, and all such projects have to compete with those already under way. However, last December $ 35 million were earmarked by Congress for family planning and could not be used for anything else. More than $ 50 million of project requests came in from the field.

Draper proposed to Paul Hoffman and U Thant that a new fund should be set up, consisting of voluntary contributions specifically for population, and administered through UNDP. Working closely with Phil Claxton as Special Assistant to the Secretary of State for Population Matters, with Leighton Van Nort and John McDonald in the International Organisation Bureau, and counting on earmarked funds available from AID, Draper unofficially conveyed to Hoffman, U Thant, and other high UN officials the message that the U.S. and other governments would support a UNDP population assistance programme based on separate voluntary contributions. While the various policy-making organs of the UN system continued under U.S. and Swedish pressure to approve increasingly favourable resolutions, the wheels began to turn in the secretariat. In May 1968 Richard Symonds, a British expert in development policy, was appointed as a consultant, first to the Population Division and then to the Secretary-General, to study how the Population Fund could best be developed into a flexible UN technical assistance programme. Finally in July 1968, ECOSOC, upon U.S. initiative, provided an official green light and recommended by a vote of 12 to 7 that UNDP give technical assistance to population programmes. Shortly thereafter negotiations began between the Secretary-General and Paul Hoffman on the management of the fund.

Symonds's report, presented to the Secretary-General in September 1968 although not released until June 1969, emphasised the problems of coordination and responsibility in a still sensitive field. Ideally, he suggested, an international population agency should be created, but if that proved impossible, Symonds recommended that a commissioner for population be appointed to give visible priority to population.

His role would be defined by agreement between the Secretary-General and the administrator of UNDP. He also suggested an interagency division, to foster a "positive coordination," an International Interdisciplinary Training Institute, joint arrangements at the regional level, and a brochure explaining what assistance the United Nations could provide. Whatever institutional arrangements were devised, Symonds emphasised the need for "an identifiable point of responsibility for the mobilisation of resources. . ." Symonds's report echoed the same arguments that Leona Baumgartner had made to David Bell in 1965 – flexibility was needed above all to react quickly to national needs, to solve interdisciplinary problems, and to take advantage of new technologies.

Nevertheless, even as the climate of support for population programmes grew warmer throughout the UN system, that "identifiable point of responsibility" remained missing through 1968 and much of 1969 since Macura lacked means or authority to influence programmes in other UN agencies. During that period, the specialised agencies received encouraging new mandates to expand their professional involvement in the population field, always with due respect for the sovereign rights of governments. Voluntary family planning was thoroughly accepted as "a basic human right". An important convert to the population cause was Robert S. McNamara, President of the World Bank, who in 1968 announced that the Bank would devote new attention to population growth as a major obstacle to economic development. At the same time, the debate over the Second United Nations Development Decade focused the attention of all governments again and again on the relationship between population growth and per capita income. Although U.S. officials had hoped for even stronger language, in fact, the International Development Strategy for the 1970s included for the first time a per capita annual economic growth target of 3.5 per cent based on an

> average annual increase of 2.5 per cent in the population of developing countries, which is less than the average rate at present forecast for the 1970s.

Reducing population growth was undeniably a relevant policy for many developing countries.

Outside the United Nations system, other strong pressures for institutional change were building up. A Population Policy Panel of the private United Nations Association of the United States was established with Ford Foundation funding under the chairmanship of John D. Rockefeller 3rd and including Richard Gardner, David Bell, George Woods, Frank Notestein, Oscar Harkevy, John Hannah, William Rogers, and other notables. The study, prepared after Symonds's review by Stanley Johnson, a young British economist, came to much the same conclusions about UN bureaucracy but in bolder, more picturesque language:

> Although the population cake has been sliced this way and that in an endless series of co-ordinating meetings, very few crumbs have as yet fallen into the lap of a hungry world.

The major recommendations were for a Commissioner for Population to be appointed within the UNDP with a high-calibre staff to be responsible for planning, coordinating, implementing and expediting UN population projects through the Population Trust Fund. The fund would allocate money to UN agencies, governments, or other bodies with the approval of donor and recipient governments. Under this system of "strong central coordination and direction," with the commissioner for population serving as principal United Nations representative at intergovernmental population forums, it was proposed that the fund be increased to $100 million in three years.

The plan in effect called for what critical UN Secretariat officials privately described as a population czar in the UNDP in effect downgrading the Population Division and restricting new WHO plans to finance reproductive biology research and family planning services through its own voluntary health fund. This public appeal by a private U.S. organisation was warmly endorsed in, President Nixon's Message on Population where he urged that the United Nations assume world leadership in the population field under the proposed plan. In 1969 President Nixon was urging the United Nations to do much the same thing that Congress had pressed upon AID in 1967. The U.S. State Department was also pressing for a major UNDP role.

Meanwhile, within the United Nations, de Seynes, Henderson, Macura, and others were looking for a compromise that would preserve an important role for the Secretariat and not alienate the specialised agencies. A memorandum of May 6, 1969, outlined major changes to be made by the Secretary-General, including:

1. Considerable expansion of the fund, requesting contributions of $ 5 million in 1969, $10 million in 1970 and $ 20 million in 1971 (the same sums Symonds had proposed).
2. Management of the fund "for direct assistance purposes" to be vested in the Administrator of the UN Development Programme (that is, Paul Hoffman).
3. The Population Programme and Projects Office of the Population Division to "be responsible for co-ordination and presentation of the substantive analysis and appraisal of requests in collaboration with the agencies" and to "recommend action to the Administrator of the UNDP."
4. Execution of projects in full or part "by the various agencies according to their competence and with appropriate consultation."

In other words, Paul Hoffman would manage the money but the Population Division would handle programming and the specialised agencies would do the implementation.

By the end of 1969, the fund had been effectively transferred to Hoffman's management. Rafael Salas, Senior Cabinet Member and Executive Secretary of the Philippine government, had been appointed by Paul Hoffman as Director of the fund and $1.5 million of projects formally approved for financing. Although Salas later became Executive Director at the level of Assistant Secretary-General, the title of Commissioner was deliberately avoided.

The events of 1968-69 in the UN system provided an almost exact parallel to the course of the AID programme in 1966 and 1967. During this period, officials in the UN Secretariat were considering internal measures to justify additional funding, to make funds more readily available to the specialised agencies and to develop programmes more flexibly, just as AID had done in organising the War on Hunger, but other pressures overtook them. Despite resistance from UN officials (comparable to the objections of the Bureau for Programme and Policy Coordination in AID) another mechanism was established to ensure higher priority. The new arrangements in both cases centered around generous funds to be administered by a technical assistance office but clearly earmarked only for population. In both cases the health agencies that had originally been expected to take the lead hesitated in tackling interdisciplinary problems and thus lost control of programmes which were finally accorded priority on economic grounds. But even though yielding to the power of the purse as exercised by legislatures and governments respectively, programme officials in both AID and the United Nations successfully resisted providing the full authority, the appropriate title, or the necessary staff to facilitate the new programme.

UNFPA: RESOURCES, STRATEGY, LEADERSHIP

Nevertheless, Salas and the United Nations Fund for Population Activities (UNFPA) in 1969 were in a far better position than Ravenholt had been in 1966 or Macura in 1967. UNFPA benefited from two years more of international support for the concept of family planning: UNFPA benefited from two years more of confidence that government programmes really could make a difference in fertility rates. Despite an uneasy relationship with the Population Division and specialised agencies, UNFPA also benefited from fairly clear control over the final allocation of funds. Relevance in terms of economic development and feasibility in terms of programme administration were thus established.

Priority and urgency for UNFPA programmes as for AID would depend on resources and events stimulated by outside action. Draper once again set out in 1970 at Paul Hoffman's request to raise the additional funds necessary for a major programme. The AID programme demonstrated more vividly each year that generous funds could overcome many organisational bottlenecks. In January 1970, on Draper's recommendation, the U.S. readily agreed to provide $ 7.5 million to UNFPA on a matching basis, that is, if other nations would contribute an equal amount and announced the pledge in fulfilment of President Nixon's message. The Swedish government contributed $1.5 million as did the German government, never before involved. Despite pleas from Salas and the U.S. Department of State to maintain a low profile, Draper approached either in person or by letter, every potential large contributor, including especially Germany, Japan, Great Britain, Canada, and the Scandinavian countries. Largely as a result of his insistent and uninhibited fund-raising, more than $15 million was pledged in 1970 from 24 countries and nearly $ 30 million in 1971 from 46 countries. Once again an ambitious target that was clearly based on judgments of priority rather than immediate programme requests had generated substantial support.

Therefore, the first challenge for Salas, as for Ravenholt, was not raising money but rather allocating sensibly the money Draper raised. Labouring, as AID had, with insufficient staff for programme development but equally unable in the face of UN and agency opposition to build up its own personnel immediately, the fund initially had to support any UN agencies or governments on whatever terms the recipients named. Still, as Table 12.1 shows, most of the agencies held back with their requests and even more so with their programming. WHO, which originally hoped for direct U.S. aid, turned to the fund in 1970 in hopes that there would be fewer strings attached. When in 1971 UNFPA began to ask for detailed programme submissions, WHO began to look for direct contributions from governments again. Yet, with UNFPA aid, WHO programmes in research and services

Table 12.1
International Agency Allocations, Remittances and Expenditures from UNFPA Funds, 1969 - 71

Agency	*Allocations*			*Remittances*			*Expenditures*			*Cumulative Expenditures as a Percentage of Cumulative Allocations*
	1969	*1970*	*1971*	*1969*	*1970*	*1971*	*1969*	*1970 (Combined)*	*1971*	
FAO	–	137,625	446,134	–	–	412,823	–	823	177,382	31
IBRD	–	–	440,000	–	–	–	–	–	–	0
ILO	63,000	261,730	285,300	–	63,000	170,000	–	65,742	265,811	54
IPPF	–	450,000	750,000	–	450,000	–	–	450,000	750,000	100
UN	67,000	977,636	846,827	352,670	286,219	408,311	–	529,926	736,926	67
UNOT	483,840	2,360,794	4,318,882	171,155	2,001,289	1,282,371	–	729,347	1,628,169	33
UNDP	–	84,995	133,010	–	57,523	15,943	–	84,995	133,010	100
UNESCO	–	423,860	852,350	58,000	110,000	342,000	–	158,330	349,911	40
UNICEF	–	665,400	3,124,861	–	285,000	1,905,000	–	59,500	2,096,880	57
UNIDO	–	–	42,500	–	–	–	–	–	16,448	39
WHO	500,000	1,312,590	4,116,030	–	800,000	1,800,000	–	786,534	1,945,396	46
Total	1,114,578	6,674,620	15,315,894	581,825	4,053,031	6,336,448	–	2,865,197	8,099,933	

Source: UNFPA, March 1972.

gradually expanded. UNESCO remained unwilling to alter its own internal structure so that population education or mass communications could expand as interdisciplinary programmes. The United Nations, including both the Population Division and the Office of Technical Cooperation, received the major share of UNFPA funds, most of which went to provide additional staff for Regional Economic Commissions in Asia, Africa and Latin America, regional demographic centers, and to support training, conferences, and advisory missions. Of all the agencies, UNICEF by the end of 1971 still maintained one of the best records in putting to work promptly the substantial funds allocated to it. Much of UNICEF money went into midwifery training, vehicles and contraceptive supplies.

Besides allocating money, there was at first little room for strategy. The fund was deliberately defined by the secretariat and the specialised agencies as a bank account rather than a programming or implementing agency. Its purposes as first drafted were:

1. To provide systematic and sustained assistance to countries desiring such assistance.
2. To enable the UN and agencies related to it to respond better to the needs of member countries.
3. To help to coordinate the population programmes among the various elements of the UN system.
4. To assist governments and agencies in the execution of population policies by helping the United Nations system to serve as a clearing house for information.

But even the clearing house role was questioned by other UN bodies and dropped from later statements. During 1970 Salas and Hoffman both took pains to insist that UNFPA was not an operating agency but rather a managerial group without expert knowledge in the specialised field of population. At first, the fund moved slowly, allocations going primarily to the UN specialised agencies. Only two agreements were negotiated directly with national government – Pakistan and Mauritius – totalling $1.8 million. By the end of 1971, however, agreements were signed or well under way for short or long-term assistance to six governments totalling nearly $ 24 million. A major and increasing emphasis of the UNFPA programme was to encourage medium and large scale government programmes, supported and coordinated through multilateral channels.

In order to help governments directly, however, UNFPA had to move beyond normal UN emphasis on training, advisory missions, and foreign exchange. What many developing countries wanted and needed was general budgetary support for local costs. The issue which Ravenholt had bitterly fought and won in AID over India was easier for UNFPA. By 1971 aid recipients openly advocated and donors acknowledged the need for broader forms of assistance. Unlike AID, the UNFPA was not hamstrung by local currency holdings that had to be liquidated first. Although UNFPA insisted that its funds be additive, not a substitute, and that governments pay a major share of local costs, unlike AID, it agreed from the start to provide "counterpart services and related costs normally paid in local currencies" especially "in countries with serious budgetary problems."

Private organisations like the International Planned Parenthood Federation, the Population Council, professional associations of physicians, demographers, statisticians, midwives, home economists, and the like were from the start recognised as useful channels for support. Although UNFPA, like AID, at first proposed to clear non-governmental requests through the Resident Representatives, Population Programme officers, and government, the attempt was soon dropped. By 1972, the UNFPA was ready not only to make grants to private organisations but also to consider the International Planned Parenthood Federation (IPPF) or others as executing agencies for assistance projects. UNFPA was also ready to admit openly, as AID rarely could, that it would take the initiative in promoting new programmes to fill any important gaps.

Even as the resources expanded, Salas, like Ravenholt, tried to keep the procedures simple and, above all, flexible. The priorities were not research or demography but "operational programmes and projects assisting efforts to moderate high rates of fertility where these constitute an obstacle to economic and social progress." During 1971 approximately 54 per cent of UNFPA funds were allocated to family planning, 23 per cent to demography, 8 per cent to population education and communications, 8 per cent to multisector activities and 7 per cent to infrastructure. (See Table 12.2) The programming breakdown was remarkably similar to that of AID, although somewhat more stress was placed on demographic research.

Table 12.2
UNFPA and AID Sector Programming, 1971-1972 (percentages)

	1971		*1972 (est.)*	
	UNFPA	*AID*	*UNFPA*	*AID*
Basic population data[b]	–	8	15.7	10
Population dynamics[c]	–	–	11.4	–
Population policy[d]	–	10	2.9	9
Sub-total	23.3	18	30.0	19
Family planning[a] (including new techniques)	53.9	46	30.3	39
Communication and education[e]	8.0	11	8.9	8
Multisector activities[f]	8.3	7	21.5	8
Programme development[g]	6.5	3	9.3	3
(contribution to UNFPA)[h]	–	15	–	23
Total (percentages)	100	100	100	100
Total (millions of dollars)	32.1	95.9	43.5	125

[a]Estimated April 1972.
[b]Headings given are UNFPA terminology. AID terms in parenthesis: adequate demographic and social data.
[c]Adequate population policies and understanding of population dynamics.
[d]Included for AID in (b), above.
[e]Adequate delivery systems for information and education.
[f]Multipurpose institutional development and use.
[g]AID/W support. For UNFPA in 1971 Infrastructure.
[h]AID budget only. Includes also 1972 AID unprogrammed.

Sources: UNFPA, *Tentative Work Plan*, February 20, 1972; UNFPA/PCC/IV/4; AID, *Population Programme Study*, July 1972, p. 10.

For Salas, however, the programming was less important than jurisdictional and managerial issues. Leaving many of the programme specifics to his capable, hardworking deputy Halvor Gille and Operations Officer John Keppel, Salas focused on the threats to basic UNFPA authority. As long as Macura, who had seen the fund removed from his own control, remained Director of the Population Division, that is, through 1971, personal as well as institutional rivalry prevailed between the division and the fund. Some of it centered around the Population Programme Officers in the field, reporting to the Population Division, but submitting projects for funding through the UNDP resident representatives. For a time, governments seeking aid, like Indonesia, still found that reaching agreement with WHO, the World Bank, and UNFPA took longer than formulating their own government programme. Coordination remained the most controversial of the fund's attempted roles. Another source of friction was the proposal for a World Population Training Institute (WPTI), endorsed by Symonds, but later interpreted by many as a possible rival to UNFPA that would be controlled by the Population Division WHO and UNESCO.

In fact, during 1970 and 1971 jurisdictional questions complicated every major population activity. In 1969 the Secretary-General recommended that a Third World Population Conference be held in 1974 and that 1974 be designated World Population Year. When the Population Commission, ECOSOC, and the General Assembly approved, it was assumed that the Population Division, acting for the Secretary-General, would be in charge. Yet the Division was short of staff even to manage the Conference. The special activities for the World Population Year as well as the Conference would clearly require UNFPA resources. To disentangle the Conference and the year, to secure prominent public leadership, and to finance these additional activities still disputed between two rival units, would require diplomacy on all sides and take nearly as long as the preparations themselves. Outside government pressures (mainly from the U.S. and Sweden), rather than internal UN initiatives, stressed the importance and imminence of these events.

The controversies of programming, implementing, and coordinating, technical assistance, of staffing the Population Fund itself, of maneouvering around earmarked support for WHO, and of managing the Conference and the year were aired continuously by the UN agencies in meetings of the sub-committee on population of the Administrative Committee on Coordination and of the UNFPA's own Inter-Agency Consultative Committee. In addition to these somewhat acrimonious sessions, the Fund itself established a Programme Consultative Committee of donors, foundations, and population organisations which increasingly focussed on substantive issues and technical problems. Also significant was the Advisory Board appointed by Paul Hoffman, consisting of international leaders and spokesmen such as Alberto Lleras Camargo, former President of Colombia; John D. Rockefeller 3rd; B.R. Sen, former FAO Director General; Ernst Michanek, Director of the Swedish International Development Agency; Directors of Regional Economic Commissions, and others. Draper had long urged the Secretary-General to appoint an advisory council, but U Thant, after consulting with the agency heads, was reluctant to set up such an unprecedented, ad hoc group. At first a somewhat anomalous body within the UN system, the panel served increasingly to guide the Population Fund in its major resource development and allocation policies and to counterbalance UN and agency pressures.

After its transfer to UNDP in 1969, the Fund was at first heavily dependent upon outside support – upon Draper and the U.S. government for major financial resources and upon other UN legislative bodies for legitimacy in the UN system. For example, at the Fifteenth Session of the Population Commission in November 1969 it was crucial that the commission, although not referring to the Fund for Population Activities by name, in the final draft resolution endorsed the concept that the fund be "truly international," "work closely together as a team" with specialised agencies, "be administered efficiently," and above all "provide assistance in all forms required to meet the needs of developing countries, including the financing of action programmes." Draper, who was appointed by President Nixon as the U.S. representative on the commission, not only guided the technical assistance language through the commission but also won approval for the World Population Year (which he had initially promoted as a member of the Secretary-General's advisory committee).

Yet the very success of the UNFPA in obtaining generous resources and high level advisors made it a more conspicuous target for charges by suspicious Catholic or Communist nations that it had never been formally authorised by the General Assembly or provided with an official governing body or council of governments. By the fall of 1971 continuing problems of coordination could be blamed more directly on the fund. Criticism at the Sixteenth Session of the Population Commission about delays in the Indonesian programme led to a request in the draft resolution that the Secretary-General "develop in cooperation with the United Nations agencies concerned appropriate measures needed to accelerate the review of requests for technical cooperation and implementation of technical assistance projects."

Thoroughly exasperated at this criticism and determined to strengthen the mandates of the fund directly, in December 1971, Rafael Salas moved behind the scenes to encourage an immediate General Assembly resolution that would provide full recognition and support for the fund. Bypassing the Population Commission resolution that required approval first from the Economic and Social Council, the General Assembly by a vote of 94-0 (with 20 abstentions) approved a resolution "noting with satisfaction the progress" of the fund and inviting governments to contribute. The General Assembly was "convinced that the United Nations Fund for Population Activities should play a leading role in the United Nations system in promoting population programmes. . ." With regard to administration, the resolution was:

> Requests the Secretary-General, in consultation with the Administrator of the United Nations Development Programme and the Executive Director of the United Nations Fund for Population Activities, to take the necessary steps to achieve the desired improvements in the administrative machinery of the Fund aimed at the efficient and expeditious delivery of population programmes, including measures to quicken the pace of recruiting the experts and personnel required to cope with the increasing volume of requests, as well as to consider the training of experts and personnel in the developing countries. . . .

Accordingly, early in 1972 Ernst Michanek was designated, by the new Secretary-General Kurt Waldheim, by the new UNDP Administrator, Rudolph Peterson, and by Salas to undertake a wide-ranging study of the operations and capacity of the fund, a study that would meet the needs of the Secretary-General under the General Assembly Resolution. At the same time in a parallel action Michanek was elected Chairman of a subcommittee of the UNFPA Advisory Board to consider how the fund might "more effectively discharge its responsibilities for leadership within the UN system and provide a focus for coordinated international efforts to deal with population problems."

Following the General Assembly Resolution, the UNFPA staff was also reorganised and expanded. An important addition to the staff in 1971 was Dr. Nafis Sadik, an unusually able, experienced, and outspoken Pakistani family-planning programme administrator. Designated programme coordinator early in February 1972, her role in UNFPA effectively challenged WHO's monopoly on health competence.

The UNFPA gained further ground in June 1972 when the Economic and Social Council (ECOSOC) gave Salas responsibility for preparations for the World Population Year in 1974. Additional staff was authorised. Furthermore, the Stockholm Conference on the Human Environment, held in

June 1972 under the direction of Maurice Strong, convinced not only the U.S. and Swedish governments but also UN Under Secretary Philippe de Seynes that the World Population Conference should be equally significant. Population policy was becoming a serious political concern of governments. ECOSOC therefore also called for a special Secretary-General to organise the 1974 conference, with his own secretariat. Thus, ECOSOC simultaneously enlarged the jurisdiction of the fund and diminished that of the Population Division while leaving unresolved the long-term relationship between the UNFPA and the UN secretariat, between operational technical assistance and agreed-upon population policy.

Nevertheless, by mid-1972 Salas had been remarkably successful in transforming a unit that started without programming authority, implementing power, or even a staff of its own into a major UN body with General Assembly support. He had started with many of the same difficulties as Revenholt plus the extra complications of intercultural differences as well as the extra prestige of an international base. Yet he approached them very differently. Where Ravenhold focussed with greatest interest on the substantive elements – oral contraceptives, new technologies, new evaluation methods – and only rather feluctantly on organisational factors, Salas concentrated on political and administrative problems. Where Ravenholt pressed forward, spoke his mind, and confronted his opponents directly, Salas proceeded cautiously, kept his own counsel, and tried to give his rivals as little opportunity to criticise as possible. Nevertheless, on the organisational issues that concerned him, he was just as determined to have his own way in the end. He moved, step by step, to consolidate his own position, not only against the Population Division and the agencies, but also against the insistent pressures of Draper, the U.S. government, and other donors. Benefitting tremendously from their support, he nevertheless retained his independence and guided the fund to a position of increasing international stature and influence.

Despite contrasting leadership the programmes of UNFPA and AID retained much in common besides their goal of reducing population growth. Both grew rapidly, generated by an international recognition of population problems that was rapidly translated into necessary resources. Financial priority, constantly pursued and provided by Draper, gave both programmes the momentum necessary to overcome many professional inhibitions, jurisdictional rivalries and bureaucratic bottlenecks. Furthermore, strategies aimed at modernising not only birth rates but also the channels of development assistance played a large part in both programmes. Both were new and flexible enough to abandon initial approaches that did not work for ones that did. Just as the AID programme had originally intended to support government-to-government assistance but shifted by necessity toward private intermediaries and multilateral agencies so the UNFPA objective originally was to support UN agencies but shifted by necessity toward governments and private international organisations. Both programmes became, more by coincidence than design, prototypes for new concepts of development assistance. The AID population programme fitted almost perfectly the model of a professional innovative International Development Institute described in 1970 by the Peterson Committee Report, whereas the UNFPA increasingly showed the potential of becoming the "head piece" for UN population programmes, "that central coordinating organisation which could exercise effective control" recommended by the Jackson Report in its study of the entire UN Development effort.

Yet in their common search for effective population and development strategies, the two men and programmes were also going in opposite directions. Ravenholt was looking . technological solution with better contraceptives and delivery systems; Salas was reaching for a political-economic solution by making resources broadly available under comprehensive country programming. As Ravenholt pointed out in 1969 when asked about President Nixon's call for UN leadership, "I see AID and the UN playing essentially complementary roles in the development of family planning programmes. The Agency is ahead of the UN which will follow trails blazed by AID."

The struggles that Ravenholt fought and generally won in AID – for example, on aid to private organisations, general budgetary support, and directed contraceptive research – usually strengthened Salas' hand in similar struggles on the international level. But with all the advantages of a non-political UN agency to deal with developing countries, the UNFPA was increasingly in a position to assist in large scale, sensitive, government actions, while AID, although often ahead in programme analysis and substantive measures, still had to fend off political criticism at home and overseas.

After the winter of 1971-72, when the AID population programme won its first Congressional appropriation to match earlier ear-markings and the UNFPA won its first General Assembly endorsement, both programmes moved up a notch in the organisation structure. In fact, by 1972 UNFPA had nearly caught up with the AID programme on the institutional side, if not in funding. Both had additional staff and authority, but at the same time both faced the possibility that more authority could also bring more specific guidelines, less flexibility, and less capacity to innovate in the future.

The first challenge both programmes still faced and had not yet fully resolved was how to enhance the efficiency and effectiveness of the assisting organisations themselves. In 1969 the complaint had been voiced that "public multilateral agencies tend to be too bureaucratic and inexpert, bilateral tend to be too energetic, and the private are too poor." By 1972 UNFPA and AID, together with other donor governments, possessed the necessary funds, experience, and skill to improve all three if they could cooperate sufficiently to do so.

By 1972 both UNFPA and AID faced the prospect also that their programmes would in future be judged less by the ability to obligate money, often for intermediate organisations, and win bureaucratic battles than by their power to influence fertility rates and reduce world population growth. The spotlight of outside publicity and evaluation would be increasingly focussed on the specific accomplishments of both agencies. Despite their rapid growth, AID and UNFPA programmes have benefited from relatively low salience in the political and international arena. The opportunity to achieve higher priority and greater urgency through the World Population Conference and year carries also the danger of increased hostility from Catholic opponents of abortion on the one hand and from advocates of greater redistribution of wealth on the other. Sweden, again in the lead, has called for a World Population Plan of Action. Can the UN – with AID and other public or private agencies – develop a population policy that stimulates the resources and leadership needed from the developed countries and at the same time satisfies the pressing political needs of the developing countries? A policy that is equally relevant, feasible, important and urgent to the haves and the have-nots, to governments, and to individual men and women? The continuing progress of both AID and UN programmes to and beyond 1974 will depend on those questions and answers.

13

BIRTH CONTROL AND THE POLICY PROCESS

The development of substantial government programmes to meet the challenge of population growth in the developing countries has been unexpectedly rapid, especially in the Agency for International Development. Less than a decade after President Eisenhower's blunt prohibition, a much-criticised agency that was frowned upon by Congress, government employees, and many professionals had become the largest source of family planning assistance in the world, the lead government agency in the search for improved methods of fertility control, a conspicuous example of the practices recommended for other U.S. aid programmes, and the major support of a growing UN effort.

Whether these programmes will succeed in their substantive goal – whether birth rates in AID or UN-assisted countries will decline; whether AID or UN support would play any role in such declines; whether different kinds of strategies or support might cause greater declines; even, in the long-run, whether declining birth rates will make a genuine impact on standards of living and economic development – these questions cannot yet be fully answered. But the change in policy and the growth of programmes are now undeniable.

These innovations resulted primarily from the external environment – from the established facts of world population growth, the knowledge that impoverished populations were multiplying rapidly to live in still greater poverty, the recognition that another billion people would be added between 1963 and 1975, and finally, the awareness that even in the United States population growth could threaten the highest living standard in the world. But the impact of natural population increase is necessarily long-term and highly interdependent with economic, social and technological change. Dealing with the problem directly requires massive, flexible, long-range, interdisciplinary and interagency programmes. For any organisation to initiate and operate such programmes in a political context where leaders want perceptible short-term results with minimal opposition is a peculiarly difficult task. The policy-making process in the population field at the governmental or the international level is therefore not a smooth and easy road even where private acceptance of fertility control methods has been high. The main purpose of this study has been to identify chronologically some of the different variables that seemed to influence the development of U.S. population policy. These relationships can be tested more systematically in different countries, states and policies under different circumstances.

The principal hypotheses and conclusions that emerge can be summarised under the following headings: the background of public opinion and media attention; the individuals and organisations who undertake deliberately to change government policy; the functioning of judicial, executive and legislative bodies; the development of technology; and the dynamics of population policy itself.

PUBLIC OPINION AND MEDIA ATTENTION

Public opinion is a perverse guide to the development of government birth control policy. Long before polls were devised and in fact even before governments were established, control of fertility seems to have been practiced by many individuals. Yet until the twentieth century the private practice of birth control was publicly opposed by church and state. The more publicly that opposition was proclaimed, the more widely birth control was practiced. Two decades ago Kingsley Davis pointed out:

As the birth control movement gains strength and vociferousness, the opposition will doubtless crystallise and gain strength as well. The capacity of a movement to evoke opposition is inevitable. It does not mean that the movement itself will fail. The very controversy itself will tend to spread contraceptive knowledge. In no country in the world has religious opposition been able to stop the diffusion of birth control any more than it has been able to stop the use of tobacco or alcohol.

Certainly that statement has proved true in the United States. Since the 1950s controversy and publicity have spotlighted the population problem. Public opinion since it was first measured in the 1930s has favoured the availability of birth control information. The practice of birth control is virtually universal in the United States. The method most widely publicised became within five years the method most widely used. Ever since the population growth problem of the developing countries was identified, nearly two-thirds of the U.S. population have favoured birth control assistance as one solution to the problem.

Yet the perception of Washington policy-makers has been very different from the quantitative measure of public opinion. Even in 1962 a congressman could assert that "the great majority of our Americans would be against birth control." The organised opposition of the Catholic Church, based on theological teaching but strongly reinforced by ethnic politics, carried more weight than public opinion or private practice. Until the mid-1960s "the intense minority" opposing government tolerance of birth control was able to "frustrate the ambitions" of the intense minority favouring birth control "with the passive acquiescence or indifference of a majority of adults or voters."

The poll data suggest that in the United States as elsewhere whenever birth control advocates were able to confront the opposition publicly, their popular support even among Catholics increased; when they or government leaders remained quiet, Catholic popular disapproval seemed to gain strength. Ironically, government policy-makers tended at first to react in an opposite way, avoiding the issue when it was controversial and taking it up only when controversy seemed to have died. But by the mid-1960s even Catholic opinion no longer showed any semblance of following its ecclesiastical leaders.

In this as in other fields not public opinion itself but the political leaders' perception of it and especially of its intensity was decisive. Only on two occasions did survey data on public opinion – Catholic opinion, in both cases – have immediate impact on the policy process. When President Johnson's first public reference to "the explosion in world population" was followed four days later by a Gallup poll indicating that over three-fourths of American Catholics (a 50 per cent increase since 1963) favoured making birth control available, that specific information at that specific moment heartened supporters and discouraged the opposition. Again, when the papal encyclical of 1968 was immediately followed by surveys showing that most Catholics disagreed, the political impact of church spokesmen was undermined.

Basically the leaders on both sides of the issue became mediators of public opinion to one another. They were more influenced by one another's statements and interpretations than by public opinion directly. When Catholic organisations seemed to represent "millions of taxpaying Catholic voters" they carried weight in the political arena. When ethnic loyalties prevailed they also carried weight. When Catholic officials began publicly feuding with their constituency, however, their influence as political spokesmen diminished. Recognising this, they became less vocal, thereby permitting proponents like Senator Gruening to redefine and shift the issue.

The influence of the news media, promptly publicising polls like these and making the subject familiar, was critical. As long as threats of Catholic boycott, feelings of impropriety, or doubts that the issue was relevant could impose a "conspiracy of silence on the media," government policy did not develop. The "publicity explosion" that began in 1959 survived the political controversy of the 1960 election and promoted the policy shift.

After 1960, James Reston's critical columns, if they did not influence the country at large, did circulate widely through Catholic officialdom as well as through the "ever-nervous State Department" and the politically sensitive White House. Kennedy, according to Sorenson, read the newspapers not to learn the facts but to learn what the press thought was important enough to write about. After 1960 the opinion-setting media seemed to take a special delight in emphasising this "once taboo subject" and chiding government officials for neglect or "timidity". Once again, it was a case of elites influencing elites as the media deliberately challenged government leaders to catch up with the people they were supposed to be leading.

During the policy process the broad purpose of birth control and population legislation was publicised in relation to world hunger and poverty to such an extent that other, potentially more controversial aspects were smothered. The major legislation Congress passed on population in the 1960s was not widely covered by the media. Washington officials, including Catholic organisations, were aware of the proposed family planning amendments to AID, OEO, and Social Security legislation but the absence of wider publicity on those provisions and the considerable controversy over other provisions, may, as the study of abortion repeal in North Carolina suggests, have contributed to final passage. There was no time for opposition to mobilise. When publicity was deliberately sought, for example, by advocates of the Family Planning Services and Population Research Act in 1970, to bypass individual congressional leaders, or by abortion advocates in 1972 when Catholics tried to repeal the liberal New York law, such publicity often emphasised jurisdictional and procedural rather than substantive issues.

INDIVIDUALS

Policy studies uniquely combine the role of the individual and the role of the system." The policy process, in fact, takes place at the boundary of interaction between the two. How individuals shape institutions to meet their goals and then in turn find those goals modified by the needs of the institution is a classic dilemma of leadership. Max Weber's formulation of the "routinisation of charisma" describes the growth of the population movement in and out of government. Organisations that proved influential were founded by women and men who possessed to some degree the charismatic qualities of personal self-confidence, unshakable conviction in the rightness of their cause, and ability to perform enough "miracles" to maintain the faith of their followers. Some also possessed the charismatic liabilities of antagonising non-believers, insisting on personal control and credit, and thereby to a degree weakening the very institutions that they had built. For the charismatic leader, the problem *will* be solved, the honeymoon will never end, and the task of institution-building will always seem secondary to the cultural revolution that is just around the corner.

In their extreme forms, charismatic leadership and institutional competence are contradictory qualities. Over time, the building of any institution creates pressures for institutional maintenance that challenge and often displace the original goals. For this very reason many professionals, for instance the physicians, already organised into their profession, found it hard to concede that birth control might help to achieve their goals. Yet, in the short-run the rapid turn-about of government policy must in part be attributed to the considerable number of interested individuals who combined some of the qualities of charisma with the more prosaic ability to build, finance and maintain lasting institutions. Many of these individuals could be classified as political elites. Their success in influencing foreign policy more than HEW domestic programmes might be predicted from previous studies of the influence the elites and "attentive publics" exert in foreign affairs.

Yet not only do elites create policy but also the policy process itself helps to create new elites. Those who were once looked down upon because of their active or professional involvement with "an immoral issue like birth control" rose in personal status as they won the moral support of government policy and the financial support of government programmes. Initially or in the short-run, elite status, based on income, professional background, and family contacts enhances a person's ability to gain access to high officials and an initial hearing, but the long-term influence of individuals and organisations depends both on the status of the policy area and on their ability to provide the kind of information and assistance that policy-makers in government want at a particular time.

Even in a bureaucracy "the likelihood of personal impact increases to the degree that the environment admits of restructuring." Like an idea whose time has come, birth control was ready to emerge as a public policy issue. Those who took the lead in promoting the new policy found not only that the time was propitious but also that in many instances the opposition was a deterrent only to those who perceived it as such.

ORGANISATIONS

In the United States the birth control and population movement was from its inception uneasily divided between the activists, around Margaret Sanger, and the social scientists and physicians. Characteristically forming separate groups, they moved slowly into an uneasy alliance. Influencing public policy was a long-range goal for each, for the activists by rousing public demand and mobilising a direct appeal and for the professionals by defining the problem and documenting the facts.

The activists like Margaret Sanger were the first to aim at government. In the typology of interest groups they started as an "attitude group". Like the proponents of Prohibition in the United States or abolition of capital punishment in Great Britain, "They are pressure groups based on shared attitudes and the advocacy of changes in public policy rather than interest groups held together by the desire to obtain benefits for their section of the community." Such ad hoc groups often look weak, poorly financed, and unstable in comparison with sectional or economic interest groups. In their single-issue approach they seem to lack the prerequisites for political bargaining and influence. But as the history of British birth control movement suggests, "If the ideological commitment implied a certain rigidity – always a weakness in a pressure group – it also entailed an emotional attachment of a peculiarly tough and lasting nature."

As social reformers the birth control activists proceeded at first by "upsetting the balance" and "polarising the issue". Then they faced the triple task of recruiting a coalition of power (which was increasingly done by men like Hugh Moore and William H. Draper, Jr., through the business community); respecting democratic traditions of participation (which was increasingly done by including the patient communities in the organisation itself); and offering an objective scientific rationale for the programme (which was increasingly done by closer cooperation with the professionals.) This long-term process gradually transformed some of the first activist groups into established or professional institutions, critised by the next generation of activists for their willingness to negotiate and compromise.

In the few areas where Catholic opposition was minimal, family planning could be quietly incorporated into policy without public or emotional confrontations, as Measham has described in North Carolina. Yet in North Carolina counties as in U.S. government agencies or international UN bodies, family planning programmes seemed to achieve highest priority and greatest impact when promoted by outside activists with extra-budgetary resources.

The professional organisation in the population field, closely linked to the foundations and university centers, were slower in trying to influence policy. They were first pushed in that direction by the activists, who stimulated a government demand for their services and a government support for their work that made some of the professionals nervous. In 1968 a leading public health physician wrote, "Professionals who have long been frustrated by public apathy as they warned about and worked on population problems, now find themselves in the anomalous position of having to urge reasonable caution and careful planning." As with most policy problems, the issue became fashionable before the solutions were proven.

The foundations, too, did not seek directly to influence policy, only to educate the policy-makers broadly toward certain problems. Congress they avoided completely but in the population field as in other areas of social policy the foundations and professionals discovered that "a national philanthrophy becomes a prestigeful and uniquely well placed broker of new ideas." To the extent that ideas and information are the currency of government those who could deal with them moved closer into the policy-making process.

As government interest and policy developed in response to the problem itself but stimulated by outside organisations the role of some of those organisations shifted gradually, too. From the agitation of the outside pressure group, distributing pamphlets on street corners and engaging in publicised confrontations, the techniques of influence changed to more persuasive, rational and personal contact. "The transition from a 'fringe' cause to a semi-consultative status does represent very considerable progress" for any organisation in its relations with government. Similarly, the power of government agencies to exclude population experts as "non-professional" or "special interests," which NIH did in 1962, is a sign that either the organisation or the policy is still in its infancy. Unless purely personal rivalries are involved the progress of an organisation from agitation to consultation to contractor or client relationship seems to be a natural part of the policy process, whether the policy is regulative like the Interstate Commerce Commission or distributive through grant-making procedures, whether the field is economic or more distinctly scientific or social. What Lowi condemns as "interest group liberalism" and Bernstein attacks as agency degeneration can from a different point of view represent the government acceptance of a social movement.

In discussing interest group Eldersveld lists six different types, a typology that can also be applied to measure not only the status of the organisation but also the progress of the policy. His categories of power and influence are, from the top down:

1. Penetration into formal policy roles.
2. Maintenance of close political support and referral.
3. Unchallengeable veto status.
4. Attention, representative and pressure relationship.
5. Political reprisal relationship.
6. Rejection by the power structure, agitation and resistance.

During the 1930s birth control organisations were at the bottom of the ladder. By 1970 some professionals or representatives of professional organisations had reached the top. Thus, Oscar Harkavy of the Ford Foundation was invited to review HEW policies and he in turn invited Frederick Jaffe of Planned Parenthood to help him. By the late 1960s many activists were just moving into the formal policy process, to perform the tasks that they and their organisations had persuaded the government were necessary.

THE JUDICIARY

In the development of government birth control policy to date, the judiciary began to play a significant role in the 1930s. At a time when religious opposition still deterred legislative and executive bodies, only the courts were sufficiently insulated from political processes to look at the policy issues.

The first major court action after World War II was the *Griswold* v. *Connecticut* (1956) decision of the Supreme Court, acknowledging the legitimacy of birth control beyond the confines of professional, medical consultation. Justice Douglas proclaimed a new marital "right of privacy" for all. In birth control decisions, as later in abortion decisions, the first generation of cases had recognised professional and institutional rights. Only later – in birth control 30 years later – were the rights of ordinary, non-professional women and men equally recognised.

The thrust of the *Griswold* decision, repudiating claims of church and state alike as sexual arbiters, was as much a warning as an encouragement to government policy-makers. Catholic lawyers have already attempted to define those limits of privacy to exclude even government support for a voluntary service. Those very efforts, although not successful now, emphasise that the rights that the *Griswold* decision confirmed for individual citizens represent at the same time a basic limitation on the scope of any government policy.

Similarly in the abortion cases the first decisions emphasised the professional rights of physicians. Later decisions were based on the individual woman's right to privacy and choice. Restrictions on the distribution of contraceptives to minors and unmarried persons were also invalidated later on the same grounds of personal freedom. Thus, just as some population control advocates were beginning to argue the social need for restraints on individual fertility the courts seemed to be setting new limits on government interference with reproduction for any social purpose.

THE PRESIDENCY

The power of the presidency in policy-making on an issue of low priority that does not directly affect national security is checked by many restraints, not least of which is the President's own reluctance to use it. The four Presidents of the United States who served between 1959 and 1969 all played a personal role in the development of population policy, using in different ways the presidential power to publicise, to persuade, to legitimise, or to condemn new programmes. None of the four significantly utilised the budgetary, personnel, or command powers of the presidency even within the confines of government.

Eisenhower, for instance, interjected his own influence and prestige deliberately to keep birth control out of the partisan political arena. He succeeded in displacing the issue and perhaps strengthening national unity, at the cost of personal and perhaps party approval. He also proved Sorenson's point that "Presidential decision is usually the beginning, not the end of public debate." Whether one agrees with Eisenhower's action or not, it was an effective public use of presidential power under the circumstances. There is no evidence to suggest that he or his immediate staff took any further steps to implement this near-command.

President Kennedy clearly did not want to invest his own time or his own influence in the issue except to the extent that was politically necessary. He used the birth control issue to prove other points – his own objectivity, his concern for the national interest, and later his support for research and the spread of scientific knowledge. He did not encourage the executive agencies, but neither did he or his aides oppose initiatives that others in government were ready to take. He hoped that government could avoid a major role.

President Johnson was the first American President to take a positive stand favouring birth control. He was prepared to utilise the publicity and prestige of major presidential statements to advance an issue he believed both relevant and important for the U.S. government. Through nearly 50 statements he assumed an educational and legitimising role that helped to transform birth control from an uncomfortable taboo into a fully appropriate tactic in the wars on hunger and poverty.

But at the same time neither President Johnson nor his aides assumed a personal responsibility to implement those bold words at the programme level. Seeing his role as a preacher not as a practitioner and increasingly absorbed by issues of higher priority, Johnson perforce allowed the agency heads to determine their own programmes. Because the agency heads too saw birth control as less vital than other needs of their large, complex organisations they did not provide the "clear signal" from above that could have mobilised their staffs. As a result, during the Johnson administration a government policy in support of birth control was fully developed and articulated but programmes were implemented only where Congress insisted.

President Nixon took more important substantive steps than did any of his predecessors. By issuing the first presidential Message on Population and appointing a commission to study the problem, he gave to population an urgent yet unmanageable status comparable to such issues as student unrest and drug abuse. Immediately thereafter he encouraged budget increases for research and domestic family planning programmes. But at a time when zero population growth was a popular slogan, protecting the environment a new national pastime, and abortion an obvious solution to unwanted population growth, President Nixon like his predecessors did not give the issue top priority. He allowed others to promote it instead of doing so himself. On what seemed to be mainly personal and political grounds he went out of his way to condemn abortion.

In each administration outside individuals, advisory groups, presidential committees, White House conferences, task forces, and in one case a UN debate raised the issue to government attention. By setting targets or proposing organisational changes that executive agencies often would not suggest, these groups became a source of innovation in each administration that led more directly to the White House and Congress than to the specific agencies. The statements of Kennedy, Johnson and Nixon ultimately provided a cloak of greater legitimacy under which congressional and outside supporters could advance.

The strongest support for population policy initiatives was voiced by Presidents Johnson and Nixon each at the beginning of a term in office, when it was undoubtedly easier both to consider long-term problems and to disregard short-term political repercussions. The greatest opposition or lack of interest occurred at the end of a term or just prior to a new election – examples are Eisenhower's repudiation of the Draper proposal in 1959, Johnson's waning interest in the Cohen-Rockefeller report in 1968, and Nixon's criticism of the Population Commission in 1972.

To stimulate favourable actions, Congress and the federal agencies joined with the outside advocates in praising presidential leadership, even reconstructing history to give credit for more than had actually been done. But while publicly praising the President, the very same agencies were often privately frustrating his intent in small ways and large. Even the Bureau of the Budget, designed to strengthen the President's hand, could set its own management and budgeting norms above the priorities of the President. With limited time, limited information, and even more limited political resources, no President did much more on the population issue than express his opinion with appropriate pomp and circumstance and "wonder if the government will go along."

On the international level, the UN Secretary-General, U Thant, even more than Presidents Johnson and Nixon, moved beyond previous leaders and official mandates to deal with the population problem. First in 1965, and more emphatically in 1966, he called public attention to the issue. Furthermore, by creating the first Population Trust Fund in 1967, and by transferring it to the UN Development Programme in 1969, he acted largely on his own initiative to help the programme expand. Yet, like Johnson and Nixon, burdened with many more immediate crises, he, too, did not prevent the imposition of bureaucratic constraints by his own subordinates upon the new programme he had encouraged.

THE ADMINISTRATIVE BUREAUCRACIES

If the great anonymous bureaucracies appear to be the villians of this account, blocking at every turn the development of new policy, it is because such agencies offer built-in resistance to innovation of all kinds. The bureaucratic habits of both national and international agencies that first hindered population programmes, then reluctantly incorporated them, and finally began to defend them, bear much resemblance to the propositions developed by Anthony Downs in *Inside Bureaucracy*. Certainly, growth of the population programme with AID confirms the basic outline Downs suggests of a new activity bitterly opposed by the programming and budgeting offices of the agency, established under zealous leadership with more concern for content than organisation, gradually establishing greater internal autonomy, wider external support, and a more precise strategy.

AID innovation in the population field did not originate at the top of the agency or even in the agency at all but rather from outside or from what in AID was the bottom, the technical professional level. In part this was the result of a declining budget. With no slack, with every decision on priority a verdict against other programmes, the power to allocate resources became more important than the resources themselves or the uses to which they were put.

In part too AID reluctance to move into any new field was a function of sunk costs, the unwillingness to cut back on started but unfinished projects. It was also a function of lack of confidence in the ability of the agency to develop a new programme and lack of confidence to judge the substantive merits of a proposal. In an attempt to measure programme efficiency against the annual yardstick of a hostile appropriations committee, the concept of programme adequacy, difficult at best in foreign aid, was most readily sacrificed.

It is significant that the one innovation that developed strictly within the bureaucratic structure, with the typical secrecy of executive agency processes, was clearly related to what Edward Banfield describes as "the maintenance and survival needs of large complex organisations." The establishment of the Office of the War on Hunger strengthened the administrator of AID by providing new leverage, both internally and externally. From Gaud's point of view it was justified by the same arguments of relevance, feasibility, priority and urgency that marked outside initiatives. But, under increasing outside pressures Gaud's principal goal was to maintain and preserve rather than carve out new territory.

A most conspicuous feature of the AID population programme was rapid expansion on a crash basis with a very small staff. Not since the European Recovery Programme often cited as the most successful modern foreign assistance effort, had an economic assistance programme – although on a very much lower level – grown so rapidly. By 1969 the virtues born of necessity in the population programme were being extended to other activities. In both AID and the UNFPA, initial emphasis was on gathering and deploying substantial resources rather than building up internal staff or training new experts. Both programmes emphasised interdisciplinary problem solving rather than professional skills per se. In both cases, the need to allocate funds in a limited time forced policy to become more flexible. For both, coordination was achieved not by organisational structure or hierarchy, but by control over funds. The activist, resource-oriented growth of AID and UNFPA contrasts with the more professional but less effective efforts of the UN Population Division and U.S. HEW programme to expand in an slow and orderly manner, emphasising first training and infrastructure. It remains to be seen whether slow-moving, professionally oriented agencies like the U.S. Department of HEW and the World Health Organisation will be able, in the long-run, to support or maintain family-planning programmes more effectively than problem-oriented but politically insecure agencies like OEO, AID and the UNFPA.

THE LEGISLATURE

Deeply involved in the population policy process in the U.S., Congress moved ahead of parties, agencies, and often the White House to develop this new issue. In a sense, the role of Congress was residual because others failed to move, but in the overall progress Congress was a critical factor.

"The informing function of Congress should be preferred even to its legislative function," Woodrow Wilson observed. Certainly, with respect to population policy "the informing function" of Congress was fully exercised. Senator Gruening's deliberate and organised hearings educated official Washington to a remarkable degree, in the process defining the birth control issue and giving it public legitimacy. Hearings on the world food crisis and family planning as part of the poverty programme suggested a new framework in which the issue could be treated by government policy-makers. Later, environmental problems and the implications of zero population growth were explored also and publicised by hearings.

At first through committee exhortations and reports Congress set broad policy direction, treating birth control as a necessary ingredient for economic development and for adequate world nutrition. Then through the broad authority of Title X of the Foreign Assistance Act Congress made it clear that population programmes should have greater flexibility, variety and discretion. None of the domestic legislation and none of Title X (except the loan-to-grant provision), provided any new statutory power, but all served to direct emphasis toward a specific policy. In addition to such guidelines, through Title X Congress established fixed funding. Despite the reluctance of officials who believed that programming and budgeting were their responsibilities, Congress insisted on action. The separate amendments on domestic programmes and the major policy thrust contained in the Family Planning Services and Population Research Act of 1970 were all to some degree enacted in spite of rather than because of executive agency concern.

Congress has so far used very little of its powers of personnel action, administrative oversight, or investigation in respect to the population programme. Early efforts at administrative oversight by Senator Gruening and Congressman Moss were designed to reinforce rather than criticise the programme, but being divorced from funding powers they carried little weight. More recently, Senator Cranston's and Congressman DuPont's hearings on research and family planning services are a start toward programme review, but are still several steps removed from the purse strings.

Within Congress the impetus came from single individuals like Fulbright, Clark, Gruening, Todd, Scheuer, Bush, Tydings, Cranston and Packwood, who on this as on other issues have often assumed the role of innovators in government. To the degree that by coincidence or seniority they were also committee or subcommittee chairmen, their power to achieve results was greatly enhanced. The frequent combination of high support for population policy and opposition to administration foreign policy, which would not hold true for the older generation of population advocates outside Congress suggests that these legislators may have a different, more independent view of congressional roles in the policy process than do their colleagues. Although the majority of senators and representatives are lawyers, Fulbright, as a former university Professor and President, and Gruening, as a former journalist, came from an educationally oriented background. With the exception of Robert Byrd, none of those who promoted birth control have sought or gained roles of political leadership except through specific policy issues.

The congressional impetus for birth control programmes came from the substantive authorising committees and was usually discouraged by appropriating committees. Partly because funding was involved on a crash programme basis but partly also because birth control did not coincide precisely with established agency objectives, the appropriating committees often played a negative or neutral role. Where annual or frequent authorisations reduced the influence of appropriating committees' influence, birth control, as an innovation stemming from broad policy reassessments, seemed to proceed faster.

Is it the changing structure of Congress and the new roles assumed by different members that made an innovation like birth control policy depend largely on legislative action? Or is it the character of birth control itself as an issue that tends to emphasise the legislative route to policy?

The important role of Parliament in formulating British policies toward birth control (and also toward capital punishment) – even though party discipline and executive control are stronger in Britain than in the United States – suggests that "this type of controversy" may have a "greater likelihood of being played out in the legislative branch of government than is true of other types of public decision-making." A British study on the abolition of capital punishment concludes: "Emotional issues that plumb deep-seated moral codes – for example, birth control, prostitution, homosexuality and hanging – are 'hot potatoes' that party leaders find unpredictable and often diversionary in character." Whether or not birth control really was a "hot potato" as an issue in the United States in the 1960s, the executive agencies though that it was and left the initiative to Congress.

Similarly, in the UN system the legislative bodies of the various agencies were often ahead of the international civil servants. Ironically, U.S. bureaucracies like AID, the State Department, and even HEW, requiring pressure from Congress to step up their own programmes, worked vigorously on the legislative, or policy and financial, level in the UN to step up UN programmes. Administrative agencies, both national and international, needed the independent pressures of outside bodies controlling financial resources in order to undertake new population programmes.

THE POLICY-MAKING PROCESS

The study of change apart from substantive content and social and economic environment may well prove to be the ultimate intellectual will of the wisp. Whether the process is called God's will, natural law, philosophy of history, evolution, thesis-antithesis-synthesis, challenge-and-response, incrementalism, or the policy process, generalisations prove all too often specific for one time, one place, one field – at best one very small part of a much larger whole.

Over the last generation the so-called policy sciences have become the "policy process". Change has become routine and stability unusual. There remains no control to measure change against. The specific changes documented in this study took place against a rapidly changing background that included:

1. The change in the world environment, that is, the population growth phenomenon itself, without which neither the policy nor the programme would have developed at all.
2. The change in the role of the U.S. government, which assumed new social and economic responsibilities both in the United States and overseas.
3. The change in public attitudes toward, first, the practice, and then the public discussion of birth control and human reproduction.
4. The change in the opposition to birth control from Catholic enforcement of prohibitions on all toward increased tolerance and Catholic practice of birth control.
5. The change in the supporters of birth control from charismatic roles toward institution-building roles, including the activation of the professionals and the professionalisation of the activists.
6. The change in birth control technology that made government programmes feasible yet sufficiently difficult to require massive effort.

Against that background the issue of birth control was first incorporated into U.S. government policy only as it appeared relevant, feasible, significant and urgent in relation to national goals of economic development. Population and birth control policies at the government level were, like military weapons, means to another end, not an end in themselves.

Under the pressure of facts, theories, technology, argument, persuasion and outside trigger events a population policy was defined in the public forum of Congress and to varying degrees implemented. The arguments progressed through various phases of relevance from optimum size to density to resources to rate of growth. Feasibility developed in relation to diminishing Catholic opposition and new improved technology. Priority was set from above in terms of financial resources by a dissatisfied Congress. Urgency was first the product of unexpected food gaps.

But even as population policy was being defined at the U.S. government level in relation to economic objectives other, non-economic, goals were being articulated and defined for government policy-making. These included better health care, elimination of pollution, concern for environment, liberation of women, and freedom from government interference in private sexual activities. In advancing each of these strategies, birth control and population policy could also be useful tactics. As improved health care was increasingly recognised in the United States to be a government responsibility, family planning could be increasingly incorporated within the health network. As concern for the total environment challenged arguments based on individual economic benefit, reduced fertility could be justified as a natural, ecological imperative. To the extent that equality for women and reduced government control over sexual behaviour were acceptable, restrictions against birth control and abortion on social grounds could be removed. In each instance, as new national goals or strategies were developed by various groups, support for fertility control measures could be strengthened to the extent that they were proven relevant, feasible, important and urgent in achieving those goals.

The original government objective that justified birth control support, economic development, was based on an optimistic assessment of man's capacity for continued rapid economic and social improvement. To the extent that a basic strategy becomes less confident, less over-reaching less of a recognised panacea for many ills, a tactic based on limitation or control gains force. Population control, like arms control, is rooted in its supporters' perception of a finite world, with limited space, resources and funds. Just as in the military field measures of arms control have become increasingly relevant as the cost of a full deterrent is no longer acceptable, so the tactics of population control may be more easily assimilated into government policy at a time when economic strategies are revised downward or limited.

As long as the role of government remains primarily the enhancement of national power and the improvement of citizens' welfare, a government population policy will have to be related to the sources and objectives of that role. The more directly a population policy is related to the most valued government objectives, the more important it will become as a government policy.

On the international level, population control programmes are increasingly viewed as a tactic in the strategy of economic development. But for some of the Communist and the developing nations other tactics, such as a greater redistribution of wealth, may be considered more relevant; for some of the developed nations environmental protection may become at least as important a strategy as economic development. Only when population control or arms control are seen by all nations as necessary tactics to achieve their other major strategies — whether they be prosperity, security, or survival — will they achieve higher priority on the policy level. Long before that day comes, individuals and couples in many countries may conclude for themselves, as they have already done in Europe and Japan and are now doing in the United States, that individual fertility must be controlled regardless of government policy.

14

NUTRITIONAL STATUS IN INDUSTRIALISED SOCIETIES: EUROPE AND NORTH AMERICA SINCE 1750 AND POPULATION EDUCATION

In the less developed countries of the world today, the association between human physical growth and the physical, economic and social environment is clear for all to see. Poverty, malnutrition, and disease shape the bodies of the people from birth to death. Both at the micro level, where the health of individual children is monitored, and at the macro level, where group or population means are calculated, physical growth is clearly seen to be responding to changes in the environment and to social and medical intervention.

For these reasons, the study and monitoring of physical growth is of particular interest in developing countries. It is also worth considering, however, whether physical growth is of interest in the industrialised and more developed societies, and how far insights from the developing countries can reasonably be applied to countries where levels of income and of health are far different. This chapter, therefore, first considers the meaning of anthropometric measures of physical growth; it then describes the history of physical growth in the industrialised world and suggests some explanations for the patterns that can be observed.

Why should We Study Human Physical Growth?

Human physical growth is studied for many reasons. To paediatricians and other medical researchers, the primary focus is on the impact of the environment on the individual or the small group and the aim is the cure or alleviation of ill-health or distress. To human biologists, growth is a central concern in understanding the complex of nutritional and hormonal mechanisms that control change in the human body. To the epidemiologist, growth is of interest as a summary measure of environmental influences and increasingly as a proxy for environmental influences during childhood and adolescence which may affect later health. To the practical nutritionist, growth is a measure of the success of intervention in diet. To the economist, physical growth and strength help to determine individual labour productivity. To the anthropologist, growth is a measure of man's adaptation to his physical environment. To the historian, growth is a measure of changing nutritional status which is closely related to the concept of the 'standard of living', the subject of many historical controversies.

These different concerns of social and biological scientists are naturally reflected in their modes of investigation of the phenomena of physical growth. The different aims determine the questions that are asked, the variables that are measured, and the period of growth that is studied. Thus, the vast majority of medical investigations are concerned with the first years of life, few with adolescence, and fewer still with the later phases of growth and then shrinking in middle and old age. Studies of nutritional intervention and of the impact of malnutrition on growth are concerned almost entirely with the less developed countries, studies of height differences between occupational groups almost entirely with the more developed countries. Economists concentrate on contemporary societies, historians and some anthropologists on societies of the past.

In addition, auxologists (as students of human growth are called) study many aspects of growth and use many indicators – height, weight, height-for-age, weight-for-height, and skinfold thickness, to name but some. The most frequently used indicator, however, is height; and, since that is also the indicator most commonly available from historical sources, it is height that is the focus of this chapter.

It is useful to distinguish at the outset between two ways in which height may be viewed. First, it can be seen as an indicator of the past and present; second, it can be seen as an indicator of the future. In both cases, height links a group of people to the environment in which they have grown up and in which they are to live.

Height as an indicator of the past and present

There is ample evidence from history, from both the developing world and the industrialised world, of the value of height as an indicator of the past or present environment of an individual or of a group of people. Studies of the efficacy of nutritional supplements provide striking evidence of the rapidity of response of growth to an improved environment. Martorell found that children provided with a high-protein, high-calorie beverage grew significantly taller and heavier than a control group; moreover, 'the higher the supplement category, the larger are the children in all four dimensions (supine length, weight, head circumference and arm circumference)'. As they commented,

> the results of the present study suggest that simple and well-known measures such as weight and supine length (height) should be utilised in evaluating public health programmes. These are not only among the most sensitive of measures but also among the most reliable.

At the level of whole societies, Eveleth and Tanner introduced their monumental study within the International Biological Programme of *Worldwide Variation in Human Growth* with the following words:

> A child's growth rate reflects, better than any other single index, his state of health and nutrition; and often indeed his psychological situation also. Similarly, the average values of children's heights and weights reflect accurately the state of a nation's public health and the average nutritional status of its citizens, when appropriate

allowance is made for differences, if any, in genetic potential. *This is especially so in developing or disintegrating countries.* Thus, a well designed growth study is a powerful tool with which to monitor the health of a population, or to pinpoint subgroups of a population whose share in economic and social benefits is less than it might be. Indeed as infant mortality rate goes down during a country's development, so the importance of monitoring growth rate increases.

The link between environment and physical growth was also plain in the developing countries of the past. As today, the connection was often clearest to visitors, who see with fresh eyes distinctions that have become so familiar as to be invisible to residents. In 1833, for example, one of the British Factory Commissioners, Dr Bisset Hawkins, commented that:

> I believe that most travellers are struck by the lowness of stature, the leanness and paleness which present themselves so commonly to the eye at Manchester, and, above all, among the factory classes. I have never been in any town in Great Britain nor in Europe in which degeneracy of form and colour from the national standard has been so obvious.

It was also clear, as in Guatemala and other less developed countries today, that social intervention in the form of feeding programmes and medical programmes could have significant effects. The trustees of the Marine Society, a London charity, described in the late eighteenth century how the boys in their care, drawn from the slums and stews of London, grew rapidly when given food and shelter; while, later in the nineteenth century, enquiries into recruiting for the army were told of the rapid physical growth of recruits after their induction into the army and the receipt of regular meals.

It was, no doubt, because he could see with his own eyes the correlation between environment and physical growth that L.R. Villermé could produce, in 1829, one of the earliest but also one of the most complete and perceptive accounts of the link:

> Human height becomes greater and growth takes place more rapidly, other things being equal, in proportion as the country is richer, comfort more general, houses, clothes and nourishment better and labour, fatigue and privation during infancy and growth less: in other words, the circumstances which accompany poverty delay the age at which complete stature is reached and stunt adult height.

Despite these early comments, and despite the modern experience of physical growth and deprivation in the less developed countries, many people in the more developed countries instinctively reject the association between height and the environment which Villerme observed. Either they are incredulous at the suggestion that there are significant differences in physical growth between distinct groups in the community, or they are unwilling to accept that such distinctions have an environmental origin. Why is this so?

In part, it stems from the Darwinian inheritance which has predisposed us to accept genetic or at least pseudo-genetic explanations for human differences. In part, also, it must stem from the fact that, as I shall show below, differences in the patterns of physical growth and their results in terms of height and weight are now much less dramatic than they were, both within and between the more developed countries.

In part, however, the difficulty stems from the lack of an adequate scientific model of the causation of growth. Summaries of the literature present a lengthening list of the correlates of physical growth; in summarising studies made before 1974, Eveleth and Tanner identified, among environmental influences on variation in growth, the following: nutrition and disease, socioeconomic level, urbanisation, seasonal and climatic variation, psychosocial stress, and the 'secular trend' for which 'factors such as improved nutrition, control of infectious disease through immunisations and sanitation, more widespread health and medical care, and population mobility (both geographically to urban areas and socially upwards) appear to be responsible'.

More recently, studies such as that by Rick Steckel have emphasised economic variables such as per capita income and the level of inequality, while sociologists have emphasised the possible effects of education and 'health behaviour' in relation to diet.

Despite the much more sophisticated techniques on which individual studies of this kind are now based, in many ways we have not advanced very much further than Villermé in understanding, for any particular population or point in time, the relative contribution of each of these multifarious factors to human growth. Some progress has been made; Martorell has convincingly shown, for example, that illness now seems to play little role in determining growth in the developed countries, while studies 'from developing nations report that common childhood ailments, in particular diarrhoeal diseases, are clearly associated with poor physical growth'.

But such cases are rare, and the absence of a general causal model vitiates many of the individual studies that have been made: they make use of a variety of statistical methods and do not report the results in a consistent form. Moreover, in the absence of a comprehensive model linking all the variables, the correlations that have been reported are necessarily misleading, since the functional relationships that have been estimated do not take account of other variables that have been shown or at least alleged to be of relevance. The separate correlations are not equivalent to partial correlations, since they are not controlled for other relevant variables. In addition, there is a strong likelihood of collinearity between some of the variables; the well documented synergistic relationship between nutrition and some diseases is an obvious and highly relevant example. If both malnutrition itself and diseases such as infantile diarrhoea cause stunting in growth, and if malnutrition predisposes children to diarrhoeal diseases and exacerbates their effects, then the statistical disentangling of their separate contribution to growth is likely to be a task of monumental difficulty.

In one sense, this problem of identifying the contribution of various environmental factors to human physical growth can be disregarded – finessed might be a better word – by invoking the concept of growth as an index of nutritional status. Height is probably best seen as an indicator of a complex of environmental factors that affect the human body and together determine the nutritional status of a person at a moment in time. For obvious reasons, height is not an indicator of such status at each moment: rather, it sums up the successive states of the human body during the growth period from conception to the cessation of height growth in adulthood. As Robert Fogel puts it,

> In considering the relationship between nutrition and height, it is important to keep in mind that height is a net rather than a gross measure of nutrition. Moreover, although changes in height during the growing years are sensitive to current levels of nutrition, mean heights reflect the accumulated past nutritional experience of an individual over all of his growing years including the fetal period. . . .
>
> The measure of net nutrition represented by mean heights depends on the intake of nutrients, on the amount of nutrients available for physical growth after the necessary claims of work and other activities (including recovery from infections), and on the efficiency with which the body converts nutrients into outputs. The body's ability to generate a surplus for growth will vary with such factors as age, the climate, the nature of the available food, clothing and shelter, the disease environment, the intensity of work, and the quality of public sanitation. In other words, the same nutritional input can have varying effects on physical growth, depending upon environmental conditions. Consequently, mean height . . . is a measure of the balance between food consumption and the claims on that consumption.

Such a generalised index of human welfare is well worth having. In *Measuring the Condition of the World's Poor,* Morris

David Morris discusses objections to all the conventional measures of socioeconomic performance and sets out six criteria that a composite measure of such performance must satisfy:

1. It should not assume that there is only one pattern of development.
2. It should avoid standards that reflect the values of specific societies.
3. It should measure results, not inputs.
4. It should be able to reflect the distribution of social results.
5. It should be simple to construct and easy to comprehend.
6. It should lend itself to international comparison.

Morris himself advocates, as satisfying these criteria, the 'physical quality of life index' with three components: infant mortality, life expectation at age 1, and basic literacy. Each component is scaled and then combined with equal weights. It would appear, however, that height as an indicator of nutritional status meets all six of Morris's criteria without the need for any scaling or weighting, which, as Morris himself admits, is inevitably somewhat arbitrary.

Height and nutritional status are therefore analogous to measures of welfare. Indeed, to many economic and social historians, the interest of anthropometric measures of nutritional status lies primarily in the light that they can shed on variation in the standard of living of populations in the past. There are important ways, however, in which measures of height differ from conventional measures of welfare such as real income levels, and even from conventional measures of health such as are collected in surveys of the health of a population.

First, as Fogel has frequently emphasised, nutritional status is itself a net rather than a gross measure: it reflects not the gross value of inputs in the form of consumption of food, warmth and shelter, but the balance between those inputs and demands on the body for maintenance, growth, and work effort, including the defeat of disease. 'Moreover, although changes in height during the growing years are sensitive to current levels of nutrition, adult height reflects the accumulated past nutritional experience of an individual over all of his growing years including the fetal period'. Similarly, the mean height of a population represents the cumulated nutritional status of that population during the periods of height growth of its members.

Cumulated nutritional status, represented by height, is thus very unlike conventional measures of welfare which describe the welfare of an individual or a nation at one moment in time, irrespective of past experience or, indeed, of the likely future welfare of that person or nation. Height, by contrast, is closer in many ways to a measure of human capital. First, it represents accumulated experience, the balance between inputs and outgoings up to the time of measurement. Second, however, it represents future potential.

Height as an indicator of the future

Military recruiters in the past explicitly sought tall recruits; they did so on the grounds that such men would be healthier and better able to withstand the stresses and strains of military life. Slave-owners, too, were prepared to pay more for taller slaves and selected relatively tall slaves for elite tasks:

> other things being equal, a male who was three inches taller than the typical adult male was 62 per cent more likely to be a driver than one who was three inches shorter than the typical male. On average, drivers were an inch-and-a-half taller than the men (and five inches taller than the women) who laboured in the gangs.
>
> Advantage in height also increased the likelihood that men would be selected as craftsmen and that women would be chosen as domestics.

As Fogel points out, increased height in this instance gave both a physical and a phychological advantage. The same seems to be true in modern developed societies. First, psychological advantage is suggested by a number of studies which have shown that relatively tall men and women are more likely to be upwardly socially mobile, whether by occupational mobility or through marriage. This relationship has been shown by Illsley in studies based on women in Aberdeen and by Knight and Eldridge in their survey of British adults. It has also very recently been demonstrated in an analysis of the British National Child Development Study by Power: they show that there is a clear class gradient in height at age 23, and that this persists even after controlling for the social class of the parents.

> Thus, social mobility between birth and 23 was selective with respect to height, but mobility did not account for the social class gradients in height; indeed, there was some suggestion that the differences in the proportions short might be wider by social class at birth than by social class at 23.

The exact mechanisms relating social mobility to height, and thus to cumulated nutritional status, have not yet been explored within this or other studies. But it seems likely that the health of the child and young adult must be an important factor; that is, healthier and (probably) richer children have a better chance of achieving upward social mobility than their poorer, less healthy peers, perhaps because relative poverty and ill-health detract from education. It is even possible that such poverty affects brain development and thus intelligence, although such a connection is highly speculative at the income levels that are achieved in the more developed countries.

Second, physical advantage has been suggested in a number of studies which have shown that, after controlling for other variables, height has an independent effect on life expectation and, probably, on morbidity. Marmot, in a study of the British civil service, found that height was a significant predictor of cardio-vascular mortality, even after controlling for social class, smoking behaviour, and other variables; and Waaler demonstrated the same relationship for both cardio-vascular and respiratory diseases, while showing that it did not hold for accidental death. Waaler is prepared to argue that the increased height of the Norwegian population, betokening higher nutritional status during the growth period, is likely to result in declining mortality levels in the future.

If, as these studies suggest, cumulated nutritional status as represented by height experts a long-term influence on life chances in a variety of ways, then the analogy between height and human capital seems close. On the other hand, height has an aspect that differentiates it both from conventional measures of welfare and from measures of human capital: once growth has ceased, or (in most developed societies) much earlier, nothing can be done to increase it. Nor, in fact, given the economic and general dependence of most children upon their parents, can any individual do anything to increase his height, though it is conceivable that the parents might be able to do so. There is little evidence, however, that food supplementation programmes or even protection from disease can make any difference to height or growth in the developed world. It remains possible, of course, for nutritional status to be maintained or improved after the period of growth ceases, but such improvements will no longer be reflected in anthropometric measures.

The measurement of height thus offers great potential for the description and exploration of the changing nutritional status of peoples in the past and in the present; if also offers the potential to contribute to the explanation of many changes, in morbidity, mortality, and even in social and occupational mobility, which have long intrigued social scientists. But can height in the past be adequately measured?

The Measurement to Height in the Past

The measurement of height is not straightforward. First, there are numerous documented sources of measurement error; although methods of measurement have been improved and standardised over the years, early methods were crude in the extreme. Second, there are problems that arise from the sources of information that are available to us. Our primary source of evidence on height during the past two centuries stems from the operations of military forces and in particular from military recruitment, whether voluntary, as was characteristic of the English-speaking nations, or by conscription, as was the case in most of the rest of Europe. Other sources do exist; the slave trade to the Americas, and in particular the effort to regulate and then abolish the trade and slavery itself, provides evidence of the heights and other physical characteristics of Africans forcibly transplanted to the new world. Finally, there exist a number of surveys of the heights of populations carried out mainly in the twentieth century, either explicitly for commercial use or by governments interested to provide information useful to designers of clothing and furniture.

However, the primary source of data on changes in the physical growth of populations remains the recruitment records. This gives rise to some pitfalls and difficulties of interpretation. It was normal for volunteers to be recruited between the ages of 15 and 30, although preponderantly between the ages of 18 and 22; with volunteer data, therefore, it is usually possible to build up a description of the last years of physical growth and to estimate the age at which growth typically ceases. Conscripts, on the other hand, were typically recruited only at a single age, normally 18, 19, or 20, although it varied between countries and over time within countries.

Such conscript data can give only a snapshot, at one moment in time, of the complex process of human growth and, moreover, of a moment at which the process of growth in those measured has largely but not entirely ceased. Ideally, one should be able to observe the whole growth process from birth to maturity, since it is known that environmental factors affect not only the absolute height achieved at a given age but also the tempo of growth. It is well known, for example, that the age at menarche in girls has become earlier since the nineteenth century, and the same applies to the timing of the adolescent growth spurt in boys and girls and to the age at which final height is achieved. This last point is highly relevant to conscription data; whereas in the past an 18-year-old might well not have achieved his final height when he was measured for military service, today he would almost certainly have done so. A comparison of the mean height of a cohort of 18-year-olds today with a cohort of 18-year-olds from one century ago will therefore probably overestimate the change in final height. On the other hand, even if we knew the change that had occurred in final height, that change would itself be an underestimate of the effect of changing environment on growth, since some of that impact would have been reflected in the earlier maturity – perhaps at the same absolute height – of the modern cohort as compared with that of the past. The problem arises because, although the tempo of growth and the final height are linked, the two phenomena are to some extent independent of each other; there are some fast-growing, early maturing groups who are short, and some slow-growing, late maturing groups who are tall. I will return to this problem below.

Military conscription data must, therefore, be interpreted with great care. Nevertheless, they offer by far the largest and the most consistent set of evidence available for the description of changes in mean height; they therefore form the principal source that is used below, although they have been supplemented by survey data and, most importantly, by data from volunteer recruiting in Britain, in its American colonies, and in the USA. Such data have their own problems of statistical estimation and interpretation, stemming from the frequent omission of those shorter than the prevailing height standard required by the army, which have been discussed and largely resolved in a number of papers.

While this is probably not a serious problem in the calculation of mean heights from large samples, more severe difficulties arise from cases in which particularly short recruits were excluded altogether from measurements; as mentioned above, it has been necessary to develop special statistical procedures to cope with this problem.

Even more problematic, however, is the difficulty, referred to briefly above, that there is no single appropriate summary measure of the height of a person or a group. Absolute height can be measured at a particular age – in late teenage years as it normally was in the case of conscription or at birth, at age 2, or when growth can be assumed to have ceased entirely. But the interpretation of the result of that measurement can only be made within the context of the whole profile of growth relevant to that person or group. As Tanner puts it,

> within a given, well-nourished population, there is no correlation between tempo and final height; tall men are as likely to have been late as to have been early maturers. Even between populations at different levels of nutrition, the correlation is far from close. A population which is short at age 14 may be so either because its children are delayed in growth (in which case they may reach a considerable height as adults) or because they are simply short – before, then and later with average tempo. As for trends within a single population, in historical data increasing mature size usually is accompanied by increasing tempo of growth. But the two should certainly not be regarded as inseparable; at least in theory, a trend in tempo might continue beyond the point at which a trend in mature size finished, or even *vice versa*.

Since this is so, no single measure of height can be relied upon to summarise the entire growth experience, as it might be required to do when entering as the single dependent variable into an estimation of the determinants of nutritional status. It is probable that, as Tanner indicates, final height in adulthood comes closest to serving as such a summary measure. On the other hand, differentials in adult height between populations and between groups within populations are typically much smaller than are differentials in height at, for example, the time of the adolescent growth spurt; evidence from maximum likelihood estimates of socioeconomic differentials in the heights of male adults in Britain in the early nineteenth century suggest a range of not more than 3-4 inches in adult heights, but the range at age 14 between boys from the London slums and boys from the upper classes who entered the Royal Military Academy was as much as 10 inches.

Faced with this situation, it is possible to argue that final height provides the most conservative estimate of height differences and that it is, therefore, the safest indicator of nutritional status. It is tempting to dismiss adolescent height differences as 'merely' the product of differences in the timing of the adolescent growth spurt. But the height at adolescence is not a spurious indicator: differences in tempo do reflect differences in nutritional status, and, by implicitly subsuming them within adult height, we may be not only substantially underestimating the changes in nutritional status that have occurred, but also depriving ourselves of variance which should be of use in statistical analysis. It is true that in practice we rarely have the luxury of choice, since the data usually do not permit us to observe the whole growth profile or even more than one part of it; but we should not therefore forget how partial or inadequate one single measure of height may be.

Despite these difficulties, it is sensible to try. What can we discover about heights in the past?

Human Height in the Industrialised World, 1750 – 1980

It is unfortunately necessary, because of the availability of data, to confine our attention to the countries of western Europe and North America. Evidence from military records shows that the average height of European male populations at the age of conscription has varied, during the last two hundred years, between 159 and 181 cm. The shortest mean height yet recorded or computed for conscripts recruited on a national basis is that of 159.1 cm for recruits aged 18 to the Habsburg armies in the eighteenth century, while Kiil estimated that the height of recruits aged 18.5 to the Norwegian army in 1761 was 159.5 cm; the *Historical Statistics of Italy 1861 – 1965* (Italy, 1978) shows that the mean height of 20-year-old recruits born in 1854 was 162.39 cm; Spanish recruits, as late as 1913, had a mean height of 163.6 cm.

Since growth would probably have continued after the age at which these recruits were measured, it is likely that these measurements are a slight underestimate of final adult heights for those communities. On the basis of modern populations in the less developed world, who have similar mean heights, it is reasonable to add an estimate of about 3 per cent for further growth after the age of 18, giving an estimated minimum mean final height for European national populations of about 165 cm.

Measurement of the upper end of the observed range can rely on modern data. Army recruits aged 17.5 in the Netherlands had a mean height of 180.7 cm in 1982 (Netherlands, 1983). These men, the tallest recorded in Europe, were closely followed by Norwegians with a mean of 179.4 cm in 1983 (Norway, 1984). In the absence of survey data, it is not clear how much further growth before final height is reached should be assumed for such tall populations, but it is unlikely that more than 1 per cent more could possibly occur, giving an estimate for final height of not more than 182.5 cm.

The range of final heights for whole national populations observed in Europe has thus been between about 165 and 183 cm during the past two hundred years. As would be expected, the range over sub-groups of national populations has been somewhat wider. The shortest geographical group of all appears to have been recruits from the town of Murcia in Spain, whose mean height was only 158.8 cm in 1895. At the upper end of the scale, the tallest geographical group yet recorded within Europe appears to be the inhabitants of Aust-Agder in Norway at 180.8 cm (Norway, 1986), although it seems likely that some Dutch areas would have higher means; the Dutch statistical yearbook unfortunately ceased to record regional height data after the Second World War. If we again allow 3 per cent further growth after conscription for the shortest recorded group and 1 per cent further growth for the tallest, we can estimate the range for large geographical sub-groups of national populations to have been between 163.6 and 182.6 cm. There is, unfortunately, too little evidence to make similar statements about the range across different socioeconomic groups, although, once again, one would expect the range to widen somewhat if economic and occupational factors could be taken into account. Some variation of this type is, presumably, proxied by geographical variation, and I have used height material to discuss inequality within Europe in another publication.

All the European and North American societies for which evidence on physical growth is available have experienced increases in mean height during the past two centuries, or at least since records have become available. So ubiquitous is this phenomenon that it has simply been called 'the secular trend' by auxologists and human biologists. Study of the evidence, however, shows that different societies have approached their modern mean heights by very different routes. It is possible to distinguish three broad groups, although the divisions between them are often slight.

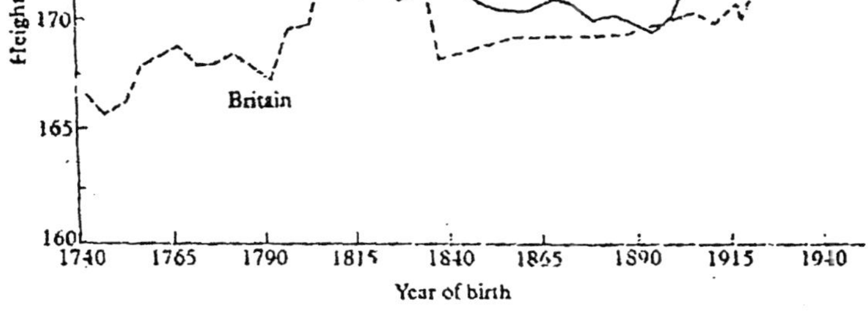

Fig. 14.1 : Adult Height: America and Britain, 1740 – 1940.

The first group (Fig. 14.1) consists of Britain, its North American colonies, the USA, and, probably, Australia. Estimated height means for North America and Britain are shown in the figure. These countries exhibited heights that were relatively great, both by modern standards and, as we shall see, by the standards of Europe as a whole as early as the eighteenth century; thereafter heights followed a cyclical path without a marked upward trend until the twentieth century. Substantial increases in height then took place, particularly after the Second World War, with some evidence that mean heights ceased to rise during the 1960s, although this is still in dispute.

The second group (Fig. 14.2) consists of a number of northern European nations, in particular Denmark, Norway, the Netherlands and probably Sweden. These countries all had significantly lower mean heights than the English-speaking nations in the eighteenth and early nineteenth centuries but grew rapidly, particularly in the twentieth century, and have now become among the tallest peoples in the world.

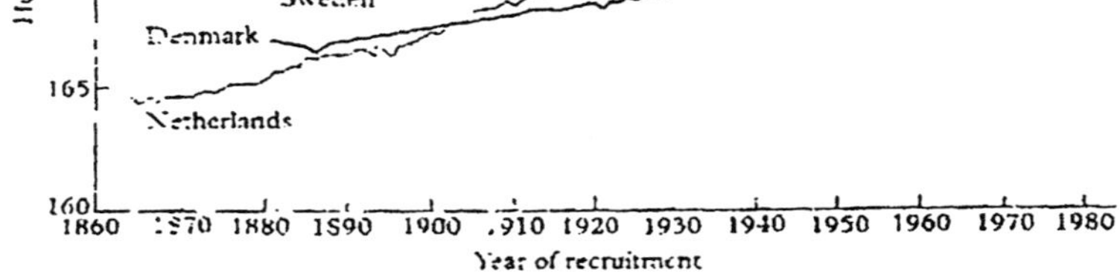

Fig. 14.2 : Height at Conscription Age: Sweden, Norway, Denmark and the Netherlands, 1860 – 1980.

The third group (Fig. 14.3) consists of a number of southern European nations, in particular France, Italy and Spain, which have had mean heights consistently below those of northern Europe, but have seen increasing growth, particularly since the Second World War.

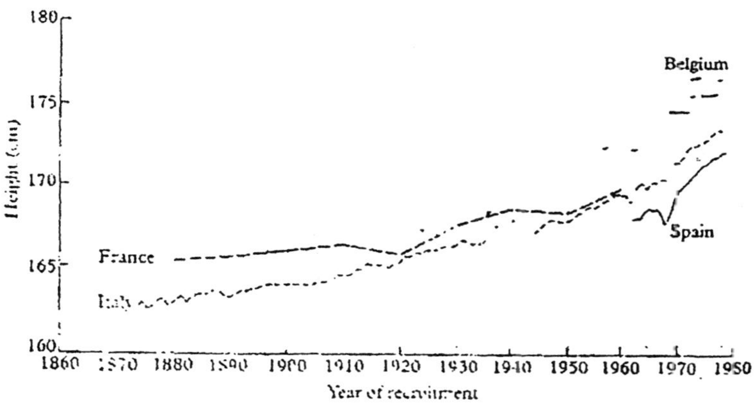

Fig. 14.3 : Height at Conscription Age: Belgium, France, Italy and Spain, 1860 – 1980.

The difference between the second and the third group is of particular interest, since it shows that, despite the common growth overall, the process has not so far been one of convergence to a common European mean height. Indeed, the gap between the mean height of Italian and Dutch male conscripts, for example, has grown consistently, both in absolute and in relative terms, over the last century. In 1874 Italian recruits averaged 162.4 cm and Dutch 164.9 cm, a difference of 2.5 cm, while in 1982 the averages were respectively 172.8 cm and 180.7 cm, a gap of 7.9 cm. Although Italians are now growing taller at a rapid rate, it would be rash to predict when, if at all, the gap will be closed.

It is important to put the growth in European heights over the last two hundred years in perspective. It is a matter of considerable psychological interest – although it is not a

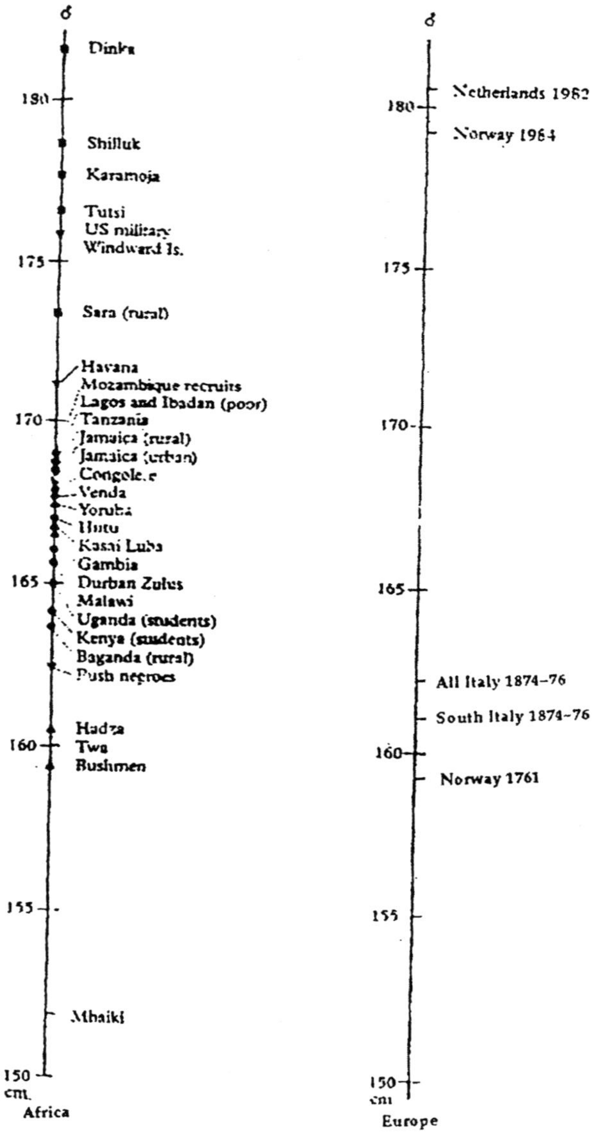

Fig. 14.4 : The Contrast between the Range of European Heights over Time and of African Heights Today.
Source: Eveleth and Tanner (1976).

subject that seems to have received explicit attention from psychologists – that apparently small differences in height, of the order of a centimetre or two, are very clearly perceived as significant differences by observers. As a consequence, and because we presumably carry in our minds a concept of the usual range of human heights that we are likely to encounter, we also tend to overestimate the actual size of height differences between different groups. Figure 14.4 therefore reproduces a diagram from Eveleth and Tanner of the modern heights of African adults and juxtaposes this with the range of European heights over the last two hundred years. It can be seen that the European range over time spans almost the whole of the African range over space, with the exception of some, though not all, bushmen and pygmy tribes.

As a specific example, the Norwegian recruits of the 1760s were as short as African bushmen, while today they are as tall as the Dinka of the Sudan. This comparison is not meant to imply that it is to be expected that, given adequate nutrition, bushmen will ultimately grow as tall as the Dinka, for we do not know whether this will be so, but rather to emphasise by analogy how different the Norwegians of the eighteenth century would have looked from the Norwegians of today.

Despite the overall increase in heights in Europe and America, there is abundant evidence of the persistence of differences in mean heights within national populations, related both to geography and to socioeconomic status, and to the interaction of these two influences with each other and with other environmental factors. Such differences persist even in the countries with the greatest mean height; in Norway in 1985, for example, the region of Troms had a mean height of 178.1 cm while that of Aust-Agder averaged 180.8 cm. In other countries the differentials are still wider; in France in 1960 there was a gap of 6.35 cm between the shortest department, Morbihan at 166.2 cm, and the tallest, Seine at 172.55 cm. Survey evidence also shows that in Britain there is still a significant difference in mean height not only by region but also by social class; as the authors of the government survey comment,

> it is clear that there is a class effect on height independent of age and sex. In almost every age group people from households headed by a manual worker were shorter, on average, than people from non-manual worker households. Overall, the average height of men was 175.5 cm (5' 9") in Social Classes I and II but 172.3 cm (5' 8") in Social Classes IV and V. Similarly, female height in Social Classes I and II was 162.5 cm (5' 4") compared with 159.6 cm (5' 3") in Classes IV and V.

It is, however, often asserted that in countries such as Sweden, which have less marked income and wealth inequality than Britain, such class gradients have now disappeared.

The evidence of change in the heights of Europeans thus presents social scientists with a number of problems. What has caused, first, the overall increase in heights; second, the differing patterns seen in different national countries; and, third, the persistent height differences that are still found even in countries that have very high levels of income and correspondingly low levels of mortality and morbidity?

An Interpretation of the Increase in European Heights

The thousand or more studies reported by Eveleth and Tanner, together with the many more performed since 1974, make it clear that height variation is a reflection of a multiplicity of possible environmental influences interacting with genetic factors. In the less developed countries, it is possible to assert that the primary causes of heights that are low by the standards of the more developed countries are poverty and disease, associated in the familiar synergistic relationship.

In addition, it seems likely that the overall disease environment, worsened by the extreme poverty of the bulk of the population, accounts for a phenomenon that Robert Fogel has named the 'peerage paradox'. This stems from the observation, first made of the British peerage in the eighteenth and nineteenth centuries, that high-wealth and high-income groups in society – presumably able to command whatever food and comfort they wished to consume – nevertheless had life expectations significantly worse than similarly wealthy groups in developed countries today. I have observed a similar phenomenon in the case of height: the sons of the aristocracy who attended the Royal Military Academy in the nineteenth century, although far taller than working-class boys, were yet shorter than the modern mean for the entire British population and shorter still than the modern upper-class mean. Although it is possible that both life expectation and height could be accounted for by poor treatment of aristocratic children in the nursery, it seems much more likely that the general level of infectious disease, from which they could be only partially isolated, was responsible for the poor nutritional status of the upper classes. Similar conclusions have been drawn from modern studies of high-income families in the developing world today.

Thus, there is little mystery about the causes of the poor nutritional status and low height of the bulk of the population of less developed countries or of their relatively low average nutritional status; the low average income and the extreme inequality in the distribution of incomes experienced in those countries is bad both for those suffering from poverty malnutrition, and disease and for those who, though apparently rich enough to avoid such deprivation, yet suffer from living in such a society.

But can the same be said of the more developed, industrialised countries that are the focus of this paper?

The most striking feature of the change in mean height in Europe and North America shown in Figs. 14.1 – 14.3 is clearly the overall increase in all countries in the twentieth century, compared with a stable rate, a much slower rate of increase, or even a temporary decline in the nineteenth century. As I have shown elsewhere, height growth in the countries of western Europe, excluding Britain, during the late nineteenth and twentieth centuries is highly correlated with movements in GDP per capita and the rate of infant mortality. I have not yet attempted a similar analysis of British and

North American data, but it seems reasonable to expect that the same ecological relationship would apply. Since we know that, in most of the countries studied, infant mortality has fallen to low levels since the beginning of this century, it seems likely that movements in GDP have recently been a more significant influence. This is particularly so if one includes within those movements changes in the distribution of national income and wealth.

The situation in the nineteenth century is much more complex. Although the movement of gross domestic product per capita in Britain and the USA in the eighteenth and nineteenth centuries is still the subject of hot debate, it seems almost certain that, in terms of the conventional measures of welfare, both Britain and its American colonies, later the USA, were the wealthiest countries in the world. This is, indeed, borne out by the height data. It is somewhat surprising that, between those two countries, the American colonies should have exhibited such an advantage in mean heights over Britain in the eighteenth century, but this can probably be accounted for by very high levels of food consumption in the rural colonies. It appears that this advantage disappeared during the first quarter of the nineteenth century, perhaps as a result of the early stages of British industrialisation and the rising real incomes which it and the agricultural revolution brought to the British working class.

What is most puzzling, however is the failure of either the American or the British mean heights to rise significantly during the nineteenth century, when it is commonly thought that the impact of industrialisation, after some lags, led to an increase in the real incomes of the populations. Indeed, in both countries mean heights appear to have fallen from the levels reached early in the second quarter of the century, and not to have regained those levels until almost a century later. This is despite the fact that conventional measures of real income show very marked increases in both countries.

While it is impossible to be certain, it seems highly likely that this check or reverse in height growth can be attributed to the later stages of the impact of industrialisation, when the growth of industry led to massive urbanisation and a worsened disease environment. Both Fogel and Komlos, in work so far unpublished, have suggested that the American evidence is compatible with such an explanation, particularly since there seems to be some ground for thinking that the reverse came first in the urban areas and then spread to the countryside. In Britain, it is known that infant mortality and life expectation, which had improved in the latter part of the eighteenth century, show little significant change for much of the nineteenth century: while child and adult mortality declines from the 1870s, infant mortality, which is particularly relevant to growth, does not improve markedly until the twentieth century. There is also abundant impressionistic evidence of the poverty, disease and degradation of the urban areas of industrialising Britain. Moreover, detailed analysis of British military records shows clearly that birth and residence in the urban areas, in particular London, was associated with shorter height, and that the positive association between urban residence and tallness that is a feature of twentieth-century data was negative in the eighteenth and nineteenth centuries.

It also seems possible, although much more detailed research would be needed to confirm this, that differences in the disease environment contributed to the differences between northern and southern European countries seen in Figs. 14.2 and 14.3, although both Italy and Spain also had, until recently, much lower income levels than the northern European countries. It seems likely that the very rapid recent increase in mean heights in Italy and Spain represents the recent increases in the wealth of those countries and the conquest of endemic and epidemic disease.

Another feature of the western European data deserves more discussion. In the several countries for which annual data are available, the growth in heights appears extremely smooth, a rising trend undisturbed by the various cataclysms that have affected Europe during this century. By contrast, both British and American data for the eighteenth and nineteenth centuries show marked fluctuations. It is possible, of course, that the contrast reflects in some way the different methods of military recruitment used in each group of countries. It is unlikely, however, that statistical procedures used on the British recruitment data, to compensate for the effects of the lower height limit, could be at fault. Such procedures are of little importance in the North American case, where the distributions were little affected by the rejection of the shortest potential recruits. Sampling variability may be a problem, since much of the British and most of the North American data are based on samples; but in most cases the sample sizes are large.

It seems likely, however, that one major distinction between the European and, at least, the British data may be of importance. As mentioned above, the conscription data include most if not all of the male populations, while in Britain recruits were drawn almost entirely from the working class, many of whom were living in or brought up in poverty, and who would exhibit more fluctuation in mean height as a result of environmental variation than would recruits drawn from the upper and middle classes. It may be, therefore, that variations in height in the European countries have been dampened by the inclusion of upper- and middle-class recruits in their height statistics, and that this leads to the relatively smooth pattern of change over time in those countries. Only detailed research in the military archives, as opposed to the use of published statistics, can settle this issue.

Even if the overall trend in European heights is not too difficult to explain some problems remain. In the industrialised countries extreme poverty has long been avoided by income support schemes of various kinds, infant mortality and morbidity has been enormously reduced, and the general income level of the population is both far higher and more equally distributed than in less developed countries. It thus seems clear that, although the overall trends in height over time may indeed reflect the elimination of much poverty and disease in the developed world, neither the current variation in height and nutritional status within that world nor, to some extent, the trend in the most recent past can owe much to the traditional causes of such variation. These countries are today so rich, and they have been so rich for so long, that malnutrition and epidemic or endemic disease seem unlikely determinants of height variation. One is faced, in fact, with the modern version of the 'peerage paradox'; instead of needing to explain the low heights of the rich within a poverty-stricken society, we now need to explain the low heights of the poor within an affluent society.

It can be argued that the matter is one for empirical study; after all, the statistical estimation of the determinants of height will presumably reveal the most influential variables. In principle this is so, but such estimation is likely to be extraordinarily difficult because of problems of measurement of many of the variables and of multicollinearity. In addition, such studies as that of Martorell on the relationship between disease and growth emphasise the view that, as Steckel puts it in discussing his modern cross-sectional study.

> it is likely that different coefficients would be obtained from data for earlier time periods. Improved medical technology probably shifted the relationship between average height and per capita income. Knowledge of the germ theory of disease, for example, enabled individuals to improve health, and therefore increase height, with no change in income.

Nevertheless, there are persuasive arguments for the view that, even in the more developed countries, differences in income, wealth and health still exert a measurable and significant influence on nutritional status and therefore on height. The strongest support comes from the analysis of differentials in height by social class, which are clear in Britain but greatly attenuated, if present at all, in Sweden. The survey by Knight and Eldridge (1984) shows these differentials for adults in Britain, but numerous studies of children demonstrate their pervasiveness and the early age at which they become established. Rona, for example, showed that there is an association in British children between height and parental social class, sibling size, and the unemployment of parents; while Smith showed that such associations and the resulting differentials are established before children enter school at the age of 5. By contrast, Lindgren found for Sweden that 'No significant differences between socio-economic strata defined by father's occupation and family income were found either for height and weight or for ages at PHV, PWV and menarche'.

It is possible, of course, that income differences are not responsible for such class differences in height; other possibilities might be the extent of psychological and emotional support for children, differences in the amount of work effort or other physical activity required in different classes, or even inherited characteristics. But, of these, only the last could conceivably affect children as young as the age of 2, when class differences in height can be found, and it seems most unlikely that genetic inheritance could explain marked class differences in countries such as Britain which have high levels of social mobility. The evidence of Sweden, where income differences have been much reduced but where behavioural differences between white-collar and manual workers are still evident, also suggests the primacy of income as a determinant. But exactly how income exerts its influence – whether through the quality or quantity of diet, warmth, housing density, or other mechanism – still remains undetermined.

If we look forward rather than back, the main implication of Figs. 14.1 – 14.3, so far as the contemporary developed world is concerned, is that we have not yet experienced the full effects of the improvement in nutritional status which is shown by measurements of height to have occurred in recent decades. If, as Waaler's work suggests, such improvements have direct consequences for mortality levels, in particular for mortality from respiratory and cardio-vascular diseases, then it is likely that significant improvements in mortality and associated morbidity have still to occur in most of the countries of western Europe. This is particularly so if such improvement is combined with the independent effects of reductions in tobacco consumption and an increase in exercise, which are both known to affect such diseases.

Further improvement in the overall nutritional status of the populations in the more developed world is unlikely, however, without a decrease in inequality. Steckel found that, in a cross-sectional analysis of contemporary societies, the extent of inequality was a significant determinant of mean height, and this is confirmed by the evidence, quoted above, which links height to class structure in Britain and, presumably, in other developed countries. Unfortunately, in Britain at least, the combined effects of fiscal measures to increase income and wealth inequality and the increase in unemployment are militating against such an improvement: it may indeed be true that, for the first time since the nineteenth century, a developed nation is experiencing a decline in the mean height of its population.

15

THE EUROPEAN ESCAPE FROM HUNGER: FAMINES, CHRONIC MALNUTRITION AND MORTALITY RATES

During the late 1960s a wide consensus emerged among social and economic historians regarding the causes of the decline in the high European death rates that prevailed at the beginning of the early modern era. The high average mortality rates of the years preceding the vital revolution were attributed to periodic mortality crises which raised 'normal' mortality rates by 50 – 100 per cent or more. It was the elimination of these peaks, rather than the lowering of the plateau of mortality in 'normal' years, that was believed to be principally responsible for the much lower mortality rates that prevailed at the end of the nineteenth century. These crises, it was held, were precipitated either by acute harvest failures or by epidemics. Some scholars argued that, even if the diseases were not nutritionally sensitive, famines played a major role because epidemics were spread by the beggars who swarmed from one place to another in search of food. Whatever the differences on this issue, it was widely agreed that many of the mortality crises were due to starvation brought on by harvest failure.

A mechanism by which a harvest failure was transformed into a mortality crisis was proposed by Hoskins in two influential papers published in the 1960s (1964, 1968). Noting that it was possible to identify harvest failures by looking at the deviations in grain prices from their normal level, Hoskins computed the annual deviations of wheat prices from a 31-year moving average of these prices. Normal harvests were defined as those with prices that were within ± 10 per cent of the trend. He found that, over the 280 years from 1480 to 1759, good harvests (prices 10 per cent or more below trends) were about 50 per cent more frequent than deficient harvests (prices 10 per cent or more above trend). His most important finding, however, was that good and bad harvests (as shown by prices) ran in sequences, so there were frequently three or four bad years in a row. These sequences, he argued, were due primarily not to weather cycles but to the low yield-to-seed ratios, which he put at about 4 or 5 for wheat at the beginning of the sixteenth century. Thus, one bad harvest tended to generate another because starving farmers consumed their reserve for seeds. The consequence of several bad harvests in a row was a mortality crisis.

The interpretation of the European escape from hunger and high death rates embodied in this train of research was brought into question with the publication of The Population History of England, 1541 – 1871: A Reconstruction by E. A. Wrigley and R.S. Schofield (1981). Using data from 404 parish registers widely distributed throughout England, these scholars and their associates constructed monthly and annual estimates of the English population over a 331-year period, as well as monthly and annual estimates of the national birth rates, mortality rates, and nuptiality rates. Although important issues have been raised about various assumptions employed in the analytical procedures that transformed the information on baptisms and burials contained in the Anglican registers into national estimates of birth rates and death rates, it is widely agreed that the reconstruction was carried out with meticulous care, and that the various adjustments for deficiencies in the record were judicious. Whatever the shortcomings of the reconstructions, the new time series produced by Wrigley and Schofield have become the foundation for all further research into the demographic history of England.

In addition to presenting their basic time series and describing the complex procedures employed to produce them, Wrigley and Schofield began the processes of relating these demographic rates to underlying economic and social phenomena. They determined that both fertility rates and marriage rates were strongly correlated with measures of real wages and the cost of living, but that mortality rates were not. A chapter of the book contributed by Lee reported a statistically significant but weak relationship between short-term variations in death rates and in wheat prices; but Lee, as well as Wrigley and Schofield, concluded that short-run variations in English mortality were 'overwhelmingly determined' by factors other than the food supply. In so far as the long-term trend in mortality was concerned, Wrigley and Schofield reported that they were unable to find even a weak statistical correlation between mortality rates and the food supply.

Since the findings of Wrigley, Schofield and Lee appear to be so sharply in conflict with the train of research that has linked the escape from high mortality rates to the escape from hunger, it is tempting to declare that one of the research trains must be wrong, and to choose sides. I believe that such a conclusion is not only premature but very likely wrong. The aim of this chapter is to reconsider the older line of research in the light of the findings of Wrigley, Schofield, and Lee in order to see where they are compatible and where the evidence tilts towards one or the other side.

In the next section, I present evidence indicating that the elimination of crisis mortality accounted for only a small part of the decline in national mortality rates during the nineteenth century. The text under Heading Measuring the Variability of Food Supply argues that some previous attempts to infer the extent of the shortfall in the quantity of foodgrains harvested from movements of prices have exaggerated that shortfall because of overestimates of the elasticity of demand for foodgrains. Text under heading Families Amid Surpluses presents an alternative hypothesis which makes sharp changes in the distribution of foodgrains, resulting from relatively small shortfalls in output, the principal cause of periodic famines. A mechanism underlying such distributional changes is proposed. It is then argued in heading The Long Struggle to Repair the System of Food Distribution that famines could have been avoided, and apparently were avoided during 1600 – 40 in England, by proper government policies. Text under heading Chronic Malnutrition and the Secular Decline in Mortality deals with the effects of chronic malnutrition on mortality rates. It presents evidence which suggests that most of the secular decline in mortality in England, France and Sweden before 1875, and about half of the decline between 1875 and 1975, was due to the reduction of chronic malnutrition.

The New Findings on Mortality Crises

One of the most important aspects of the *The Population History* is the new light it sheds on mortality crises over the 331 years it covers. Wrigley and Schofield are the first scholars who have had a sample of parishes large enough in number and wide enough in geographic coverage to permit an estimate of the national impact of mortality crises on the annual crude death rates in early modern England. Following established procedures, they measure mortality crises as deviations from a 25-year moving average, and define a crisis year as one with an annual CDR (crude death rate) that is more than 10 per cent above trend. That criterion yielded 45 crisis years, a bit less than 14 per cent of the years in their study. They also computed national crisis months (months with monthly death rates at least 25 per cent above trend), and found that 94 years contained at least one such crisis month. Their analysis confirmed many of the findings of scholars working with less complete data. The year 1558/9, for example, emerged as by far the worst year for mortality in the entire period. They also found that the most severe mortality crises were concentrated during 1544 – 1658, although there was a lethal recurrence during the late 1720s.

Perhaps the most important aspect of the new time series on mortality, however, is that these data drastically diminish the role of crisis mortality as an explanation for the high mortality rates that generally prevailed between 1541 and 1800. This conclusion emerges from two tables in *The Population History*, which together provide the data needed to compute the crisis component of total mortality. The results of the computation are presented in Table 15.1 by quarter-centuries (or fractions thereof) as well as by centuries (or fractions thereof). In no quarter-century did crisis mortality account for as much as 10 per cent of the total mortality. Even after crisis mortality is factored out, the 'normal' mortality remains above 25 per thousand for the sixteenth, seventeenth and eighteenth centuries. Indeed, the 'normal' mortality rate of the eighteenth century was as high as the total mortality rate of each of the two preceding centuries, despite their many crises. Consequently, the escape from high mortality rates was due primarily not to the elimination of crises, as many have previously argued, but to the reduction in so-called normal mortality levels. Nearly three-quarters of the decline of mortality between 1726 – 50 and 1851 – 71, despite the relatively high level of crisis mortality at the beginning of this period and its negligible level at the end of it, was due to the reduction of 'normal' mortality.

It follows that, even if every national mortality crisis identified of Wrigley and Schofield was the result of a famine, the elimination of periodic famines cannot be the principal explanation for the secular decline in mortality. This is not to deny that famines in particular localities at particular times produced great increases in local mortality rates: too much evidence of local disasters induced by food shortages has accumulated to rule out such phenomenon. However, in light of the Wrigley-Schofield data, it now seems clear that, dramatic as they were, mortality crises, whether caused by famines or not, were too scattered in time and space to have been the principal factor in the secular decline in mortality after 1540.

Table 15.1
The Impact of Crisis Mortality on the Average Crude Death Rate: England, 1541 – 1871

Period	*(1) CDR per 1000 person-years*	*(2) Crisis mortality per 1000 person-years*	*(3) CDR after factoring out crisis mortality (per 1000)*	*(4) Crisis mortality as % of average mortality*	*(5) Crisis mortality as % of 'premature' mortality*
By quarter-centuries					
(1) 1541 – 50	30.33	2.25	28.08	7.42	9.64
(2) 1551 – 75	28.28	2.35	25.93	8.31	11.04
(3) 1576 – 1600	24.21	1.22	22.99	5.04	7.09
(4) 1601 – 25	24.61	2.05	22.56	8.33	11.64
(5) 1626 – 50	26.36	0.99	25.37	3.76	5.11
(6) 1651 – 75	28.07	1.58	26.49	5.63	7.50
(7) 1676 – 1700	30.29	1.66	28.63	5.48	7.13
(8) 1701 – 25	27.79	0.06	27.73	0.22	0.29
(9) 1726 – 50	30.57	2.34	28.23	6.40	9.93
(10) 1751 – 75	27.28	0.40	26.88	1.47	1.97
(11) 1776 – 1800	26.85	0.55	26.30	2.05	2.77
(12) 1801 – 25	25.40	0.15	25.25	0.59	0.82
(13) 1826 – 50	22.58	0.13	22.45	0.58	0.83
(14) 1851 – 71	22.42	0.13	22.29	0.58	0.84
By centuries					
(15) 1541 – 1600	26.93	1.87	25.06	6.92	9.38
(16) 1601 – 1700	27.33	1.57	25.76	5.74	7.72
(17) 1701 – 1800	28.12	0.83	27.29	2.95	3.93
(18) 1801 – 1871	23.53	0.14	23.39	0.59	0.85

Notes :

Lines (1)–(4): col. (1) Each entry is the average of the quinquennial rates for the period given in Wrigley and Schofield (1981: 528–9). *Col. (2)* Each entry is the difference between the corresponding entries in cols (1) and (3). *Col (3)* Wrigley and Schofield (1981: 333) give the CDR (D_{c}) for each of the 45 years they identify as a crisis year, as well as the percentage deviation of the crisis CDR from a 25-year moving average, which is taken to be the normal CDR for that year. Hence, by dividing 1 plus the percentage deviation into the crisis CDR, it is possible to obtain the 'normal' CDR for the crisis year (D_{nc}). It is also possible to solve the following equation for the normal CDR in non-crisis year (D_{nn}) :

$$D = \theta D_{c} = (1-\theta)\, D_{nn}$$

Where D is the average CDR for the time period (as shown in col. (1) and θ is the share of crisis years during the time period. The average CDR with the crisis mortality factored out (D_n) is then given by

$$D_n = \theta D_{nc} + (1-\theta)\, D_{nn}.$$

The entries in col (3) are the values of D_n *Col (4)*. Each entry is 1 minus the ratio of the col. (3) entry to the col. (1) entry.

Lines (15) – (18): cols. (1) and (3) The entries for each period are average of the corresponding figures for the sub-periods in lines (1) – (14), weighted by the number of years in the sub-periods. *Col. (2)* Each entry is the difference between the corresponding entries in cols. (1) and (3). *Col. (4)* Each entry is 1 minus the ratio of the col. (3) entry to the col. (1) entry. *Col. (5)* 'Premature' mortality is defined as the crude death rate of a given period minus the English death rate of 1980 standardised for the English age structure of 1701 – 5 (see Fogel 1986*a*: Table 1).

Measuring the Variability of Food Supply

The Population History does not provide the same challenge to previous thought on the scope of subsistence crises as it does on the question of mortality crises. Indeed, the periods that Wrigley and Schofield identified as the major subsistence crises generally coincide with those identified by Hoskins. That outcome is not surprising, since the procedures used in the identification and measurement of subsistence crises by Wrigley, Schofield and Lee are quite similar to those of Hoskins. Wrigley and Schofield used annual deviations in an index of real wages from a 25-year trend to identify subsistence crises. Because of the procedure for smoothing the wage series, as they pointed out, nearly all the variability in the index came from the price deflator which was dominated by grains (broadly defined). Lee, like Hoskins, relied on wheat prices alone, on the grounds that the price of wheat was so highly correlated with other food prices that wheat was 'a good proxy for food prices in general'.

The tradition of judging the shortfall in the food supply by price is an ancient one dating back at least to Gregory King, who first formalised the systematic relationship between the yield of a harvest and the subsequent price of the grain.

Called 'King's Law', his schema (see Table 15.2) has been employed as an estimate of the elasticity of demand for wheat. Later economists, such as Jevons and Bouniatian, formulated quite similar laws in equations. All three laws are closely approximated by constant elasticity demand curves with ε ranging between 0.403 and 0.422. As Table 15.2 shows, the equation

$$Q = 1.00P^{-0.403} \tag{1}$$

gives a very close fit to King's Law in the specified range of prices. It seems quite reasonable, therefore, to use the deviation in price to infer the deviation in the yield of a harvest from its normal level, as numerous analysts have done ever since King's time.

Table 15.2
A Comparison Between King's Law and a Constant Elasticity of Demand Equation
(1 = normal price and yield)

King's Law		$Q = 1.00P^{-0.403}$	
Q	*P*	*Q*	*P*
1.0	1.0	1.00	1.0
0.9	1.3	0.90	1.3
0.8	1.8	0.79	1.8
0.7	2.6	0.68	2.6
0.6	3.8	0.58	3.8
0.5	5.5	0.50	5.5

Source: Slicher von Bath (1963: 118 – 19) presents King's Law and compares it with those of Jevons and Bouniatian.

When King's Law is combined with the proposition that the yield-to-seed ratios of wheat was about 4 – i.e. that one-quarter of the crop was needed for seeds – the interpretation of harvest failures developed from price series by Hoskins and numerous other scholars during the past three decades follows immediately. Wheat prices 50 per cent above normal imply a harvest that is 15 per cent below normal, a situation presumed to have put heavy pressure on farmers to dip into their seed reserve. With two such years in a row, even if farmers succeeded in maintaining the normal proportion of the crop for seed reserves, consumption in the second year would be cut by more than a quarter – pushing the average food intake of the lower classes to perhaps 1340 calories per equivalent adult or less per day. How devastating, then, must have been years such as 1555 and 1556, when a 51 per cent deviation of the price of wheat above normal was followed by a 105 per cent deviation above normal – suggesting a decline of lower-class consumption to the neighbourhood of 1180 calories.

The problem is that the implied level of caloric consumption in 1556 is too low to be believable, since it is well below the requirement for basal metabolism. We know, both from controlled semi-starvation experiments and from actual conditions in underdeveloped countries today, that even levels of 1300 – 1500 calories produce protein-energy malnutrition (PEM) serious enough to incapacitate a large proportion of the population and also lead to so many cases of kwashiorkor that death rates increase significantly among those affected. A population forced to consume less than basal metabolism for a whole year would have produced noticeable increases in mortality. Yet the Wrigley-Schofield time series, while confirming Hoskin's finding that 1555 and 1556 were years of extreme dearth, report that the mortality rates during these two years averaged about 10 per cent below normal. Indeed, after searching for a correlation between extreme annual deviations in prices and in mortality rates, they concluded that no significant contemporaneous relationship existed, although there was evidence of a weak lagged relationship.

This puzzle is not necessarily without a solution. One possibility is that government intervention prevented a subsistence crisis from turning into a mortality crisis. Another possibility is that defects in the Wrigley-Schofield estimates of mortality may explain the anomalous results. Yet their ingenious procedures for correcting the undercount of deaths, if less than perfect, seems to have produced a series quite adequate for the particular analysis they have undertaken. The problem, I believe, lies not so much in the data but in a series of implicit assumptions that have gradually crept into the analysis of the data, assumptions made so often that they hardened into an unquestioned procedure. It was only with the discovery of the Wrigley-Schofield paradox that the need to reconsider the analytical procedures became evident.

The crux of the problem lies with the application of King's Law which as has been indicated, is well described by a simple demand equation of the form

$$Q = P^{-\varepsilon}. \tag{2}$$

When P (price) and Q (quantity) are measured as proportional deviations from trend, (2) becomes

$$\overset{*}{Q} = -\varepsilon \overset{*}{P}, \tag{3}$$

where an asterisk over a variable indicates percentage deviations from trend, and ε is the elasticity of demand. Equation (3), which is the definition of that elasticity, is thus a simple linear equation in which the value of the coefficient of the right-hand variable is given by

$$\varepsilon = \frac{\sigma_q}{\sigma_p} r_{pq} = -\frac{\overset{*}{Q}}{\overset{*}{P}}, \tag{4}$$

where σ_q is the standard deviation (s.d.) of $\overset{*}{Q}$, σ_{*p} is the s.d. of $\overset{*}{P}$, and r_{pq} is the correlation coefficient between $\overset{*}{Q}$ and $\overset{*}{P}$. It follows that the value of ε will be greatest when r_{pq} is assumed to equal 1, which is the assumption generally made in the application of King's Law. Since this assumption is not at issue in the analysis that follows, and because a value of r_{pq} less then 1 would strengthen my argument, I will assume that $r_{pq} = 1$ in the balance of the discussion.

It follows from (4) that one can estimate an elasticity for wheat by obtaining estimates of σ_p and σ_q. The estimate of σ_p

for wheat is readily available from the wheat prices used by Lee and is about 0.22 for the period 1540 – 1840. The value of σ_q (measured as a proportional deviation from trend), computed for the first 30 years for which data on the physical yield of wheat in England are available, is 0.040. Assuming, as a first approximation, that the climatic factors affecting the variability of yield were similar between the seventeenth century and the end of the nineteenth, the preceding figures imply that the demand elasticity for wheat was 0.183 (0.0402 ÷ 0.220), which is more than 50 per cent below the elasticity of the demand for wheat implied by King's Law, or at least by the way that it has been interpreted.

Table 15.3
The Effect of Allowing for Carry-over Stocks in the Supply of Wheat at the End of the New Harvest

(1) *Deviation from normal yield of current harvest* Q_j	(2) *Price*	(3) *Deviation from normal supply if carry-over is 5 months* Q'	(4) *Deviation from normal supply if carry-over is 4 months* Q''
1.0	1.0	1.00	1.00
0.9	1.3	0.93	0.92
0.8	1.8	0.86	0.85
0.7	2.6	0.79	0.78
0.6	3.8	0.72	0.70
0.5	5.5	0.65	0.62

Note: Cols. (1) and (2) are from Table 15.2; cols. (3) and (4) are computed from

$$Q_j^i = \theta I + (1-\theta) Q_j,$$

where I is the carry-over inventory, which is assumed to be constant for each value of Q_j (taken from col. (1), and θ is the share of carry-over inventories after the close of a normal harvest ($\theta = 0.294$ with 5-mo. carry-over and 0.250 with 4-mo. carry-over.

The problem with some previous interpretations of King's Law is that investigators implicity assumed that carry-over stocks of wheat from the previous harvests were nil. This assumption was an unintended but necessary consequence of treating the deviations from normal annual yields [column (1) of Table 15.2] as the total supply – as when I used the series in columns (1) and (2) of that table to estimate equation (1). However, the annual supply is not just the harvest in a given year, but the harvest plus the carry-over stock from previous years. Davenant estimated that in normal times carry-over stocks varied between four and five months (i.e. between 33 and 42 per cent of a normal crop). Consequently, when estimating the demand curve, the proper quantity is not Q but Q' or Q'' (Table 15.3). When those series are substituted for Q, the estimated values of are given by :

$$Q' = 1.00P^{-0.248} \quad \text{(when carry-overs are five months);} \quad (2a)$$

$$Q'' = 1.00P^{-0.272} \quad \text{(when carry-overs are four months).} \quad (2b)$$

Thus, when one corrects for the neglect of carry-over stocks, King's Law implies an elasticity of demand that is not only between 33 and 38 per cent below the level often presumed, but also a good deal closer to the estimate obtained by using the standard deviation of proportional deviations of physical yields from trend at the end of the nineteenth century.

Table 15.4
The Normal Distribution of the Supply of Grain (New Crop Plus Carry-over Inventories) at the Close of Harvest

	%
(1) Carry-over stocks	29.4
(2) Animal feed	8.5
(3) Seed for the next crop	17.6
(4) Human consumption	44.5

Source: Lines (1) and (2) Davenant (1699 : 71 – 4. 82); line (3). Hoskins (1968: 25 – 6).

Before pursuing the implications of this finding, one other implicit assumption needs to be made explicit. This stems from the neglect of grains fed to livestock as a reserve for human consumption. Although the feeding off of grasses, clover, vetches, turnips, lentils, other meadow crops, and hay provided the bulk of animal feed, Davenant estimated that about 12 per cent of annual grain production was normally fed to livestock. In other words, human consumption of grains (see Table 15.4) normally constituted only about 45 per cent of the available supply at the close of a harvest. Even if we add the 17.6 per cent reserved for seeds, there was still normally a reserve of 37.9 per cent (carry-over plus feed) that could serve as a buffer before a deficient harvest required a restriction of human consumption or an encroachment on the seed reserve.

It follows from (3) that not even a 100 per cent deviation of wheat price above trend, which occurred only once in the entire period examined by Hoskins, implied a physical shortfall of wheat (standing here for a typical grain) so large as to eliminate carry-over stocks, let alone the combination of carry-over stocks and animal feed. Even the worst pair of years identified by Hoskins would still have left more than 10 per cent of the normal carry-over inventory as a buffer without encroaching on feed, seed, or human consumption in either year.

The point of the preceding exercise is that, even for a single grain, and even assuming a low yield-to-seed ratio, the physical shortfall in the worst pair of years was not so great as to require a general encroachment on seeds in order to maintain human consumption, although such encroachments undoubtedly occurred in some localities in some years, especially among the poorer farmers. This is not to say that the high prices did not cause sharp reductions in consumption, especially among the lower classes, or to deny the existence of famines. I mean only to call into question the proposition that *nationwide* subsistence crises after 1541 were the consequence of natural disasters.

Indeed, even the preceding discussion overemphasises the part played by natural factors, since until now I have accepted the common assumption that, because wheat prices were highly correlated with other food prices, wheat prices alone are an acceptable proxy for an index of all food prices. However, when one is attempting to infer the variability of the quantity of food from the variability in wheat prices, the critical question is not the strength of the correlation but the size of the elasticity between these two variables. Since the elasticity (α) of all food prices with respect to wheat prices is given by

$$\frac{\overset{*}{P}_f}{\overset{*}{P}_w} = \alpha = \frac{\sigma_f}{\sigma_w} r_{fw}, \tag{5}$$

it follows that, if α is less than 1, σ_f (the s.d. of deviations around the trend in food prices) will be less than σ_w (the s.d. of deviations around the trend in wheat prices) even if correlation between wheat and food prices is perfect ($r_{fw} = 1$). As it turns out, the estimated value of α is 0.346 (and $\bar{R}^2$ is 0.61) over the years 1540 – 1738, so that use of wheat prices, and their conversion within the context of King's Law into a measure of supply, greatly exaggerates the variability of the food supply during the early modern era (see the Appendix to this chapter).

If the deviations around trend in the food supply (σ_{fq}) are to be estimated from the deviations in wheat prices, what we need to know is the elasticity of the food supply with respect to wheat prices (ε_{fw}) rather than the King's Law which, even when properly interpreted, gives only the elasticity of the quantity of wheat demanded with respect to wheat price. Unfortunately, the time series needed to estimate σ_{fq} (the s.d. of deviations in the annual quantity of the food supply) for England is not yet available even for recent times, but it is possible to estimate σ_{gq} (the s.d. of deviations from trend in an index of all grain yields) after 1884. With this change, the desired elasticity ε_{fw} can be estimated from equation (6):

$$\varepsilon_{fw} = \frac{\sigma_{gq}}{\sigma_w} r_{gq,w}, \tag{6}$$

where σ_w is the s.d. of proportional deviations from trend on wheat prices. If we assume $r_{gq,w} = 1$, only σ_{gq} needs to be estimated, since as indicated earlier $\sigma_w = 0.220$. When σ_{gq} is estimated from data over the period 1884 – 1913, it turns out to be 0.0300, which puts ε_{fw} at 0.136.

This provisional estimate of ε_{fw} implies that even the largest deviation of wheat prices above trend in Hoskin's entire 280-year period (or Wrigley and Schofield's 331-year period) involved a manageable shortfall in the supply of food. Although carry-over stocks were diminished, more than two-thirds of the normal amount – more than a three-month supply – remained over and above all claims for feed, seed and human consumption.

Famines Amid Surpluses: A Suggested Mechanism

There does not, then, appear to have been a single year after *c.* 1500 in which the aggregate supply of food was too low to avoid a subsistence crisis. These crises were man-made rather than natural disasters, and clearly were avoidable within the technology of the age, as Davenant and other contemporary men of affairs pointed out. Famines amid surpluses remain a phenomenon even today, as Amartya Sen recently emphasised, not only because foods on a world-wide scale are ample enough to prevent famines, but because famines have broken out in certain underdeveloped nations despite good harvests. These famines were caused not by natural disasters but by dramatic redistributions of 'entitlements' to grain. The events that promoted the redistributions of entitlements were sharp rises in the price of grain relative to wages or other types of income received by the lower classes. In the 'great Bengal famine' of 1943, for example, the exchange rate between wages and foodgrains declined by 86 per cent, despite an 'exceptionally high' supply of grain. In this case the rise in grain prices had nothing to do with the bountifulness of the harvest, but was driven by forces outside the agricultural sector. The Bengal famine, Sen points out, was a 'boom famine', caused by 'powerful inflationary pressures' unleashed by a rapid expansion of public expenditures.

The relevance of the entitlement approach to the interpretation of the social and economic history of the early modern era does not depend on the source of the rise in grain prices that triggers the redistribution of entitlements. It is the similarity in the structural characteristics of traditional societies of the past and of low-income countries today that makes the entitlement approach pertinent. At the root of these structural similarities is the highly unequal distribution of wealth and the over-arching importance of land as a source of wealth. These twin characteristics lead directly to two other structural features. First, they cause the price elasticity of the total demand for grains to be quite low. Second, they drive a large wedge between the grain demand elasticities of the upper and the lower classes, with the elasticity of the lowest classes having a value that may be 10 or 20 times as large as the elasticity of the class of great land magnates. It is these large class differences in demand elasticities (caused by social organisation), rather than wide year-to-year swings in harvest yields (caused by variations in weather or other natural phenomena), that were the source of the periodic subsistence crises that afflicted late medieval and early modern England and the Continent.

The remainder of this section sets forth a mechanism that may have produced a world with famines amid surpluses that were more than adequate to have prevented the famines. I have endeavoured to make the following model conform as closely as possible to the known facts of English society during the early modern era. The Appendix describes my procedures for estimating the key parameters and the sources for these estimates. It also gives the derivations of equations (7) – (11).

Equation (7) is a convenient starting point for the estimation of the relevant elasticities.

$$\varepsilon_i = [\theta (1 - \varepsilon_t) - \beta_i] \psi_i - \bar{\varepsilon}_i \tag{7}$$

where

ε_i = price elasticity of the demand for grain

ψ_i = income elasticity of the demand for grain

$\bar{\varepsilon}_i$ = income-adjusted price elasticity of the demand for grain
β_i = share of grain in total consumption expenditures
θ_i = share of income arising from the ownership of grain
ε_t = price elasticity of the total aggregate demand for grain [See (10)]
i = subscript designating the ith class

Equation (7) states that the price elasticity of demand for grains of a given class depends not only on $\bar{\varepsilon}_i$ (the income-adjusted price elasticity, which is often referred to as the 'substitution' elasticity) but also on the relative magnitude of $(1 - \varepsilon_t)\theta$ (which is the elasticity of nominal income with respect to the price of grain) and of β_i. It follows from (7) that wealthy landlords would have a much more inelastic demand for grain [because the share of their income arising from the ownership of grain-producing lands equalled or exceeded the share of their income that was spent on the consumption of grains – i.e. because $(1 - \varepsilon_t)\theta_i \geq \beta_i$] than landless labourers (for whom $\theta_i = 0$ and β_i is large).

Table 15.5 divides the English population at the middle of the Wrigley-Schofield period (*c.* 1700) into four categories or classes, which correspond roughly to the aristocracy and gentry, the yeomanry, artisans and petty shopkeepers, and common labourers (including the unemployed). Out-servants working in the households of the upper classes are included with these classes, since their masters provided the food they consumed. In other words, the population embraced by the landlords (class 1 in the table) includes not only the landlords and their immediate families, but all of their retainers, high and low. The category titled 'farmers and lesser landlords' includes such other owners of food inventories as bakers, brewers, innkeepers and grain merchants. The categories are thus defined so that virtually all inventories are owned by the two top classes and virtually none by the two bottom ones.

Table 15.5 also presents my estimates of the share of the English population represented by each of the classes, the normal share of each class in the annual consumption of grain

(φ_i) and and of $\theta_i(1-\varepsilon_t)$, β_i, ψ_i and ε_i (see the Appendix for sources and procedures). The values of φ_i shown in column (2) imply that landlords consumed nearly two-thirds more, and yeomen about a sixth more, grain per capita than the national average (much of it as ale and spirits); that shopkeepers and craftsmen consumed the national average; and that common labourers and paupers consumed about three-quarters of the national average. These values of φ_i imply that the average caloric intake of the poor was at about the mean level of Ghana or Chad today (World Bank, 1984), while that of the landlords was at about the level of US farmers *c.* 1850.

One important implication of Table 15.5 is that, although labourers comprised about 44 per cent of the population, they accounted for only 33 per cent of the normal consumption of foodgrains. Another implication of the table is that the effect of a rise in grain prices on elasticities was quite different for different classes [see columns (6) and (7)]. In the case of landlords and farmers (classes 1 and 2), the rise in prices had two effects: as owners of surpluses, the rise in prices increased their income, while as consumers, it reduced their income. Since the producer's effect is stronger than the consumer's effect, the income component of the price elasticity (i.e. $[(1-\varepsilon_t)\,\theta-\beta]\,\psi$) is negative and so offsets the income-adjusted elasticity ($\bar{\varepsilon}$), making the price elasticities of these two classes quite close to zero. In the case of labourers, however, only the consumption, effect operated. In this case the income component of the price elasticity augments $\bar{\varepsilon}$. Although $\bar{\varepsilon}$ is already relatively high, the total price elasticity (ε) is more than twice as high.

The values set forth in Table 15.5 make it possible to estimate the aggregate elasticity of the foodgrain demand for grains (ε_c) by making use of the following relationship:

$$\varepsilon_c = \varphi_1\varepsilon_1 + \varphi_2\varepsilon_2 + \varphi_3\varepsilon_3 + \varphi_4\varepsilon_4. \tag{8}$$

Substituting the appropriate values of φ_i and ε_i in (8) yields

$$\varepsilon_c = (0.18)\,(0.01) + (0.39)\,(0.01) + (0.11)\,(0.32)$$

Table 15.5

Estimates of the 'Normal' Shares in Foodgrain Consumption and of the 'Normal' Price Elasticities of the Demand for Foodgrains, by Socioeconomic Class in England *c.* 1700

Class of household head	*(1) Share in population*	*(2) Normal share in consumption of the foodgrains*	*(3) Share of grain in total expenditure of a class*	*(4) Elasticity of nominal income with respect to the price of grain*	*(5) Income elasticity*	*(6) Income-adjusted price elasticity*	*(7) Price elasticity*
		φ_i	β_i	$\theta_i(1-\varepsilon_i)$	ψ_i	$\bar{\varepsilon}_i$	ε_i
(1) Landlords (incl. servants and retainers)	0.11	0.18	0.15	0.23	0.10	0.02	0.01
(2) Farmers and lesser landlords (incl. servants)	0.34	0.39	0.15	0.35	0.19	0.05	0.01
(3) Shopkeepers, minor professionals, and crafesmen (incl. servants)	0.11	0.11	0.35	0.00	0.36	0.19	0.32
(4) Labourers and the unemployed (not incl. servants covered in lines (1), (2) and (3)	0.44	0.33	0.70	0.00	0.92	0.41	1.05

Sources: see Appendix.

$$+ (0.33)(1.05) \qquad (9)$$
$$= 0.387$$

Thus, the estimates of class elasticities in Table 15.5 imply that the elasticity of the aggregate foodgrain demand was below 0.5, even though common labourers and paupers, who accounted for nearly half the population, had an elasticity in excess of 1. However, as (8) indicates, it is shares in consumption rather than in population that determine the value of ε_c: if it were the population shares that mattered, ε_c would be nearly 30 per cent larger than the indicated size.

Although ε_c is the price elasticity of the aggregate foodgrain demand, it is not the price elasticity of aggregate demand for all grain, which is given by

$$\varepsilon_t = \delta\varepsilon_s + (1 - \delta)\varepsilon_c, \qquad (10)$$

where

ε_s = the price elasticity of demand for grains used as seed, feed and carry-over inventories

δ = the share of the total supply used as seed, feed and carry-over inventories.

Since about 55 per cent of the supply of grains was reserved for carry-over, seed and feed, the estimation of ε_s is critical. If ε_s were 0, ε_t would be only 0.174. There is much commentary in the literature which suggests that that was the case. There was, for example, virtually no long-term variation in the amount of wheat seed planted per acre, which appears to have stood at about 2.5 bushels from the fourteenth century to the nineteenth. During the Irish famine it was noted that many farmers starved to death while holding on to the stocks of potatoes and grains they had set aside to pay their rents. Farmers also were apparently loath to dip into grain set aside for animal feed. It is not possible with the data currently at hand to estimate ε_s directly, but it is possible to estimate ε_t, and then to solve for (10) for ε_s. Using the estimate of σ_{gp} (the s.d. of deviations in grain prices around trend) for the period 1540 – 1738, and of σ_{gq} for 1884 – 1913, ε_t can be estimated from

$$\varepsilon_t = \frac{\sigma_{gq}}{\sigma_{gp}} r_{gq,gp}, \tag{11}$$

again assuming $r_{gq,gp} = 1$. The resulting value of ε_t is 0.178, which tends to confirm the belief that during the early modern era the elasticity of the demand for stocks held in reserve to ensure feed, seed, rental payments, and other contingencies was close to 0.

An important implication of the model set forth in this section is that a relatively small decline in the supply of grain could have produced a sharp rise in prices. Because of the highly inelastic demand for inventories, virtually all of the adjustment in entitlements would have taken place among consumers. As Table 15.6 shows, even a shortfall of supply as small as 5 per cent triggers significant shifts in the shares of grain consumed by different classes. In the case of landlords, the rise in their share largely offsets the decline in output so that their per capita consumption is virtually unchanged. In the case of labourers, however, the decline in their share reinforces the decline in output so that their per capita consumption is down by 32 per cent. It is worth noting that, although output declines by 5 per cent, aggregate foodgrain consumption declines by 11 per cent. Because the demand for grain reserves for feed, seed and rentals is so inelastic, virtually the entire shortfall is borne by foodgrain consumption.

The sharp decline in consumption of the labouring class (when $Q_s = 0.95$) is due to the combination of its high elasticity of demand ($\varepsilon_4 = 1.05$) and the sharp rise in price (P goes to 1.44). It should be noted that about a quarter of the indicated price rise is due not directly to a decline in Q_s from 1 to 0.95, but to the decline in the value of ε_t as the price increases. If ε_t had remained constant, the decline in Q_s would have led to a 33 per cent increase in prices instead of a 44 per cent increase. In other words, one of the effects of the shifting distribution of entitlements is to reduce ε_t, both because ε_c declines and because δ increases. It follows that an initial rise in prices tends to feed on itself even in the absence of

Table 15.6
The Consequence of Shifting 'Entitlement' Exchange Ratios on the Share of Each Class in the Reduced Crop and on the Per Capita Consumption of Each Class

	Normal share (%) of each class in foodgrain crop $Q_d = Q_s = 1$ $P = 1$ $\varepsilon_t = 0.178$ *(1)*	*Case where* $Q_s = 0.95$: *Share of each class in reduced output of foodgrain at market-clearing price (%)* *(2)*	*Case where* $Q_s = 0.95$: *% decline of each class from normal per capita consumption of foodgrains* *(3)*
(1) Landlords (incl. servants and retainers)	0.18	0.201	0.2
(2) Farmers and lesser landlords (incl. servants)	0.39	0.436	0.2
(3) Shopkeepers, minor professionals, and craftsmen (incl. servants)	0.11	0.110	10.9
(4) Labourers and the unemployed (not incl. servants listed under (1), (2) and (3)	0.33	0.252	31.9

Source: See Appendix.

speculative hoarding, by increasing the share of grain entitlements held by classes with a highly inelastic demand.

The Long Struggle to Repair the System of Food Distribution

Reductions in the national supply of grain by as much as 5 per cent were rare events during the early modern era, occurring about once a century. However, deficits of 4 per cent in the grain supply were more frequent, occurring about once a generation. When such events occurred, their impact was devastating on labourers and the unemployed, among whom the subsistence crisis was largely confined. Such great events, which reduced a normally poor diet to starvation levels, were social disasters. Whatever their impact on mortality, they could not be ignored by either local or national authorities.

Nor were they. In England during the Tudor and Stuart eras, containing the damage caused by grain shortages was a primary objective of the state. Famines were viewed not only as natural and economic disasters, but also as political ones. The basic strategy of the Crown was to leave the grain market to its own devices during times of plenty, except to guard against abuses of weights and measures and to foil plots to corner markets. (Even these measures provoked hostility from provincial justices and traders, who resented the attempts of the central government to usurp local rights; as a result of their pressure, the Long Parliament passed legislation which made it impossible for a uniform system of weights and measures to be established up until the nineteenth century).

In years of grain shortage, however, the state overrode the complaints of traders, merchants, brewers, bakers, and other processors. In 1587 and in subsequent years of dearth, the Privy Council issued a 'Book of Orders' which instructed local magistrates to determine the grain inventories of all farmers, factors, maltsters and bakers; to force holders of inventories to supply their grain to artificers and labourers at relatively low prices; to suppress unnecessary taverns and unnecessary expenditures of corn in manufacturing; and to prevent all export abroad and limit transportation at home.

It was, of course, easier to issue such orders than to enforce them. Despite the spectre of popular upheaval that spurred the authorities, they found it difficult to grain control of inventories or to curb the rise of prices. Despite the attempts of magistrates, corn continued to be exported abroad and sold to brewers. Innkeepers who had contracted for their supplies before the harvest insisted on the enforcement of their contracts. When maltsters complied with suppression orders they often found themselves prosecuted by customers who had sent barley to them to be malted. Caught in the middle, many tradesmen and processors were driven to poverty by regulations intended to prevent just that. The procedure enraged farmers and tradesmen who were subject to the inquisitional searches of bailiffs and constables, often for no better reason than the testimony of a common informer.

Because of the resistance of landlords, farmers, merchants, maltsters, and other owners of stock, it has been argued that government efforts to gain control of grain surpluses and to reduce the volatility of prices were a failure. Some hold that the paternalistic restrictions of the government were actually counter-productive, since the effort to uncover hidden stocks of grain served to foster alarm and push prices up. Instead of promoting greater efficiency in the market, these restrictions thwarted the activities of middlemen, whose function was to balance demand and supply by moving grain from places in which it was abundant to those in which it was scarce. Others believe that Tudor-Stuart paternalism actually worked. Although it might have taken a while for the scheme to ration grain on behalf of the poor to become effective, numerous instances can be cited during the reigns of James I and Charles I in which concealed grain was brought to market and sold to the poor at reduced prices.

Evidence bearing on this debate can be obtained by relating the variance in deviations of wheat prices from trend to the dominant policies of government in particular periods of time. For this purpose I have defined four periods. The first is 1541 – 99, which represents the years before the paternalistic apparatus for controlling grain supplies during dearth was in place or became effective. Although precedents for the intervention of the Privy Council during a subsistence crisis may be found during the reign of Henry VIII, it was not until the end of the third decade of Elizabeth's reign that a potentially effective system was spelled out. The *Book of Orders*, published in 1587, listed 33 measures aimed at giving the authorities enough control over the supply to permit the sale of grain for consumption directly to labourers at moderate prices. It set forth a mechanism at the local level for enforcing the regulations, assigned specific roles to sheriffs, justices of the peace, and mayors, and called for special juries of the leaders in each community to oversee the search for surplus stocks.

Devising a minute system of regulations and making it work are two separate matters, especially since the local justices, who were the lynchpin of the system, were lukewarm to the policy. The system did not become effective until the Privy Council provided the zeal and the administrative pressure required to mobilise local authorities. The turning point came in 1597, with the passage of a series of new laws aimed at alleviating poverty, laws framed in response to three years of turbulence set off by a combination of a depression and severe dearth. Fearing spontaneous insurrections, the Privy Council not only promoted the new legislation but sought to enforce vigorously its 'Book of Orders'. Beginning about 1600, the Council brought increasingly heavy pressure to bear on the local authorities. Proclamations were much the same as they had been, but the orders were more detailed and the follow-up more systematic. Local authorities responded. In some cities and towns public granaries were established so that stores would be available to sell grain to the poor below market price; the making of malt was regulated by quotas; and searches for surpluses were more thorough. By 1631 the sale of grain to the poor below market prices had become widespread.

This paternalistic system began to unravel with the Civil War. Indeed, the heavy-handed intervention of the Privy Council with local authorities in order to relieve poverty was one of the grievances of the opposition to Charles I. However, although the victory of Parliament over the King enabled those who sought free markets and the protection of property to have their way, the paternalistic system did not collapse at once. The same inertia at the local level that made it so difficult for Elizabeth and the early Stuarts to effect their reforms now operated in the opposite direction. Although the landholders and merchants who dominated Parliament developed a legislative programme aimed at unshackling farmers, producers and merchants from the restraints that had been imposed on them, local authorities continued to prosecute those who sought to profit from dearth at the expense of the poor. However, as Parliament implemented its new programme, local authorities veered in the new direction and the paternalistic apparatus atrophied.

The motivation for the switch in government policy has been debated by historians but not resolved. Some investigators believe that after the Civil War landowning classes, unrestrained by the bureaucratic paternalism of the Tudors and the early Stuarts, lifted restrictions on producers and merchants and placed a tariff on imports as acts of self-aggrandisement. That process was, in this view, abetted by a grateful William III, who supported export bounties on grain as one of his favours to the class that put him in power. Others, noting that the principal economic problem after the Restoration was economic stagnation and unemployment,

Table 15.7
Analysis of the Variance in the Deviations of Wheat Prices from Trend During Four Periods Between 1541 and 1745, England

Period	*Dates*	S^2 *(measured as % deviations from trend)*
(1) The years preceding paternalist regulation or during which the machinery for regulation was being put in place	1541 – 99	935
(2) The apogee of regulation	1600 – 40	270
(3) The dismantling of the regulatory machinery	1641 – 99	625
(4) The dominance of government policies aimed at promoting agricultural growth and diversification by raising prices and developing markets	1700 – 45	633

Source : Wheat prices are from Hoskins (1964, 1968).

believe that new measures were aimed at stimulating a depressed agriculture, promoting the reclamation of the fens and other waste lands, improving the system of marketing and transportation and promoting industry. According to this view, it was not so much the landlords but the ordinary tenant farmers who would have been impoverished by outworn policies that continued to drive prices down. In the face of an agricultural depression that gripped not only England, but the Continent as well, the key issue was the encouragement of agricultural diversification and the industrial production of agricultural products, including beer and spirits.

Whatever the motivation for the switch in policy, it was the abandonment of the Tudor-Stuart programme of food relief, and not natural disasters or the technological backwardness of agriculture, that subjected England to periodic famines for two centuries further. That conclusion is implied by Table 15.7, which shows that during the period 1600 – 40, when government relief efforts were at their apogee, the variance of wheat prices around trend declined to less than a third of the level of the proceeding era. That large a drop cannot be explained plausibly by chance variations in weather, since the *F*-value is statistically significant at the 0.0001 level. Nor is it likely that the sharp rise in the variance of wheat prices during the last six decades of the seventeenth century was the result of chance variations in weather.

In the absence of government action to reduce prices during grain shortages, workers took to the streets and price-fixing riots became a standard feature of the eighteenth century. During the early decade of the eighteenth century the government sought to cope with such out breaks by enforcing vagrancy and settlement laws and by force. During the late 1750s, however, after food riots of unprecedented scope and intensity, proposals for the government to intervene vigorously in the grain market (to return to the Tudor-Stuart policies), including proposals to re-establish public granaries, re-emerged. As the battle over these questions ebbed and flowed during the next half-century, the government, at both local and national levels, gradually shifted towards more vigorous intervention in the grain market. However, it was not until the nineteenth century that government control over stocks became adequate to reduce the variance in wheat prices to the level that prevailed at the apogee of Tudor-Stuart paternalism. By the middle of the nineteenth century famines had been conquered, not because the weather had shifted, or because of improvements in technology, but because government policy (at least with respect to its own people) had unalterably shifted back to the ideas and practices of commonweal that had prevailed during 1600 – 40.

Chronic Malnutrition and the Secular Decline in Mortality

Had the political will been present, a system of public relief adequate to deal with grain crises could have been in place long before the nineteenth century. So much of the famine-related mortality, and much related suffering short of death between 1640 and 1815, could have been avoided. However, as Table 15.1 shows, even complete success in the struggle to eliminate famines would have left the level of mortality in 'normal' times shockingly high. Indeed, that table undoubtedly exaggerates the extent of famine mortality, since the available evidence suggests that in the English case less than 10 per cent of all crisis mortality between 1541 and 1871 was due to famines.

Although the possibility that famines might have had only a small impact on aggregate mortality had been anticipated, Wrigley and Schofield provided the data needed to measure the national impact. By demonstrating that famines and famine mortality are a secondary issue in the escape from the high-aggregate mortality of the early modern era, they have indirectly pushed to the top of research agendas the issue of chronic malnutrition and its relationship to the secular decline in mortality. It is clear that the new questions cannot be addressed by relating annual deviations of mortality (around trend) to annual deviations of supplies of food (from their trend). What is now at issue is how the trend in malnutrition might be related to the trend in mortality, and how to identify the factors that determined each of these secular trends.

The new problems require new data and new analytical procedures. In this connection one must come to grips with the thorny issue of the distinction between diet (which represents gross nutrition) and malnutrition (which represents net nutrition: the nutrients available to sustain physical development). I will not dwell on this distinction here (which is set forth in Floud's paper), but will only emphasise that when I mean gross nutrition I will use the term 'diet', and that such other terms as 'malnutrition', 'undernutrition', 'net nutrition' and 'nutritional status' are meant to designate the balance between the nutrient intake (diet) and the claims on that intake.

Malnutrition can be caused either by an inadequate diet or by claims on that diet (including work and disease) so great as to produce widespread malnutrition despite a nutrient intake that in other circumstances might be deemed adequate. There can be little doubt that the high disease rates prevalent during the early modern era would have caused malnutrition even with extraordinary diets, that is diets high in calories, proteins, and most other critical nutrients. I believe that the USA during 1820 – 80 is a case in point. However, recent research indicates that, for many European nations before the middle of the nineteenth century, the national production of food was at such low levels that the lower classes were bound to have been malnourished under any conceivable circumstance, and that the high disease rates of the period were not merely a cause of malnutrition but undoubtedly, to a considerable degree, a consequence of exceedingly poor diets.

Recently developed biomedical techniques, when integrated with several standard economic techniques, make it possible to probe deeply into the extent and the demographic consequences of chronic malnutrition during the eighteenth and nineteenth centuries. The biomedical techniques include improved approaches to the estimation of survival levels of caloric consumption and of the caloric requirements of various types of labour; epidemiological studies of the connection between stature and the risk of both mortality and chronic diseases; and epidemiological studies of the connection between body mass indexes (BMIs) and the risk of mortality. The economic techniques include various methods of characterising size distributions of income and of calories, as well as methods of relating measures of nutrition to measures of income and productivity.

Energy Cost Accounting: the Case of Britain and France During the Last Quarter of the Eighteenth Century

Historical estimates of mean caloric consumption per capita have been derived from several sources, including national food-balance sheets and household consumption surveys. The various problems attendant upon using these sources have been described elsewhere. Despite their limitations, Toutain's time series of food consumption in France and the household surveys of English food consumption towards the end of the eighteenth century indicate that in each of these countries a majority of the population was malnourished.

Toutain, on the basis of a national food balance sheet, has estimated that the per capita consumption of calories in France was 1753 during 1781 – 90 and 1846 during 1803 – 12. Converted into calories per consuming unit (equivalent adult male), the figures become about 2290 and 2410 calories. Data in the household budget studies recently re-examined by economic historians indicate that English daily consumption during 1785 – 95 averaged about 2700 calories per consuming unit.

One way of assessing these two estimates is by considering their distributional implications. As noted elsewhere, all of the known distributions of the average daily consumption of calories for populations are not only reasonably well described by the lognormal distribution, but also have coefficients of variation that lie between 0.2 and 0.4 – a narrow range, which is determined at the top end by the human capacity to use energy and the distribution of body builds, and at the bottom end by the requirement for basal metabolism and the prevailing death rate. Consideration of available evidence on mortality rates and the findings of Goubert, Bernard, Hufton, Kaplan, and others on the condition of the lower classes in France during the late *ancien régime*, rule out either 0.2 or 0.4 as plausible estimates of the coefficient of variation and suggest that 0.3 is the best approximation in the light of current knowledge.

Table 15.8 displays the caloric distribution for England and France implied by the available evidence. Several points about these distributions, which lend support to Toutain's estimate for the French and the estimates derived for the English from the budget studies, are worth noting. First, the average levels are not out of keeping with recent experiences in the less developed nations. Low as it is, Toutain's estimate of the French supply of calories is above the average supply of

Table 15.8
A Comparison of the Probable French and English Distributions of the Daily Consumption of kcal Per Consuming Unit Towards the End of the Eighteenth Century

Decile	*(A) France c. 1785* $\overline{X} = 2290$ $(s/X) = 0.3$		*(B) England c. 1790* $\overline{X} = 2700$ $(s/X) = 0.3$	
(1)	*Daily kcal consumption (2)*	*Cumulative % (3)*	*Daily kcal consumption (4)*	*Cumulative % (5)*
1. Highest	3672	100	4329	100
2. Ninth	2981	84	3514	84
3. Eighth	2676	71	3155	71
4. Seventh	2457	59	2897	59
5. Sixth	2276	48	2684	48
6. Fifth	2114	38	2492	38
7. Fourth	1958	29	2309	29
8. Third	1798	21	2120	21
9. Second	1614	12	1903	13
10. First	1310	6	1545	6

Source and procedures: See Fogel (1987), esp. Tables 4 and 5 and n.6.

calories in 1965 estimated for such nations as Pakistan, Rwanda and Algeria, and only slightly less (by 39 calories) than that of Indonesia. The English estimate is above that for 30 less developed nations in 1965, including China, Bolivia, the Philippines, and Honduras, and only slightly (by 37 calories) below India (World Bank, 1987).

Second, the distributional implications of the two estimates are consistent with both qualitative and quantitative descriptions of the diets of various social classes. For example, Bernard's study of marriage contracts made in the Gévaudan during the third quarter of the eighteenth century revealed that the average ration provided for parents in complete pensions contained about 1674 calories. Since the average age of a male parent at the marriage of his first surviving child was about 59, the preceding figure implies a diet of about 2146 calories per consuming unit. That figure falls at the 47th centile of the estimated French distribution (Table 15.8, distribution A), which is quite consistent with the class of peasants described by Bernard.

The two estimates are also consistent with the death rates of each nation. The crude death rate in France *c.* 1790 was about 36.1 per 1000, while the figure for England *c.* 1790 was about 26.7. It is plausible that much of the difference was due to the larger proportion of French than English who were literally starving. The French distribution of calories implies 2.48 per cent of the population had caloric consumption below basal metabolism (the minimum energy required for the functioning of the body); Table 15.8 implies that the proportion of the English below basal metabolism was 0.66 per cent. If a quarter of these starving individuals died each year, they would account for about a fifth (6.6 per 1000) of the French crude death rate, but only about a sixteenth of the English rate (1.7 per 1000) and for about half of the gap between the crude death rates of the two nations.

What, then, are the principal provisional findings about caloric consumption at the end of the eighteenth century in France and England? One is the exceedingly low level of food production, especially in France, at the start of the Industrial

Revolution. Another is the exceedingly low level of work capacity permitted by the food supply, even after allowing for the reduced requirements for maintenance because of small stature and reduced body mass. In France the bottom 10 per cent of the labour force lacked the energy for regular work and the next 10 per cent had enough energy for less than 3 hours of light work daily (0.52 hours of heavy work). Although the English situation was somewhat better, the bottom 3 per cent of its labour force lacked the energy for any work, but the balance of the bottom 20 per cent had enough energy for about 6 hours of light work (1.09 hours of heavy work) each day.

That the English ultra-poor were better off than the French ultra-poor was due partly to the greater productivity of English agriculture (as measured by the per capita production of calories). However, the distribution of income was so unequal in England that, had it not been for the English system of poor relief, the proportion of the English that starved would have been nearly as great as that of the French. In response to the bread riots of the eighteenth century, English authorities substantially expanded the system of poor relief. Between 1750 and 1801 poor relief increased at a real rate of 2.3 per cent per annum, which was nearly three times as fast as the growth of either GNP or the pauper class. Consequently, by *c.* 1790 relief payments to the ultra-poor had become substantial, more than doubling the income of households in the lowest decile of the English income distribution. In pre-revolutionary France, on the other hand, the average annual relief provided to the ultra-poor could purchase daily only about one ounce of bread per person. The responsiveness of the British government to the bread riots of the poor, not only kept the English death rate from soaring, but may have spared Britain from a revolution of the French type.

The Implications of Stature and Body Mass Indexes for the Explanation of Secular Trends in Morbidity and Mortality

The available anthropometric data tend to confirm the basic results of the analysis based on energy cost accounting:

chronic malnutrition was widespread in Europe during the eighteenth and nineteenth centuries. Furthermore, such malnutrition seems to have been responsible for much of the very high mortality rates during this period. Moreover, nearly all of the decline in mortality rates between 1750 and 1875 appears to be explained by the marked improvement in anthropometric measures of malnutrition. This section summarises evidence bearing on the relationship between mortality and two anthropometric measures – height at maturity and the body mass index (BMI).

Height and body mass indexes measure different aspects of malnutrition and health. Height is a net rather than a gross measure of nutrition. Moreover, although changes in height during the growing years are sensitive to current levels of nutrition, mean final height reflects the accumulated past nutritional experience of individuals over all of their growing years including the foetal period. Thus, it follows that, when final heights are used to explain differences in adult mortality

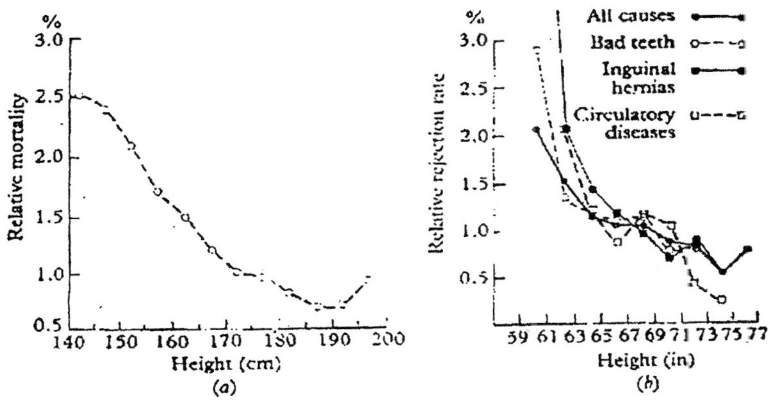

Fig 15.1 : A comparison of the relationship between body height and relative risk in two populations:

(a) Relative mortality rates among Norwegian men aged 40 – 59, 1963 – 1979.
Source: Waaler (1984).

(b) Relative rejection rates for chronic conditions in a sample of 4245 men aged 23 – 49 examined for the US Union army.
Source: Fogel *et al.* (1986).

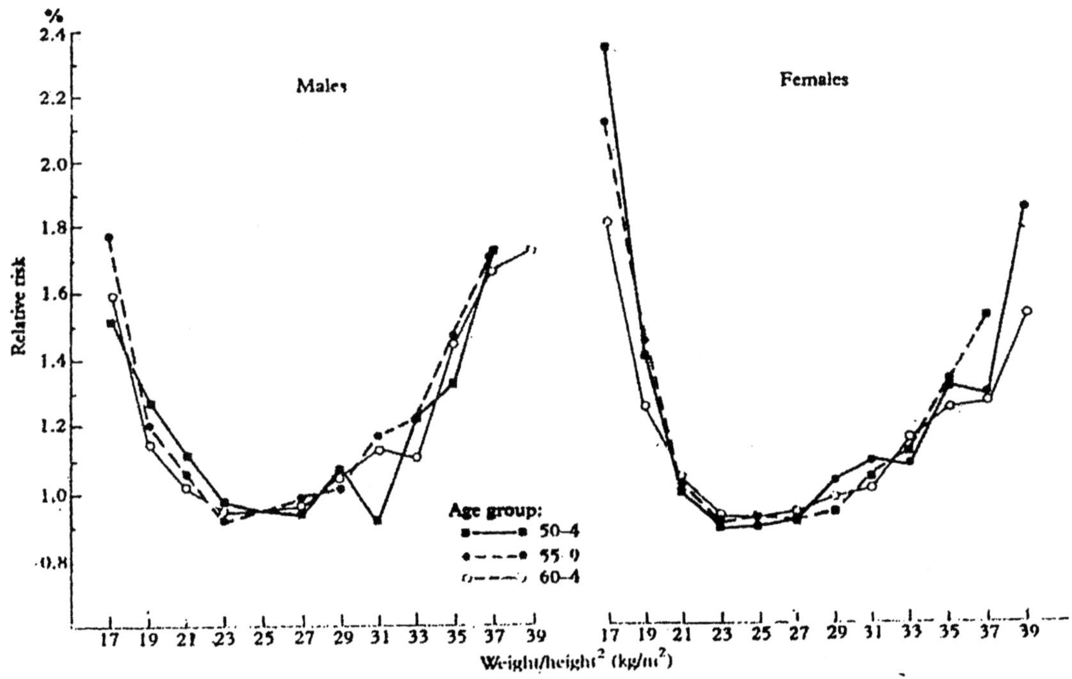

Fig 15.2 : The relationship between BMI and prospective risk among Norwegian adults aged 50 – 64 at risk, 1963 – 1979.
Source: Waaler (1984).

rates, they reveal the effect not of adult levels of nutrition on adult mortality rates, but of nutritional levels during infancy, childhood and adolescence on adult mortality rates. A weight-for-height index on the other hand, reflects primarily the current nutritional status.

A number of recent studies have established the predictive power of height and BMI with respect to morbidity and mortality. The results of two of these studies are summarised in Figs. 15.1 and 15.2. Part (*a*) of Figure 15.1 reproduces a diagram by Waaler (1984). It shows that short Norwegian men aged 40 – 59 at risk between 1963 and 1979 were much more likely to die than tall men. Indeed, the risk of mortality for men with heights of 165 cm (65.0 inches) was on average 71 per cent greater than that of men who measured 182.5 cm (71.9 inches). Part (*b*) of the figure shows that height was also an important predictor of the relative likelihood that men aged 23 – 49 would be rejected from the US Union Army during 1861 – 65 because of chronic diseases. Despite significant differences in mean heights, ethnicities, environmental circumstances, the array and severity of diseases, and time, the functional relationship between height and relative risk are strikingly similar. Both the Norwegian curve and the US all-causes curve have relative risk that reach a minimum of between 0.6 and 0.7 at a height of about 187.5 cm. Both reach a relative risk of about 2 at about 152.5 cm. The similarity of the two risk curves in Figure 15.1, despite the differences in conditions and attendant circumstances, suggests that the relative risk of morbidity and mortality depends on the deviation of height not from the *current* mean, but from an *ideal* mean: the mean associated with full genetic potential.

Waaler has also studied the relationship in Norway between BMIs and the risk of death in a sample of 1.7 million individuals. Curves summarising his findings are shown in Figure 15.2 for both men and women. Although the observed values of the BMI (kg/m^2) ranged between 17 and 39, over 80 per cent of the males over age 40 had BMIs within the range 21 – 29. Within the range 22 – 28 the curve is relatively flat, with the relative risk of mortality hovering close to 1.0. However, at BMIs of less than 22 and over 28, the risk of death rises quite sharply as the BMI moves away from its mean value. It will be noticed that the BMI curves are much more symmetrical than the height curves in Fig. 15.1, which indicates that high BMIs are as risky as low ones.

Although Figs. 15.1 and 15.2 are revealing, neither one singly nor both together are sufficient to shed light on the debate over whether moderate stunting impairs health when weight-for-height is adequate, since Fig. 15.1 is not controlled for weight and Fig. 15.2 is only partially controlled for height. To get at the 'small-but-healthy' issue, one needs an iso-mortality surface that relates the risk of death to both height and weight simultaneously. Such a surface, presented in Fig. 15.3, was fitted to Waaler's data by a procedure. Transecting the iso-mortality map are lines which give the locus of BMI between 16 and 34, and a curve giving the weights that minimise risk at each height.

Fig. 15.3 shows that, even when body weight is maintained at what Fig. 15.2 indicates is an 'ideal' level (BMI = 21), short men are at substantially greater risk of death than tall men. Thus, an adult male with a BMI of 25 who is 162 cm tall is at about 55 per cent greater risk of death than a male at 183 cm who also has a BMI of 25. Figure 15.3 also shows that the 'ideal' BMI (the BMI that minimises the risk of death) varies with height. A BMI of 25 is 'ideal' for men in the neighbourhood of 176 cm, but for tall men (greater than 183 cm) the ideal BMI is between 22 and 24, while for short men (under 164 cm) it is a bit under 26.

Before using Fig. 15.3 to evaluate the relationship between chronic malnutrition and the secular decline in mortality rates after 1750, three issues in the interpretation of that figure need to be addressed. First, since an individual's height cannot be varied by changes in nutrition after maturity, adults can move to a more desirable BMI only by changing weight. I, therefore, interpret the x-axis as a measure of the effect of the current nutritional status of mature males on adult mortality rates. Moreover, since most stunting takes

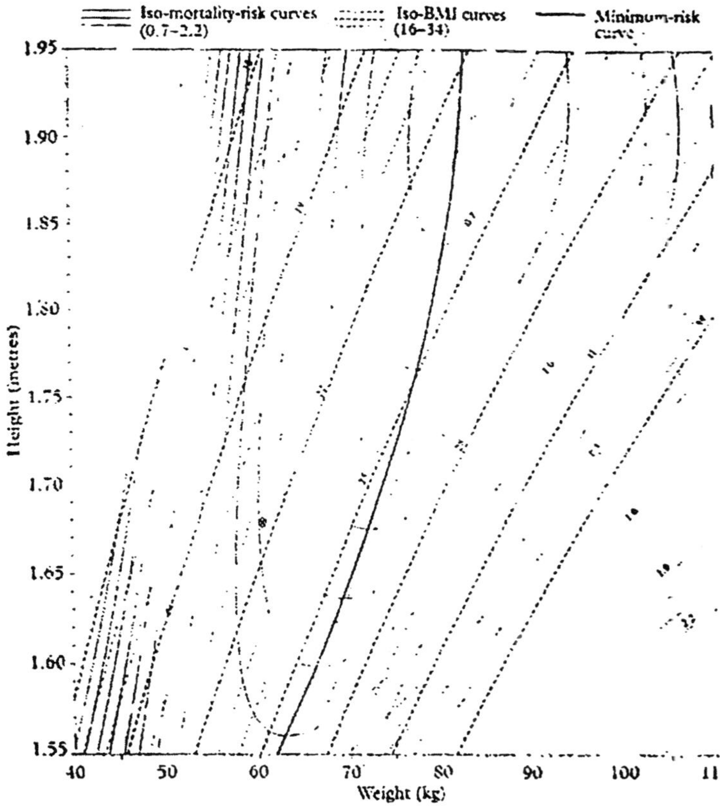

Note:

⊕ = the possible location of adult French males aged 25 – 34 *c.* 1790 on the iso-morality map. The predicted risk for French males is 1.63.

⊗ = the possible location of comparable English males *c.* 1790. The predicted risk for English males is 1.18.

All risk are measured relative to the average risk of morality (calculated over all heights and weights) among Norwegian males aged 50 – 64.

Fig 15.3 : Iso-mortality curves of relative risk for height and weight among Norwegian males aged 50 – 64, 1963 – 1979.

Source: Fogel (1987).

place below the age of 3, I interpret the *y*-axis as a measure of the effect of nutritional deprivation in *utero* or early in childhood on the risk of mortality at middle and late ages.

Second, in applying Fig. 15.3 to the evaluation of secular trends in nutrition and mortality, I assume that for Europeans environmental factors have been decisive in explaining the secular increase in heights, not only for population means, but also for individuals in particular families. The reasonableness of this assumption becomes evident when one considers the issue of shortness. If shortness is defined as a given number of standard deviations below a changing mean (i.e. if 'short' is 2 standard deviations below the mean, whether the mean is 164 cm or 183 cm), then genetic and environmental factors may be difficult to disentangle. If, however, shortness is defined in absolute terms, say as applying to all males with heights below 168 cm, then it is quite clear that most shortness in Europe and America during the eighteenth and much of the nineteenth centuries was determined by environmental rather than genetic factors.

The point at issue can be clarified by considering the experience of the Netherlands. Shortness has virtually disappeared from that country during the past century and a half. Today, less than 2 per cent of young adult males are below 168 cm. but in *c*. 1855 about two-thirds were below that height. Since there has been little change in the gene pool of the Dutch during the period, it must have been changes in environmental circumstances, nutrition and health that eliminated about 95 per cent of all short males from the Dutch population. Given current growth rates in the mean final height of the Netherlands, the remaining men shorter than 168 cm may yet be virtually eliminated from the Dutch population.

The Dutch case illustrates the general secular pattern of physical growth in the nations of western Europe. The secular increase in mean final heights, which ranged between 10 and 20 centimeters (4 and 8 inches) over the past 200 years, cannot be attributed to natural selection or genetic drift, since these processes require much longer time-spans. Nor can it be attributed to heterosis (hybrid vigour), because the populations in question have remained relatively homogeneous and because the effects of heterosis in human populations have been shown, both empirically and theoretically, to be quite small. Only the top 6 per cent of the Dutch height distribution *c.* 1855 overlaps with the bottom 6 per cent of the current distribution of final heights. Since the Dutch mean is still increasing, and we do not yet know the maximum mean genetically obtainable (often referred to as the genetic potential), it may well be that even the 6 per cent overlap between the distribution of final heights in the *c.* 1855 generation and that of the latest generation will be cut in the next few decades, perhaps by as much as half.

Third, even if the Norwegian iso-mortality surface is applicable to European populations generally, the surface may not have been stable over time. Since height-specific and weight-specific mortality rates are measured relative to the crude death rate (CDR) for the population as a whole, short-term shifts in the CDR by themselves will not shift the surface. However, fundamental shifts in environment, including changes in medical technology, may shift the risk surface. One way of ascertaining whether there has been a shift in the risk surface is by determining what part of the decline in mortality rates can be explained merely by movements along the surface (i.e. merely by changes in height and weight on the assumption that the surface has been stable since 1750).

The average final heights of men in several European countries over the period from 1750 to modern times are reported in Table 15.9. It will be seen that during the eighteenth century these Europeans were severely stunted by modern standards. The French cohort of 18-IV is the most stunted, measuring only 160.5 cm (63.2 inches). The next two shortest cohorts are those of Norway for 18-III and Hungary for 18-IV, which measured 163.9 cm (64.5 inches). Britain and Sweden were the tallest populations between 1775 and 1875, although by the end of the period Norway nearly matched the leaders.

France was intermediate in its early growth rate, with stature increasing about 0.73 cm per quarter between 18-IV and 19-II. However, the French rate of increase sagged slightly over the next half century and hovered between 165.3 and 166.7 cm until the turn of the twentieth century. British heights increased more rapidly (1.90 cm per quarter century) and for a longer period than the French. The accumulated increase over the first 75 years (18-III to 19-II) was 5.7 cm, more than three-fifths of the total increase in British heights between 18-III and the current generation of adults. However, British heights declined slightly with the cohort of 19-III and also remained on a plateau for about half a century. Swedish heights appear to have declined during the last half of the eighteenth century but then to have risen sharply beginning with the second quarter of the nineteenth century, initiating the marked secular increase in Swedish heights that has continued down to the present day.

Indeed, over the last century the three Scandinavian countries shown in Table 15.9 and the Netherlands have had the most vigorous and sustained increases in stature in the western world, outpacing Britain and the USA. Hungary's growth pattern differs from that of all the other European nations: its cohort of 18-III was taller than that of Sweden, but then Hungarian heights declined sharply for half a century; and, despite a turnabout in the nineteenth century, Hungary remains one of the shortest populations in Europe: its mean height today is below the level achieved by the British cohort of 19-II.

Data on body mass indexes for France and Britain during the late eighteenth and most of the nineteenth centuries are much more patchy than those on stature. Consequently attempts to compare British and French BMIs during this period are necessarily conjectural. It appears that *c*.1790 the average English BMI for males about age 30 was between 21 and 22, which is about 10 per cent below current levels. The corresponding figure for French males *c*.1790 may have been only about 19, which is about 25 per cent below current levels. The conjectural nature of these figures makes the attempt to

Table 15.9
Estimated Average Final Heights of Men Who Reached Maturity Between 1750 and 1875 in Six European Populations, by Quarter-centuries (cm)

(1) Dat of maturity	(2) Britain	(3) Norway	(4) Sweden	(5) France	(6) Denmark	(7) Hungary
(1) 18–III	165.9	163.9	168.1	—	—	168.7
(2) 18–IV	167.9	—	166.7	169.0	165.7	165.3
(3) 19–I	168.0	—	166.7	164.0	165.4	163.9
(4) 19–II	171.6	—	168.0	166.7	166.8	164.2
(5) 19–III	169.3	168.6	169.5	165.2	165.3	—
(6) 20–III	175.0	178.3	177.6	172.0	176.0	170.9

Source: Fogel (1987): Table 7 for all columns except 5. Column 5: rows 3–5 were computed from Meerton (1989) with 0.9 cm added to allow for additional growth between age 20 and maturity (Gould 1869: 104-5; cf. Friedman 1982: 510 n. 14). The entry to row 2 is derived from a linear extrapolation of Meerton's data for 1815 – 36 back to 1788, with 0.9 cm added for additional growth between age 20 and maturity. The entry in row 6 is from Fogel (1987), Table 7.

go from anthropometric data to differential mortality rates more illustrative than substantive. However, Fig. 15.3 indicates the apparent location of French and English males of 18-IV on the iso-mortality map generated from Waaler's data. These points imply that the French mortality rate should have been about 40 per cent higher than that of the English, which is quite close to the estimated ratio of mortality rates for the two countries. In other words, the available data suggest that in 18-IV both France and Britain were characterised by the same mortality risk surface (i.e. the same mortality regimen), and that differences in their average mortality rates are explained largely by differences in their distributions of height and weight-for-height.

This result raises the question as to how much of the decline in European mortality rate since 18-IV can be explained merely by increases in stature and BMIs: that is, merely by movements along an unchanging mortality risk surface. For the three countries for which even patchy data are available – England, France and Sweden – it appears that nearly all of the decline in mortality between 18-IV and 19-III was due to movements along the Waaler mortality surface, since the estimated changes in height and BMI appear to explain between 80 and 100 per cent of the decline in mortality during this three-quarters of a century. However, movements along the Waaler surface appear to explain only about 50 – 60 per cent of the decline in mortality rates after 1875. After 1875 increases in longevity involved factors other than those that exercise their influence through stature and body mass.

APPENDIX

This appendix deals with the assumptions, mathematical derivations, estimation procedures and sources of data for the analysis and estimates presented in headings The New Findings on Mortality Crises and Measuring the Variability of Food Supply above. (For the assumptions, mathematical derivations and estimation procedures reported under heading Chronic Malnutrition and the Secular Decline in Morlality).

The two principal implicit assumptions that underlie the analysis in headings The New Findings on Mortality Crises and Measuring the Variability of Food Supply are traditional in the literature on the pricing of English grain during the early modern era (here taken to be 1500 – 1750), and are consistent with the available evidence. The first of these assumptions is that the average price each year was established under conditions of a completely inelastic aggregate short-run supply curve. The second is that year-to-year changes in price were due to fluctuations in this short-run supply from one harvest to another around a fixed (or relatively fixed) aggregate demand curve.

The assumption that the demand curve was relatively fixed rests on the flat trend in income and in the relative prices of complements and substitutes for foodgrains (broadly defined), and on the stability of tastes. The assumption that the short-run supply curve of grain was completely inelastic rests on (1) the observation that, once the harvest was concluded, the production of grain could not be increased until the next crop was planted and harvested, and (2) the fact that the price wedge between England and the Continent was such that net imports of grain were generally negative even during years of dearth. In the few years when net imports were positive, they were about 1 per cent of annual consumption.

When the aggregate short-run supply curve is perfectly inelastic, the usual problems of simultaneity disappear, and the estimate of the elasticity of aggregate demand curve can be obtained by regressing price directly on quantity. However, the usual econometric issues of simultaneity remain if one wishes to explain the distribution of the fixed supply between the holders and non-holders of grain inventories. That task is not undertaken in heading The New Findings an Mortality Crises. When it is undertaken in heading Measuring the Variability of Food Supply, the key parameters are not estimated by the econometric procedures since neither the time-series nor cross-sectional data needed for such estimation are available.

A third important implicit assumption for the analysis presented in heading The New Findings on Mortality is that the distribution of arable land among crops did not vary from year to year but remained fixed by conventions that changed slowly over time. Consequently, all the short-run variation in output from one year to the next in grain crops has traditionally been presumed to have been due to variations in per-acre yields rather than to variations in the number of acres sown.

The derivation of equation (7)

The demand curve for the *i*th class of consumers for a good (Q), when income is measured in real terms, may be written as

$$Q_i = \left(\frac{Y_i}{P^{\beta_i} P_m^{1-\beta_i}}\right)^{\Psi_i} \cdot P_m^{\varepsilon_{mi}} P^{-\bar{\varepsilon}_i}, \tag{7a}$$

where

$Q =$ the quantity of grain
$P =$ the price of Q
$Pm =$ the price of all other goods, Qm
$Y =$ nominal income
$\beta =$ the share of Q in consumption expenditures
$1-\beta =$ the share of all other goods in consumption expenditures
$\psi =$ the income elasticity of the demand for Q
$\varepsilon_m =$ the cross-elasticity of the demand for Q with respect to P_m
$\bar{\varepsilon} =$ the own-price elasticity of the income-adjusted demand for Q
$i =$ a subscript referring to the ith class of consumers

Differentiating (7*a*) totally and rearranging terms yields

$$\overset{*}{Q}_i = \Psi_i \overset{*}{Y}_i + \left[\varepsilon_{mi} - \Psi_i\left(1-\beta_i\right)\right]\overset{*}{P}_m - \left(\Psi_i\beta_i + \bar{\varepsilon}_i\right)\overset{*}{P}. \tag{7b}$$

Since by assumption Q_m is the numeraire, $\overset{*}{P}_m = 0$ and equation (7*b*) reduces to

$$\dot{Q}_i = \Psi_i \dot{Y}_i - \left(\Psi_i\beta_i + \bar{\varepsilon}_i\right)\dot{P}. \tag{7c}$$

Now, by definition,

$$Y_i = PQ_i + P_m Q_{mi}. \tag{7d}$$

Differentiating (7*d*) totally yields

$$\dot{Y}_i = \theta_i\left(\dot{P} + \dot{Q}_i\right) + \left(1-\theta_i\right)\left(\dot{P}_m + \dot{Q}_{mi}\right), \tag{7e}$$

where θ_i is the share of PQ_i in Y_i. Since Q_m is the numeraire and $Q_m = 0$ by assumption, (7*e*) reduces to

$$\dot{Y}_i = \theta_i\left(\dot{P} + \dot{Q}_i\right). \tag{7f}$$

If it is also assumed that all classes that own farm land suffer or benefit from random fluctuations in yields proportionately,

$$\dot{Q}_i = -\varepsilon_t \dot{P}, \tag{7g}$$

so that (7*f*) reduces to,

$$\dot{Y}_i = (1-\varepsilon_t)\theta_i \dot{P}, \tag{7h}$$

where ε_i is the aggregate price elasticity of demand over all classes of consumers of grain [*see* equation (10)]. Substituting (7*h*) into (7*c*) and rearranging terms yields

$$\dot{Q}_i = \{\Psi_i[\theta_i(1-\varepsilon_t)-\beta_i]-\bar{\varepsilon}_i\}\dot{P}. \tag{7i}$$

Hence the price elasticity of demand for the *i*th class of consumers (ε_i) is the coefficient of $\overset{*}{P}$ in (7*i*), or

$$\varepsilon_i = [\theta_i(1-\varepsilon_t)-\beta_i]\Psi_i - \bar{\varepsilon}_i, \tag{7j}$$

which is the same as equation (7).

The derivation of equations (8) and (10)

The derivation of equation (8) follows directly from the identity

$$Q_c = Q_1 + Q_2 + Q_3 + Q_4 = \sum_{i=1}^{4} Q_i, \tag{8a}$$

where

Q_c = the aggregate demand for foodgrains

Q_1, Q_2, Q_3, Q_4 = demand for foodgrains of each of the four classes defined in Table 15.5.

Differentiating (8*a*) totally yields

$$\dot{Q}_c = \sum_{i=1}^{4} \varphi_i \dot{Q}_i. \tag{8b}$$

where φ_i = the share of Q_i in Q_c. Substituting $-\varepsilon_i \dot{P}$ for $\dot{Q}_i$ in (8*b*) yields

$$\dot{Q}_c = -\dot{P}\sum_{i=1}^{4}\varphi_i \dot{Q}_i, \tag{8c}$$

Hence by definition, we have

$$\varepsilon_i = \sum_{i=1}^{4}\varphi_i\varepsilon_i = \varphi_1\varepsilon_1 + \varphi_2\varepsilon_2 + \varphi_3\varepsilon_3 + \varphi_4\varepsilon_4, \tag{8d}$$

which is the same as equation (8).

The derivation of equation (10) is symmetrical to the derivation for (8), except that the initial identity is

$$Q_t = Q_c + Q_s \tag{10a}$$

where

Q_i = the aggregate quantity demanded for grain for all uses

Q_s = the quantity demanded for grain used as seed, feed and carry-over inventories

The sources for the estimation of parameters in equations (4), (5), (6) and (11)

The estimate for σ_q was obtained by fitting a normal distribution to the ratio of the residuals to trend values of annual wheat yields obtained from a linear regression of yields on time. Per-acre yields, rather than annual wheat production or wheat production plus net imports, were used because of the assumption in the literature that the distribution of arable land across crops remained fixed from year to year by conventions that changed only very slowly over time.The estimated standard deviation of the residuals around yields is greater than those around the production or around the annual production plus net imports. The data on wheat yields for the period 1884 – 1913 are from Mitchell and Deane. The root mean square errors around quadratic trends were lower than those around the linear trends.

The estimates of α were based on two time series of prices that were spliced at the overlap to provide a continuous series for the period 1540 – 1738. The series for 1540 – 1649 are from Bowden, and the series for 1640 – 1749 are from Bowden. 'Grains' was defined to include wheat, barley, oats, rye and peas and beans. 'Food' was defined to include the preceding crops plus livestock and animal products. The grain price index and the food price index were constructed by giving equal weight to the prices of each of the commodities. The reasons for choosing equal weights are discussed by Bowden. Plausible alternative weighting schemes (such as those indicated in Phelps Brown and Hopkins, Thirsk, Shammas and Komlos tend to reduce both α and σ_{gp} because the prices of livestock and animal products are less variable than those of grains. The data on crop yields and total output are reported in Mitchell and Deane and in the sources cited there.

The standard deviations of prices from trend during 1540 – 1738 were computed around a 25-year moving average in which the trend value of the price was standardised at 1. A similar procedure was followed in computing the standard deviation around a moving average of the real wage series developed by Wrigley and Schofield from the series of Phelps Brown and Hopkins as well as around the original price series. The estimates of the standard deviation around trend from these series over 1541 – 1871 were quite close to those computed from the Bowden all-food series for 1540 – 1738. Use of an 11-year moving average instead of a 25-year moving average also had negligible effects on the estimates of the standard deviation around trend in the several series.

Sources for the parameter estimates in Table 15.5

Column (1) The population shares are based on King's table (Laslett 1984), except that out-servants were divided among the top three classes on the assumption that there were an average of 5 out-servants for each household of a landlord ('landlords' include the gentry down through 'Persons in the Law'), an average of 0.44 out-servants for each farm and lesser landlord household (a category that includes households of freeholders and ordinary clergy in addition to farmers), and an average of 0.24 out-servant for each household in the category of shopkeepers, minor professionals, and craftsmen (including military officers). The remainder of the households in King's table, which comprise the fourth class of Table 15.5, are presumed to hire no out-servants. The analysis stemming from the table is not particularly sensitive to reasonable alternative definitions of classes or of other distributions of out-servants, nor to re-estimates of King's table like the one proposed by Lindert and Williamson, since such redistribution would have little effect on the inequality of the caloric distribution by income or social class.

Column (2) The shares of the four classes are based on the assumption that the English distribution of claories was lognormal with $\bar{x}$ = 2.700 kcal per equivalent adult and $s/\bar{x}$ = 0.3 (*see* Table 15.8 above). The means of the four classes are obtained from

$$Z_{mi} = \frac{N_i}{(2\pi)^{0.5}} \int_{Zi}^{Z_{i+j}} Ze^{-0.5Z^2}\, dZ. \qquad (A1)$$

and

$$\bar{X}_i = e^{S_{mi}\sigma + \mu} \qquad (A2)$$

where

Z_{mi} = the Z scores of the mean of the *i*th class

Z_{j+i} and Z_i = the Z scores of the upper and lower bounds of the interval for the *i*th class

$\bar{X}_i$ = the mean of the *i*th interval in the lognormal distribution

N_i = the reciprocal of the area between Z_i and Z_{i+j}.

For a further discussion of this procedure *see* Fogel (1988).

Column (3) The shares of grain in the expenditure of the four classes is based on the assumptions listed in Table 15.10.

Values in column (3) were rounded to the nearest 5 per cent. These estimates are rough approximations based on data in Stigler, Crafts, Shammas, and Phelps Brown and Hopkins Thirsk. The share of grain and of food in total expenditures for landlords may seem high, but it should be kept in mind that the majority of the persons in their households were from the lower classes and that bread and beer or ale were the main components of their ration.

Column (4) Estimates of King and Davenant indicate that foodgrains accounted for about 43 per cent of value added in agriculture *c.* 1700 and animal products about 30 per cent. The remaining 27 per cent was accounted for by feed crops, other crops (e.g. flax, hemp), timber, and firewood. It is likely, however, that non-grain products, particularly animal products, represented a larger share of the agricultural income of wealthy landholders (class 1) than of farmers and lesser landlords (class 2). I have assumed that $1 - \varepsilon_t = 0.82$, that class 1 had claims upon or produced about one-quarter of annual grain output, and that the remaining three-quarters belonged to class 2.

Table 15.10
Assumed Shares of Grain in Class-specific Expenditure

Class	*(1)* *Share of food in total expenditure*	*(2)* *Share of grain in food expenditure*	*(3)* *(1) × (2)*
1	0.30	0.50	0.15
2	0.40	0.40	0.15
3	0.60	0.60	0.35
4	0.80	0.90	0.70

Column (5) The income elasticity for grains for class 4 was estimated directly by Shammas from the Edens and Davies surveys of *c.* 1790. Her figure (0.92) is quite close to the elasticity of grain (rice) derived from Timmer's equation for contemporary Indonesia (Timmer *et al.* 1983: 59). For classes 2 and 3 I used Timmer's equation, and the income per household relatives for classes 2 and 3 computed from King's table (Laslett 1984), with the per-household income of class 4 standardised at 100. Since the relative average income of class 1 was far beyond the range of observations on which Timmer's equation was computed, I arbitrarily assumed that the value of ψ for class 1 was one-half of that for class 2.

Column (6) Timmer's procedure was followed, employing the income relatives computed from King's table, as indicated in the paragraph above relating to column (5). For the reason indicated in the previous note, and Timmer's finding that the $\bar{\varepsilon}$ declines more rapidly than ψ with income, I arbitrarily assumed that $\bar{\varepsilon}$ for class 1 was 0.02.

16

INTRA-HOUSEHOLD ALLOCATION OF NUTRIENTS

For most individuals in most developing countries intra-household food allocation is responsible for the provision of most nutrients. Since households generally include individuals of both sexes, there is the possibility of a systematic influence of gender on the nutrients that a specific individual receives; that is, the sex of the person who controls the allocation of critical resources and the sex of each individual recipient may affect the allocation of nutrients to a specific individual. A number of studies, particularly of southern and western Asian societies, conclude that females often receive fewer nutrients relative to their needs than do males. Other studies suggest that gender may have an impact in that, the greater the share of resources controlled by women, the more of a given level of resources is devoted to nutrients for children.

This chapter considers the intra-household allocation of nutrients and gender effects within the framework of household models of intra-household allocation, and surveys a number of studies of structural relations and reduced-form relations that can be interpreted within such frame works. Text under heading Analytical Frameworks considers analytical frameworks for investigating these issues, text under heading heading Measurement Problem discusses some data problems. In heading Empirical Studies of the Intra-Household Allocation of Nutrients and Gandev Effects a number of existing empirical studies are reviewed.

Analytical Frameworks

An analytical framework helps as an organising device for interpreting empirical evidence, particularly for a topic for which the available information is as imperfect as it is regarding the intra-household distribution of nutrients in poor societies. I outline two standard static economic stories about intra-household distribution of nutrients and gender.

Constrained maximisation of a unified preference function

Within this framework, the household is assumed to have a unified preference function defined over outcomes for each of the I household members. Such a preference function is consistent with there being a dictator in the household, benevolent or malevolent, as well as with the situation in which everyone in the household has the same preferences defined over the consumption of all household members. The latter might not be completely implausible if there is strong enough identification with the household or family line, whether for sociobiological, altruistic, or economic reasons. However, the requirement that each household member weigh the arguments of all other members of the household identically does seem quite strong. Nevertheless, if there is a household member close enough to a dictator or a situation does enough to identical preferences, a unified household preference function may be an adequate approximation for considering the intra-household allocation of nutrients. Moreover, for most existing data-sets, the estimable relations that come out of the constrained maximisation of a unified household preference function cannot be identified from those that come out of a bargaining frameowrk, as is discussed in sub-heading *Empirically estimable relations pertaining to the intra-househole allocation of nutrients and gender effects.*

For the purposes of the present paper, it is useful to be explicit about some of the arguments in the preference function: individual consumption (C_i), human resource quality (Q_i), time use (T_i) and assets (A_i):

$$U = U(C_i, Q_i, T_i, A_i, I, \ldots) \text{ for all } i = i, \ldots, I. \qquad (1)$$

Each of these variables has a subscript *i* to reflect that it is individual household members' consumption that enters into the preference function. Each variable is represented as a vector to reflect that there are multiple dimensions for each.

Consumption of goods and services (C_i) is included because of the standard assumption that, *ceteris paribus*, increased consumption improves satisfaction. A subset of the elements in this vector refers to food consumption (c_i^f), which is important in itself because of the direct satisfaction that food consumption provides in addition to its impact on the health component of quality and possibly on productivity. I include the whole consumption vector and not just the food component to emphasise that there generally are trade-offs between food consumption and other consumption for fixed total household resources, in addition to trade-offs among the food consumption of various household members. Further, the food consumption of some household members, through productivity effects, may alter the total resources available to the household, and thus probably both food and non-food consumption.

The human resource quality (Q_i) of each individual includes health (Q_i^h), schooling (Q_i^s), and other human resource attributes. These effect the current welfare of individuals and the household. They also have an investment dimension with effects in the future, beyond the period of immediate relevance for this static one-period framework. For example, in the absence of good capital markets and old-age pensions plans, parents may be interested in the human resource qualities of their children because they relate to the children's potentialities for providing income transfers to the parents, particularly support for them in their old age. As is discussed below, these human resource qualities may be 'produced' in part by nutrients.

The time use (T_i) of individuals affects preferences directly because different time uses provide different degrees of satisfaction (e.g. leisure versus work versus schooling). Different time uses also feed back indirectly on household welfare by altering indirectly the other arguments in the preference function, as is discussed further below.

The assets of individuals (A_i) are included for reasons parallel to the non-food consumption and the investment dimension of human resources. Asset accumulation represents an alternative use of current resources and an alternative to human resource investments regarding the future. Improvements in capital markets, for example, might make such assets relatively more attractive than human resource investments in children for parental old-age security, and could cause a shift away from human resource investments, *ceteris paribus*. While assets are indicated to be associated with individuals, if the household pools all its resources, pooled rather than individual assets enter into household preferences.

The last argument that is indicated explicitly is household size (I). This may have some immediate direct impact on household welfare if, for example, the household places positive value on pleasures of having more children (I^c). There also may be an indirect effect through changing the total resources to be allocated, the number of individuals among whom they are allocated, and the potential for exploiting economies of scale. The number of children also has an investment dimension, and there may be a trade-off among human resource investments, other assets, and number of children regarding alternative strategies for providing for parental old-age security.

One observation worth making explicit is that nutrients (N_i) do not appear directly in this preference function. That is, nutrients are not posited to attect preferences directly, but only indirectly, through their association with foods consumed $\left(C_i^f\right)$ or their impact on human resource quality (Q_i), both of which reflect production relations that are considered below.

The preference function is maximised subject to two sets of constraints. The first is the production functions, broadly defined. For the present purpose, among the most important are those for the health (Q_i^h) and schooling (Q_i^s) components of human resource quality (Q_i), nutrition (N_i), births (B), mortality (M_i), and possibly wages (W_i) and farm/firm production (Y).

The health of the ith household member (Q_i^h) is posited to be produced by nutrients consumed by that individual (N_i), other health-related inputs (C_i^h),[10] the general environment (R), endowments related to the inherent robustness and capabilities of the individual (E_i) and of the primary health care provider in the household (hereafter 'mother', E_m), the time use of the individual (T_i) and of the mother (T_m), the schooling of the individual (Q_i^s) and of the mother (Q_m^s), and the health status of all other individuals in the household $(Q_k^h, k \neq i)$:

$$Q_i^h = Q^h\left(N_i, C_i, R, E_i, E_m, T_i, T_m, Q_i^s, Q_m^s, Q_k^h\right)$$

$$\text{(for all } k \neq i\text{) for each } i = 1, \ldots, I. \tag{2}$$

Nutrients are included in this production relation because nutrient intakes presumably are a major input into the production of health status. But five observations are useful regarding the role of nutrients in producing health.

1. Nutrients are not equivalent to health status. They may not be a good indicator of health status, moreover, unless one of two conditions are satisfied. First, the health production function in (2) must have fixed coefficients between nutrients and the other inputs so that there is not substitution between nutrients and the other inputs:

$$Q_i^{h*} = \min\left[Q^{h*}(N_i), Q^{h**}\left(C_i^h, R, \ldots\right)\right]. \tag{2a}$$

Such a condition seems very strong, suggesting, for example, that nutrition inputs result in the same level of health for individuals who have much different inherent robustness (which is related to E_i) or much different time use patterns (T_i). Second, all individuals in society (or at least in the sample) must face the same relative prices for all of the inputs in the health production function (2) and therefore, in their maximising behaviour, must select the same non-nutrient and nutrient input combinations; thus, nutrients (or any other single input) are a perfect proxy for the composite input. This too seems to be a very strong condition that is unlikely to be satisfied. Relative market prices are likely to differ for individuals across space because of transportation costs and even in a given location if prices of some items are subsidised for some members of society (e.g. subsidised food, or medical services for the poor). Effective prices for endowments, moreover, are likely to vary since no market exists for, say, genetic endowments, with the result that effective prices differ even for members of the same household (with the possible exception of identical twins). Therefore, nutrients are not necessarily very good indicators of health status, nor *vice versa*. In fact, nutrients may not even be associated positively with health status. If endowments are very important in the production of health, and if nutrients are allocated so as to compensate for endowment inadequacies, for example, nutrients may be inversely associated with health status.

2. Basal metabolism also plays a role in the absorption of nutrients, apparently varying considerably across individuals, and possibly adapting to nutrient intakes. In the health production function, metabolism is reflected partially in the individual's endowments but also, if it is affected by nutrient intakes, in those intakes. The variance and possible endogeneity of basal metabolism may weaken further the association between nutrient intakes and health status.

3. Time use and associated energy expenditure also alter how a given level of nutrient intakes affects health status, at least as measured by the usual health indicators. Two persons with identical basal metabolism may absorb vastly differing

amounts of current nutrient intakes through different physical activities, and thus have much different quantities of nutrients remaining to affect longer-run health status. While the importance of time use patterns is widely recognised, empirical estimates of health production functions generally do not control for time use differences.

4. Besides nutrients, there are a number of other inputs in this health production function. For example, human resources may affect significantly the knowledge of or efficiency of use of other inputs, so these are included for both the individual himself and the household's primary health care provider/mother. To the extent that these human resources result in individuals being better informed about options, one would expect a positive association between human resources such as schooling and the use of modern inputs or good nutrition practices, as, for example, Strauss reports for the Ivory Coast. On the other hand, more human resources may substitute for other inputs if, for example, better educated food preparers boil bad water but less educated ones do not. Rosenzweig and Schultz present some evidence for Colombia consistent with this possibility. The other non-nutrient inputs include the health status of other household members. These are included primarily to capture the possibility of contagion, though that for the mother may also represent her energy and effectiveness in providing household health care services. Health-related inputs for a particular individual, including nutrients, might through contagion (as well as through other means such as labour productivity) have impact on the health of other household members.

5. There is a lot that we do not know about the biological technology of the health production function. The marginal product in terms of health status of increasing nutrients is likely to be positive for poorly nourished individuals. But at higher levels of nutrient intakes the marginal products may become negative, leading to obesity, arteriosclerosis, etc. Even at moderate nutrient intake levels, whether the marginal product is positive or negative may depend upon

exactly what dimension of health is of interest. For example, increased calorie consumption may increase current energy levels at the same time that it contributes somewhat to longer-run obesity problems. Moreover, many nutrients may interact, and all may interact with other inputs, such as the environment, endowments and non-nutrient health-related inputs. Furthermore, some effects have considerable lags, which may make them hard to detect. A casual examination of the nutrition literature over the past several decades reinforces the observation that we do not know many details of these biological processes, as indicated by changing fads about the importance of proteins versus calories, etc.

Although the individual health status production function is critical in understanding the roles of intra-household distribution of nutrients, other production functions also are important. I discuss these more briefly now.

Mortality (M_i) can be considered to result when an individual's health status falls below a critical level $\left(\bar{Q}_i^h\right)$:

$$M_i = M\left(Q_i^h\ \bar{Q}_i^h\right) \qquad \text{for each } i = 1, \ldots, I. \qquad (3)$$

The critical level, of course, may vary across individuals. Thus, in a sense, mortality is just another (albeit extreme and irreversible) health status indicator, so the comments above about the health production function and the associations between health status and nutrients carry over, except that the irreversibility of mortality limits sharply some substitutions over time.

Nutrient intakes of the *i*th individual in the household (N_i) depend on food intakes of that individual $\left(C_i^f\right)$ and on time use and capacities of the mother $\left(T_m, Q_m^e, E_m\right)$:

$$N_i = N\left(C_i^f, T_m, Q_m^s, E_m, \ldots\right) \text{ for each } i = 1, \ldots, I. \qquad (4)$$

For given expenditures on food, the nutrient intakes can vary enormously because of different food composition and different preparation.

Education of the *i*th individual $\left(Q_i^s\right)$ is posited to depend on the endowments (E_i), the number of grades $\left(S_i^g\right)$ and quality $\left(S_i^q\right)$ of schooling, the health $\left(Q_i^h\right)$, and the nutrition (N_i) of that individual:

$$Q_i^s = Q^s\left(Q_i^h, N_i, S_i^g, S_i^q, E_i, \ldots\right) \text{ for each child } i = 1, \ldots, I_c. \tag{5}$$

Health and nutrition are included because of evidence that at best the former is associated with schooling success through increasing students' productivity. The quality of schooling is included in addition to grades of schooling because of recent evidence in the developing country context that schooling quality is very important in understanding the impact of schooling on some important outcomes, and estimates that ignore it may be very misleading. Endowments are included because of similar evidence that the failure to control for the attitudes and abilities relating to the adults' childhood family backgrounds may cause misunderstanding of both the determinants of schooling and its impact in developing countries.

Births (B) are determined by a 'biological supply function' in the spirit of Easterlin and Rosenzweig and Schultz as dependent on contraceptive use $\left(C_m^c\right)$, the efficiency of the mother and father in using contraceptives as related to their education $\left(Q_m^s, Q_f^s\right)$ and endowments $\left(E_m, E_f\right)$, their fecundity as related to their health and nutritional status and their endowments $\left(Q_m^h, Q_f^h, N_m, N_f, E_m, E_f\right)$, and the frequency of intercourse (F):

$$B = B\left(C_m^c, Q_m^s, Q_f^s, Q_m^h, Q_f^h, N_m, N_f, E_m, E_f, F\right). \tag{6}$$

There is some controversy about the role of nutrition in affecting births. If there is a role, it might provide another channel through which intra-household nutrient allocations feed back upon intra-household allocations by changing the size and the composition of the household.

The number of household members (I) equals births (B) minus mortality (M) minus other net outflows (O_i):

$$I = B - \sum_i (M_i - O_i). \tag{7}$$

Other net outflows may occur because of migration, marriages, etc., that are not modelled easily within this simple framework.

To this point, I have been agnostic about whether income generation can be treated separately from consumption/demand. If it can, wages and income can be treated as predetermined variables from the point of view of the determination of individual nutrient intakes and health status. But if there are immediate impacts of health and nutrition on labour productivity, or impacts of labour time use on health (or if, for farm/firm production, there are sufficiently incomplete markets), the separability assumption is not valid. Recently, moreover, a considerable literature has developed that emphasises the integration of decisions regarding the gender allocation of a farm's production labour with those regarding the gender allocation of household consumption. In such cases, production relations must be added for wages for the *i*th individual and for farm/firm production:

$$W_i = W\left(Q_i^s, Q_i^h, N_i, E_i, \ldots\right) \quad \text{for each } i = 1, \ldots, I, \tag{8}$$

and

$$Y = Y\left(Q_i^s, Q_i^h, N_i, E_i, \ldots\right) \quad \text{for all } i = 1, \ldots, I. \tag{9}$$

These relations allow for the possible impact of health and nutritional status on individual labour market productivity, as reported in recent studies by Behrman and Deolalikar, Deolalikar, Sahn and Alderman and Strauss. If there are such effects, the total resources available to the household may increase if more resources are used for nutrients so that productivity and income increase. If such effects differ by gender, then within the maximising framework they feed back with optimal intra-household nutrient allocations favouring those individuals for whom at the margin the productivity effects are greater. Of course, in such an allocation any health and nutrient impact on household productivity, presumably primarily through the mother, given her dominance in time use for household production, also should be incorporated into the analysis.

The second constraint is on time and monetary resources, as is summarised in a full-income budget constraint in which the P_c refer to prices that incorporate money and time costs:

$$\sum_i W_i \bar{T}_i + Y = \sum_i P_c C_i + \sum_i W_i T_i^l + \sum_i W_i T_i^s + \sum_i \Delta A_i, \qquad (10)$$

subject to the constraints that the total time use for each individual must equal the total time ($\bar{T}_i$) available for that individual. The left-hand side (LHS) of (10) gives the total value of full income: the total time of each household member $\bar{T}_i$ valued at the relevant wage (W_i) plus net income from all sources other than labour of members of the household (Y). The right-hand side (RHS) gives total resource expenditures: the sum of consumption ($P_c C_c$) plus the value of leisure time $(W_i\ T_i^l)$ plus time spent in schooling $(W_i\ T_i^s)$ plus asset changes ($\Delta\ A_i$) for all individuals in the household.

Under the assumption that the underlying functions have the desirable characteristics, the first-order conditions for the constrained maximisation lead to reduced-form demand relations:

$$V = f(Z) \qquad (11)$$

where

$$V = \left(C_i, T_i, Q_i, S_i^g, S_i^q, N_i, W_i, Y, B, M_i, F, \Delta A_i\right)$$

For all $i = 1, \ldots, I$

except $i \neq m$ or f for S_i^g ans S_i^q, and

$$Z = \left(P_c, P_f, E_i, R, \bar{A}_i, S_m^g, S_f^g, S_m^q, S_f^q\right) \text{ for all } i = 1, \ldots, I.$$

The dependent variables (V) include the food consumption, health, and nutrition of all household members, in addition to the grades and quality of schooling for all children, births, mortality, unearned income, and time use, wages, and asset accumulation for all individuals. The RHS variables (Z) include all of the consumption prices (P_c), farm/firm prices (P_f), the general environment (R), and all predetermined assets of the household – all individual endownments (E_c), grades and quality of schooling for the adults $\left(S_m^g, S_m^q, S_f^g, S_f^q\right)$, and initial assets $\left(\bar{A}_i\right)$.

Bargaining model of intra-household allocation of nutrients

A number of people argue that the unified preference assumption of the framework outlined in sub-heading *constrained maximisation of a unified preference function* is misleading. Instead, they advocate a bargaining framework in which each individual has his or her own preferences and assets and bargaining occurs over the allocation of resources, including nutrients, among household members. Such a framework seems plausible on the basis of casual observation. While household members may be altruistic about one another and share important concerns about the perpetuation of the household, there generally also appears to be some differences in preferences and conflicts regarding intra-household allocation at each point in time and over the life-cycle of the household.

Manser and Brown and McElroy and Horney have developed theoretical bargaining models for intra-household allocations. A critical element of these models is the existence of threat points that relate to the possibility of an individual leaving the household if his/her utility is less than some fixed level determined by his/her options outside the household, and thus by his/her assets (both human resource and physical/financial). Within this framework, the intra-household allocation can be interpreted in terms of a generalised (i.e. non-symmetric) Nash bargaining model. In work in progress, Behrman develop this framework for the investigation of intra-household allocation of nutrients and leisure within Indian and Malaysian households.

The structural relations for the formal bargaining model are very similar to those described in sub-heading *constrained maximisation of a unified preference function*. All production functions for individual health, nutrition, wages, etc. remain. The major differences are that there are preference functions for each individual rather than the unified household preference function in relation (1), threat points (TP_i) regarding the possibility of exit from the household for all household members, and full-income budget constraints for each individual rather than the overall household budget constraint in (10). The resulting reduced forms are identical to those in relation (11) except that Z is augmented to include the threat points of all I household members. If certain household members systematically favour one gender, then increasing their threat points increases the nutrient (and other resource) allocation to individuals of that gender.

Empirically estimable relations pertaining to the intra-household allocation of nutrients and gender effects

Structural relations – One interesting question is whether equal outcomes are weighted differently depending upon the gender of the individual in the unified preference function (1) or the in individual preference functions for the bargaining framework. Direct estimation of preference functions is not possible, of course, because utility is not observed. But preference parameters can be estimated in some cases from reduced-form relations, though simultaneity and the absence of exogenous gender-specific instruments may limit the possible inferences.

Direct estimation of the structural production function relations for health status, schooling, wages, firm/farm production, and possibly time use may be informative regarding gender effects of intra-household nutrient allocations. Such estimates may suggest, for example, whether the return to marginal nutrients is greater for one sex than for the other, given markets and customs that determine those returns. At least three major problems, however, need to be surmounted in such estimates. First, most of the RHS variables in the production functions are simultaneously determined with the outcomes of interest within the frameworks described in sub-headings *constrained maximisation of a unified preference function* and *Bargaining model of intra-household allocation of nutrients*. This means that there must be a sufficient number of exogenous variables (i.e. those in Z) to permit identification of the coefficients of the endogenous variables and appropriate estimation procedures must be used to avoid simultaneity bias. Second, some of the RHS variables are not easily observed, most notably endowments. If these unobserved variables are associated with observed variables, then the failure to control for the unobserved variables causes omitted variable bias, since the observed variable partially represents the effects of the omitted unobserved one. Third, lags may be critical, but theory provides little or no guidance regarding these lags.

Finally, the alternative unified preference function versus the bargaining frameworks has no differential implications for estimating these production relations.

Reduced-form relations. – The reduced-form relations may reveal whether there are gender differences in the intra-household allocation of nutrients in response to exogenous changes in prices, the environment, and the other variables in Z in relation (11). Are nutrients adjusted more (or less) for females than for males, for example, when food prices change? Such differences may exist because of preference weights that differ according to the sex of individuals, because of bargaining among household members of both sexes, and because of differences in production functions or individual endowments by sex. Generally, reduced-form relations cannot distinguish among these possibilities. Estimation problems include possible omitted variable biases and lag structures as for structural relations, but not

simultaneity bias if the relations are truly reduced forms (since, in such a case, all of the RHS variables are exogenous). In principle, the two frameworks discussed in sub-headings *constained maximisation of a unified preference function* and *Bargaining model of intra-household allocation of nutrients* lead to different reduced-forms in that the reduced-form relations for the bargaining model include the variables that determine individual threat points in addition to the variables that are explicit in Z in relation (11). But note that these variables have to be in addition to those in Z and therefore cannot include the human capital variables that might be representing shadow prices of time rather than threat points. Since such variables are difficult (though not impossible) to obtain in most data-sets, most, if not all, existing empirical studies that claim to provide evidence in favour of the bargaining model (or *vice versa*) are not persuasive. A significant impact of women's schooling or women's wages (even if one ignores possible simultaneity problems) simply does not discriminate between the unified preference versus the bargaining model. Either further structure or predictions or else observations on variables that might affect threat points without affecting the shadow price of time (e.g. assets bought into the marriage by the husband and by the wife are required.

Quasi-reduced form relations – Sometimes estimates of quasi-reduced forms are made, in which some endogenous RHS variables are included in addition to some of the prices and other variables in Z. Such relations may be derived from the reduced-form relations by solving a particular reduced-form relation that determines one endogenous variable (say Y) for one exogenous variable (say P_f treated as a scalar) and then using that relation (say for N_i). The relation so obtained has all but one of the exogenous variables in Z plus one endogenous variable on the RHS. In the example indicated in the parentheses immediately above, for instance, nutrients could be expressed as a function of consumer prices, (endogenous) farm/firm income, and the other exogenous variables in Z (other than P_f). This basically is the standard demand relation.

Three observations about quasi-reduced forms are useful. First, to estimate them correctly requires the same information as to estimate the reduced-form relations, since the excluded exogenous variable must be used to identify statistically the influence of the included endogenous one. Second, a number of estimates that have a mixture of endogenous RHS variables and exogenous variables in Z are not truly quasi-reduced forms, in the sense that this term is used here, because they could not be derived by the above-described process of substituting endogenous variables for exogenous ones using reduced forms. It is not clear how to interpret such relations. Third, the interpretation of even true quasi-reduced forms may be murky since a given change in any exogenous variable may work in part through the included endogenous variable(s). Therefore, these estimates may reflect only the partial, not the total, effect of changes in exogenous variables.

Measurement Problems

Measurement problems may be severe for an empirical exploration of the intra-household allocation of nutrients and gender effects. For estimation of many of the possible structural, reduced-form, or quasi-reduced-form relations of interest, direct observations on individual nutrient intakes are required. Such observations are difficult to obtain and currently are available for only a few (though a growing) number of data-sets for developing countries that also include other socioeconomic data, which permits estimation of the relations of interest. There are at least six measurement problems, moreover, that are almost inherent in these data.

First, the necessary raw data are individual consumption data for different categories of food. These usually depend on direct observations by the surveyer or on recall data, sometimes from a key respondent such as the mother in the household. The basic problem is that both of these procedures well may lead to systematic biases in reported individual food consumption towards what the respondent(s) considers appropriate norms. That is, if local norms are that older males are favoured or that equality is desired, the allocations reported by key respondents or undertaken in the presence of outside observers are likely to be biased towards those norms as compared with usual allocations. The problem for the researcher is all the more severe because it is not clear *a priori* whether this bias is likely to lead towards an understatement or an overstatement of gender inequalities in nutrient allocations.

A second measurement problem is that food consumed outside of regular meals is likely to be undercounted either by key respondents or by outside observers. Such an undercount may have a systematic impact on measured allocations between the sexes. For example, food preparers (usually females) may consume relatively great quantities of food while preparing meals; on the other hand, males may eat more outside of the household. The problem for the researcher is all the more severe, once again, because the net direction of such systematic gender biases may not even be clear.

A third measurement problem is that there often is considerable variation in food intakes for a given individual over time. In part this may result in random measurement error, which should not cause problems in the estimation of gender differences for the reduced-form nutrient intake relations, though it biases towards zero the estimated impact of nutrients on other outcomes, such as health in estimates of relation (2). But there may be systematic gender biases if, for example, nutrient intakes tend to vary seasonally more for one sex than the other but data collection tends to be concentrated in particular seasons. For example, suppose that food is allocated to ensure that males receive adequate quantities, with females receiving the residual quantities, so that gender inequalities are large when food is scarce but disappear when it is relatively abundant: then, if data collection is concentrated in the seasons when food is relatively scarce (abundant), gender inequalities will be overstated (understated).

A fourth measurement problem relates to the translation of foods into nutrients, typically by using fixed food-to-nutrient conversion factors, which effectively suppress all but the first argument in the nutrient production function of relation (4). This may result in systematic bias in measured nutrient allocations, but it is not clear that it results in a gender bias. For example, suppose that actual nutrient intakes from given foods (as categorised by the researcher) are greater for households with better educated food preparers (i.e. that Q^{c}_{m} is greater in (4) and that better educated mothers allocate relatively more food to females than do less educated mothers. In such a case it is not obvious that the measured relative allocation between males and females within a household is distorted (though differences among households may be mispresented), although it might be if there are gender distinctions in the relative quantities of food consumed that happen to be associated with systematic errors in the conversion factors (e.g., males eat relatively more meat, and the conversion factors for meat involve more – or less – error than for non-meat).

A fifth measurement problem pertains to the need often to standardise for nutrient requirements in order to make comparisons among individuals of different ages and between males and females. As a number of nutritionists and economists have emphasised recently, the use of such standards is tricky because of both inter- and intra-personal variations. With respect to representing relative nutrient intakes by gender, the effective question is whether the standardisation adopted is free of gender bias. For example, often the nutrient intakes for some relatively healthy and well-off population are used to construct age- and gender-specific standards (e.g. middle- and upper-income urban residents for Indian Nutrient Institute standards); but if there is gender bias in the nutrient allocations in that reference population, then the use of the standards themselves will tend to misrepresent gender biases in the samples under study. Sen, Chen and Epstein suggest that standards based on energy use for various activity levels systematically may understate the actual energy use of women because they assume too short work-days and too sedentary activities. If this is the case, and if nutrient intakes have a non-linear impact on productivity with diminishing marginal returns after intakes above those necessary to maintain basal metabolism are consumed, then one might expect to find that measured nutrients relative to the (gender-biased) standards have larger estimated productivity effects for females than for males.

A sixth measurement problem pertains to sample selectivity. The only individuals observed at a particular point of time are those who have survived to that time. If previous nutrient and other health-care-related allocations have favoured males and the better endowed of both sexes, for example, then the currently existing pool of females may be relatively well endowed because of relatively high mortality rates among poorly endowed females as compared with those among poorly endowed males.

Such measurement problems may thus result in systematic biases in the extent of measured gender biases in nutrient allocations. Moreover, for many of these reasons, there are likely to be random measurement errors as well, which are likely to result in biases towards zero in the impact of measured nutrients on outcomes of interest.

For such reasons, reinforced by the relatively great cost of obtaining individual food data, many studies use health or morbidity indicators instead of nutrient intakes. For example, anthropometric and morbidity indicators are often used, and even referred to as indicators of nutritional status. Such indicators have some measurement problems parallel to those mentioned above for nutrients (e.g. the problem of defining standards) that I shall not go into here in the interest of brevity. But the more basic point, as is discussed above following the health production function in relation (2), is that these indicators need not be highly, or even positively, correlated with nutrient intakes. Therefore, it may be very misleading to act as if they are representing nutrient intakes, even though they may be representing health outcomes of substantial interest in themselves.

Measurement problems also may affect other variables used in the analysis of the determinants, and the impact, of nutrient intakes. I shall not discuss these at length here except to note that there may be systematic gender bias in some relevant variables that are difficult to measure (e.g. schooling quality and individual endowments), which may result in a gender-specific omitted variable bias in estimates of the impact of nutrient intakes on outcomes of interest.

Impirical Studies of the Intra-household Allocation of Nutrients and Gender Effects

I shall now survey a number of recent studies that fit into the frameworks developed in heading Analytical Frameworks.

Estimates of structural relations

Preference parameters – Preference functions generally cannot be estimated directly, of course, because utility is not observed. They are estimable from first-order conditions, however, subject to assumptions about functional forms. In Behrman I present estimates of preference function parameters relevant for intra-household nutrient distributions for rural south India, conditional on explicit assumptions about functional forms. I begin with the assumptions that there is a unified parental preference function as in (1), which has a separable CES component defined over the health cutcomes of all I_c children.

$$U_H = \left(\sum_i a_i (Q_i)^c \right)^{1/c} \qquad \text{for all } i = 1, \ldots, I_C. \qquad (1a)$$

Two characteristics of this utility function are of interest. The first is the curvature, which relates to inequality aversion of the equity-productivity trade-off. If the preference curve is L-shaped, as in Fig. 16.1(*a*), parents obtain no additional satisfaction if, starting from a corner *A*, the health of one or the other child is improved (to *B* or *C*). To increase their satisfaction, the health of both children must be improved: equity is of paramount concern. If the preference curve is

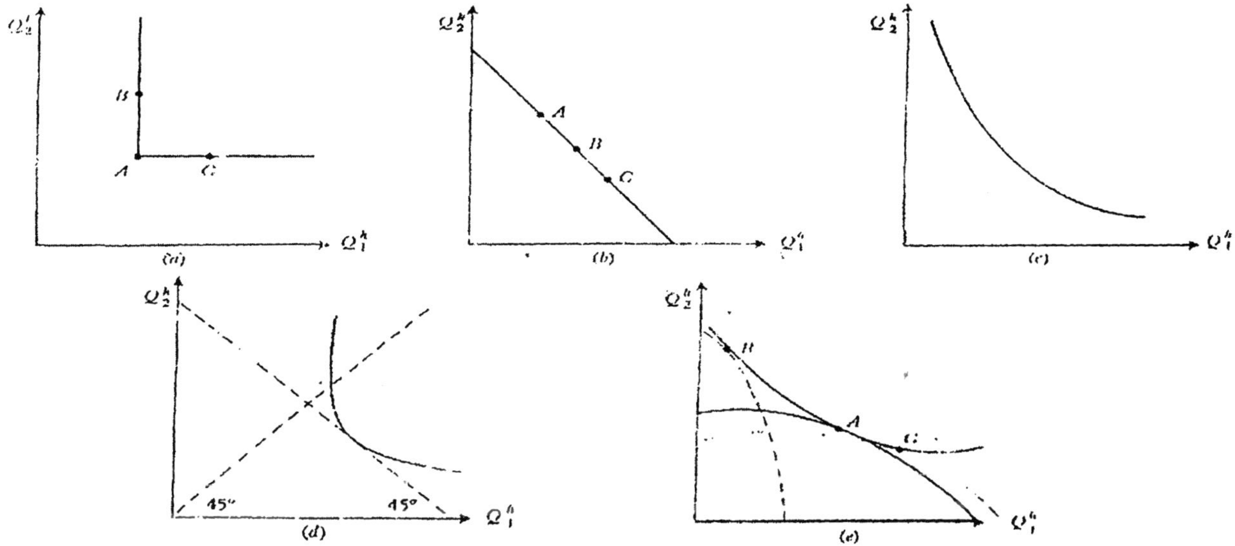

Fig. 16.1 : Model of intra-household allocation of nutrients among children to produce a distribution of expected health among the children; (a) Square-cornered parental preferences (Rawlsian or infinite inequality; aversion case) with equal concern; (b) Linear parental preferences (pure investment or no-inequality aversion case) with equal concern; (c) Equity-productivity trade-off in parental preferences with equal concern; (d) Equity – productivity trade-off in parental preferences with unequal concern favouring child 1; (e) Constrained maximisation of parental preferences at point *A* for solid health production possibility frontier (and at *B* and *C* for dashed frontiers).

linear, as in part (*b*), parents do not care about the distribution of health improvements, but only about obtaining the largest sum of the health improvements for their children: they are indifferent among *A*, *B* and C despite the very different distributional implications of these combinations of Q_1^h and Q_2^h. Between these two extremes, there are many intermediate possibilities with different degrees of equity-productivity trade-offs [as in part (*c*)]. In part (*a*), C refers to the curvature of the preferences, i.e. the degree of inequality aversion: C $\rightarrow \infty$ is the case of complete inequality aversion of Fig. 16.1 (*a*), C = 1 is the pure productivity case of Fig. 16.1 (*b*), and intermediate values of C are intermediate cases such as in Fig. 16.1 (*c*). A particularly interesting intermediate case is the Cobb-Douglas case in which C = 0. With the health production function described below, if C is less than zero, nutrients are allocated to compensate for inequality in endowments (i.e., the inherently weaker get more), and with C greater than zero, nutrients are allocated to reinforce inequality (i.e., the inherently stronger get more).

Second, preferences may be symmetrical over health outcomes of the children in the sense that equal health is weighted equally in the household preferences as in Fig. 16.1 (*a*) – (*c*). Alternatively, parents may weigh equal health outcomes differently depending on the gender or birth order or other characteristics of the children, which is called 'unequal concern'. Unequal concern implies that the preference curves are asymmetrical around a 45° ray from the origin as in Fig. 16.1 (*d*), in which case the health of child 1 is weighted more heavily than the health of child 2. The a_i refer to unequal concern; if they depend on sex, the preferences reflect unequal concern related to sex.

The next assumption concerns the technology of the health production function, which is assumed to be quasi-Cobb-Douglas. For simplicity, I write it with one nutrient and one health outcome for each child, though in the actual study both have multiple indicators:

$$Q_i^h = N_i^a g(E_i, \ldots) \tag{2b}$$

Under the assumption that there is an interior solution and that the prices of nutrients are the same for all children, the critical parameters of the preference function are explicit in the ratio of the first-order conditions for two children:

$$\frac{N_1}{N_2} = \frac{a_1}{a_2}\left(\frac{Q_1^h}{Q_2^h}\right)^c . \tag{12}$$

With data on individual nutrient intakes and individual health outcomes, the utility function parameters relating to inequality aversion (c) and unequal concern by gender (a_1, a_2) can be estimated from (12). Effectively, these estimates exploit the fact that the preference-maximising allocation of nutrients between two children is given by the tangency of the health production possibility frontier with a preference curve as at point *A* in Fig. 16.1 (*e*); but for different pairs of children the health production possibility frontiers differ in shape because of different relative endowments (perhaps in part related to sex), so a series of such tangencies trace out the shape and location of a preference curve [*B*, *C* in part (*e*)]. If ordinary least squares estimates are made, however, the estimate of C is upward-biased, since the nutrient and the health ratios are determined simultaneously.

I obtained estimates for rural south Indian households using the ICRI-SAT VLS (International Crops Research Institute for the Semi-Arid Tropics Village Level Studies) panel data. Because of great emphasis by some on seasonality, I distinguished in the estimates between the lean season (when food is in relatively short supply) and the (relatively) surplus season by effectively allowing for separability in preferences between the seasons. The estimates indicate significant inequality aversion; i.e., parents care about the distribution of health among their children and not just about the productivity of nutrients used to produce health. During the surplus season the inequality aversion is strong enough that parents adopt compensating behaviour, giving more nutrients to those children with less endowments. In other words, as is suggested as a possibility in the first point regarding the health production function in relation (2), nutrients are negatively associated with health indicators during this season because of parental efforts to compensate. During the lean season, however, the estimated inequality aversion is much less, indicating that parents may reinforce inequalities by giving more nutrients to children who are better endowed. During the lean season, moreover, the estimates indicate significant unequal concern, weighing health outcomes by about 5 per cent more for boys than for girls (and more so for lower-caste than for higher-caste households). Thus, there is substantial concern about equity and no unequal concern favouring boys when food is relatively available; but when food is relatively scarce, the less well endowed female and lower-caste children are placed at greater nutritional risk. That there is estimated gender preference in the lean season is all the more striking because for this sought Indian sample the raw nutrient intake data do not indicate sharp gender differences. Apparently, the gender differences entering through the endowments that favour girls in the health production function roughly offset the preference weights that favour boys in the lean season so that gender effects are not clear in simple bivariate associations between sex and nutrient intakes or between sex and health status, but they do appear in the structural estimates of preferences.

Health production functions – A.priori, there may be gender differences in the impact of nutrient intakes on health – as represented by anthropometric, mortality and morbidity experience indicators – in relation (2). However, I am aware of very few efforts to explore such a possibility, and those estimates that are available do not indicate much in the way of gender differences. For example, Behrman and Deolalikar present 2SLS LISREL estimates of health production functions for men, women, boys and girls for the ICRISAT south rural Indian sample, also used in the study described immediately above. While they find some evidence of significant differences across types of individuals, they do not report any significantly positive estimates of coefficients for nutrient inputs in the health production process.

Lewis presents logistic estimates of quasi-reduced-form relations that include some elements of production functions for post-neonatal mortality for 5481 male and female Jordanian infants in the mid-1970s. Her results suggest some significant gender differences in health production, with the length of breast-feeding and mother's education being of significantly greater importance in reducing male than female mortality. These results are the most compelling of any that I know in suggesting gender-specific differences in the impact of nutrient intakes on health outcomes. They must be qualified, however, because it is not clear exactly what is being estimated, and there probably is simultaneity bias arising from the failure to treat variables such as the length of breast-feeding as endogenous.

Other studies that approximate individual health-production functions have restricted themselves to additive gender effects, without interactions with nutrient intakes. For example, Magnani present estimates of production functions for weight-for-age for Philippine infants and small children (aged 1 – 59 months) with a number of inputs. They report that male children are significantly (about 6 per cent) less likely to be 25 per cent or more below Filipino anthropometric standards than are female children independent of nutrient intakes. However, the lack of control for simultaneity makes interpretation difficult. Heller and Drake estimate health production functions with additive gender effects for three anthropometric measures (weight-for-height, height-for-age, and weight-for-age) and three morbidity indicators (mild diarrhoeal disease, severe diarrhoeal disease, and number of days with illness) for 1270 children under 6 years of age in the early 1970s in Candelaria, Colombia. They find significant positive effects for weight-for-height for girls age 0 – 11 months and 12 – 23 months, significant negative effects for weight-for-age for girls age 0– 11 months, but no other significant additive effects. Their results do not appear very conclusive about possible gender discrimination, but their procedure of including the lagged endogenous variables may obscure actual gender effects. Wolfe and Behrman estimate quasi-reduced forms that are close to health production functions for child mortality and standardised child height, weight, and biceps circumference for a random area-stratified sample for 1281 households with children under 5 years of age in Nicaragua in 1977-78. For the nation and for three regions (by degree of urbanisation), they find significant additive gender effects only for males for biceps circumference in the national and other urban (i.e. other than the capital city) samples, though the quasi-reduced-form nature of their specification and the lack of control for simultaneity means that their results must be qualified. Horton presents estimates of the determinants of height-for-age and weight-for-height for 1570 Filipino children aged 15 or less in the Bicol sample with a sibling control for unobserved fixed effects. She reports significant birth-order effects, but no significance for gender. Pitt and Rosenzweig likewise report no significant additive gender effect in a production function for number of adult days ill in the previous week in rural Indonesia. Sirilaksana, finally, estimates simultaneous health production functions for three anthropometric outcomes for 1006 preschool children in north-east Thailand. She finds one significantly negative additive impact (at the 5 per cent level) for a child being female in 24 regressions for different age– anthropometric combinations – about what one would expect to occur by change if in fact there is no true effect.

Thus, there seems to be very little or no evidence that the impact of nutrient intakes on health indicators depends systematically on gender. However, this may just be part of the problem of our general ignorance of the nature of the health production technology and the failure in existing estimates to control well for metabolism, time use, and lags.

Wages – Only recently, as noted above with regard to relation (8), have there been some estimates of the impact of nutrient intakes on productivity that control for the possible simultaneity of higher wages causing better nutrition. In only two of these studies, to my knowledge, is there an exploration of gender differences. Behrman and Deolalikar present such estimates for adults in the ICRISAT rural south Indian sample. Their results suggest that the wage impact of nutrients (actually, calories) does not differ significantly between males and females but that the impact of weight-for-height does, with significant effects in the slack season for males but not for females. Sahn and Alderman also estimate wage determination relations with household calories as a simultaneously determined RHS variable for 2125 men and 625 women in rural Sri Lanka with data from the 1980/1 Labour Force and Socioeconomic Survey. They report a statistically significant elasticity of real wage with respect to calories of about 0.2 for men that is robust to different estimation approaches, but an insignificant one for women. Behrman and Deolalikar speculate that the results in these studies may reflect the gender division of tasks, with males specialising in tasks involving more physical strength (e.g. those involving the use of bullocks). If so (and if weight-for-height reflects nutrient intakes in the Behrman-Deolalikar study), then with the current division of labour there may be gains to the household as a whole from allocating somewhat more nutrients at the margin to males than to females than would be optimal without labour productivity effects. Note that these results are not consistent with the conjecture in point 5 of heading Measurement Problems that estimated nutrient impacts may be greater for females than for males because of measurement problems.

Schooling – Sirilaksana, Jamison and Moock and Leslie present recent studies which claim to investigate the impact of child malnutrition on schooling performance, but in fact consider the association between anthropometric health indicators (and, in the last case, haemoglobin count) and schooling performance. Sirilaksana estimates the determinants of school grades for 582 children aged 7 – 13 in north-east Thailand. Jamison explores the determinants of grade retardation (or 'grades behind') for a Chinese sample. Moock and Leslie investigate the determinants of schooling enrolment and grade attainment in Nepal. All of these estimates generally indicate a positive association between the anthropometric indicators and school performance. However, that better health and better schooling performance both may be due to other factors such as endowments and family background, as is suggested in heading Analytical Frameworks, is not recognised by using simultaneous estimators, so the authors' interpretation of causality must be heavily qualified. Additive gender effects are included in all of the estimates, but are significantly non-zero (negative for girls) only for schooling enrolment in Nepal. Therefore, these estimates do not provide much clarification of whether nutrient and health effects on schooling performance differ by gender.

Reduced-form relations

The reduced-form relation for nutrients in equation (11) is of particular interest for this paper. But other reduced-form relations may also be of interest if, through differential responses to food prices for outcomes of individuals identified by gender, there is evidence of the intra-household allocation of nutrients having an impact through gender effects.

Nutrient intakes – To estimate these reduced-form relations to test for most gender effects, data on *individual* nutrient intakes are required. Some of the relatively few data-sets with such information do not have much information on prices or the other RHS variables in Z in relation (11). Therefore, perhaps, it is not surprising that I am aware of only two studies that contain estimates that include prices.

The first study is for the rural south Indian ICRISAT data-set, once again, by Behrman and Deolalikar. In this study the authors first observe that the impact of a food price change on nutrient intakes may be positive for at least one food price, depending upon the extent of induced substitution to foods with higher food-to-nutrient conversion factors. That is, an increase in the price of a high-cost nutrient source may improve nutrition (though not welfare) by inducing substitution by a lower-cost nutrient source. The authors then present estimates of the price elasticities of nutrient intakes for boys, girls, men and women with a latent variable representation of nutrient intakes and with control for unobserved fixed effects through using differenced panel data. Their estimates suggest that the nutrient elasticities with respect to income are small and do not differ with the recipient of the nutrients. The nutrient elasticities with respect to price, in contrast, are large (generally greater than 1 in absolute value) and are negative for the basic staple (sorghum) but positive for the other foods. Most important for this survey, the response of nutrients to price changes differs significantly among the types of individuals, with smaller adjustments in the nutrient intakes of girls in response to changes in the sorghum price (the basic staple) and larger adjustments in the nutrient intakes of girls in response to other price changes. Therefore, nutrient intakes for girls are treated as relative 'necessities' with respect to sorghum price changes, with little significant adjustment in light of favourable or unfavourable sorghum price movements. In contrast, nutrient intakes for girls are treated as relative 'luxuries' with respect to *other* price changes, with considerable adjustments in response to favourable and unfavourable price movements.

The second such study is Garcia and Pinstrup-Andersen for a panel of 840 households in 14 villages (selected for their high incidence of malnutrition and poverty) in three provinces in the Philippines in 1983-84 to evaluate price discounts for rice and cooking oil and nutrient education programmes. Half of the households were covered by the programme; the other half were a control group. On the average, food distribution as compared with Filipino standards was biased in favour of adults, with limited evidence of pro-male biases for children; the calorie adequacy rate was 0.80 for adults, 0.60 for male preschoolers, and 0.55 for female preschoolers. Regression results are presented for reduced forms for calorie intakes for 509 individual children aged 13 – 83 months. With controls for a number of other variables (including income and some major prices and assets), boys still receive significantly more calories than girls, on the order of magnitude of 100 calories per day. Unfortunately, however, only additive gender effects are explored.

Besides there being different parameters in the reduced-form individual nutrient demand relations depending on the sex of the individual, gender may enter into the nutrient allocation decision in another way. As is discussed above in heading Analytical Framework, the nature of predetermined control of or investment in human resources by gender may affect nutrient intakes. Existing studies focus on such effects for women's schooling, and in a few cases for women's wages. The rationale for including such variables is based on the fact that better schooled women are more efficient in household production, that better schooled women bargain more effectively over household resources, and that women are more interested in nutrition than are their husbands. In any case, women's schooling is included in a number of estimated reduced-form nutrient relations. The results from these are mixed. Horton reports significantly negative effects for a sample of 366 rural households from Gujarat, India, primarily because of an inverse impact on the share of food expenditures in total expenditures. She also obtains a positive impact for the male household head's education, which in large part apparently is an income effect. Sirilaksana finds no significant impact of women's schooling (working through predicted women's wages), nor of men's schooling, on household nutrient intakes in her study of 582 north-east Thailand households, though there is a significant impact of women's schooling (through predicted wages) on food expenditure. War and Sanders report no significant effects for a north-eastern Brazilian sample, as do Behrman and Deolalikar for rural south India. Garcia and Pinstrup-Andersen report a significant positive effect of women's schooling on food expenditure, but not a significant effect on the acquisition of calories in their Filipino study cited above.

On the other hand, Valenzuela reports significant positive effects on calories and, in interaction with food expenditures, on protein and vitamin C for the Laguna Philippine data. Behrman and Wolfe and Wolfe and Behrman also report strong positive effects for their Nicaraguan data. The latter group of studies, moreover, find that the impact of mother's schooling remains strong even with random effects or with latent variable or sibling-differenced fixed-effects control for unobserved ability and attitudes related to the woman's childhood family background, in contrast to the strong effect of such controls on the estimated impact of schooling for a number of other outcomes.

Horton and Miller explore whether women have preferences favouring children and basic needs, as suggested by S.E. Brown, Dwyer, P. Engle, and others, by estimating household-level reduced-form relations for expenditure shares (including some detail for food), calories per capita, and diet quality for a low-income non-random 1984/5 sample of 145 Jamaican households, 43 per cent of which were headed by females. For aggregate expenditure shares, no difference is found between male- and female-headed households. For major food groups, female-headed households spend a significantly larger share on starch from yams, plantain, etc., a significantly smaller share on dairy products, and have no significant differences for the other nine food groups. If foods are divided by the share of luxury, necessity, and intermediate food groups (where the economic definition concerning the relation between budget share and income is used to define these categories), female-headed households spend significantly less on necessity and intermediate foods. There is no difference in calories per capita, but female-headed households have higher diet quality (as defined in an index utilising nine nutrients other than caloric). Thus, the authors conclude that there is some limited support for the hypothesis that female-headed households exhibit greater concern for basic needs and children in the diet quality results. However, their diet quality index almost seems contrived in order to find some positive impact of female headship on food and nutrients after more direct explorations did not show significant effects. For this reason, and because of their peculiar sample, it would seem inappropriate to conclude that this study provides much evidence that women are more concerned with nutrients than are males.

Health status – I am aware of nine studies that explore reduced forms for health status – once again, as measured by anthropometric and morbidity indicators – with some dimensions of gender differences that may be attributable to gender effects in intra-household nutrient allocations.

Pitt and Rosenzweig present ordered probits for the male household head being ill in the previous week and his wife being ill in the previous week and a fixed-effect logit for household head being ill relative to the wife being ill for a random sample 2347 farm households in the April-June 1978 sub-round of the National Socio-Economic Survey of Indonesia (SUSENAS). Their empirical representation of Z in relation (11) is extensive, including 13 consumption prices, 8 community or environmental variables, wages, education of the head and his wife, and owned land and farm profits. Their estimates *prima facie* suggest the possibility of some significant gender differences. At the 5 per cent level of significance, the probability of the household head being ill is affected positively by his education and the price of vegetables, and negatively by the price of sugar; the probability of the wife being ill is affected positively by the price of fish and the presence of public lavatories in the community. Such evidence is hardly overwhelming, however, given that only 5 of 56 coefficient estimates are statistically significant at the 5 per cent level, not much more than would be expected to occur by chance if there were no true associations. In part this may reflect the considerable measurement problems in using self-reported illness for only one week as the health indicator.

Bhuiya estimate separate (almost) reduced forms for weight-for-age for about 700 (each) boys and girls aged 2 – 60 months in Matlab in Bangladesh using data from the

International Centre for Diarrhoeal Disease Research Demographic Surveillance System. Their estimates suggest some definite gender differences in these relations, though the presentation of their results does not permit an easy untangling of all the effects. For example, they report a significant positive impact of mother's education (larger for Hindus than for Muslims) on boys' but not on girls' health. They also find a significantly positive impact of possession of articles, reinforced by the male head's education, on boys,' but not girls', health. However, the interpretation of this last result as a wealth effect is clouded by confusing gender effects associated with their land-tax variables. Thus, their results suggest that young boys benefit more in terms of weight-for-age from more educated mothers than do young girls, presumably because of intra-household allocations, including those for nutrients. It is interesting to note that, in this case, having more educated mothers favours sons and more educated fathers with low wealth favours the daughters (but *vice versa* if there is some wealth, as represented by the ownership of items such as a quilt, hurricane lamps, bicycle or radio).

Behrman and Deolalikar present reduced-form estimates for the determinants of individual health status (as represented by multiple anthoropometric indicators within a LISREL latent variable framework) for men, women, girls and boys in the rural south Indian ICRISAT sample, with control for unobserved fixed effects through differencing panel data. Their estimates indicate a significant impact of half of the food prices on health status, but no significant gender differences among the price, income, or wage coefficients.

Khan estimates relations for height as a function of age and simultaneously determined household nutrients (from basic grains) for males and females in four age groups (2 – 5, 5 – 14, 14 – 19 and 19 years and over) for a 1976-77 rural survey of about 6000 individuals conducted by the Bangladesh Institute of Development Studies. Significant effects are reported for males aged 19 and over and for females aged 14 – 19 and 5 – 14, but not for the other age-sex combinations considered. These results might be interpreted to mean that at the margin household nutrition allocations favour females aged 5 – 19 and males aged 19 and over, or that the marginal productivity of nutrients in terms of height is the greatest for such groups. The latter interpretation seems doubtful since the marginal health impact probably is greatest for small children, so probably these results reflect intra-household allocation patterns as much as differential nutrient productivities. If so, they constitute some evidence of intra-household allocation patterns in which sex and age interact. But the strength of the results is limited, since in the majority of cases there is no significant impact of nutrients on height, and since the instruments used for the first-stage estimates for household nutrients (i.e. land and socioeconomic status) are limited.

In addition, five other studies permit only additive gender effects. Strauss's extensive estimates for the rural Ivory Coast report no significant impact of gender. Akin present logit estimates of infant feeding in the Bicol Philippines 1978 sample and also report no significant gender effects; but Horton reports a significant gender effect favouring girls for height-for-age for children under 15 in the same sample, which Barrera also finds for the older children in this sample using different techniques. Garcia and Pinstrup-Andersen, for the same 509 Filipino children aged 13 – 83 months described above, report a significantly higher additive Z-score for weight-for-age for boys, but not for weight-for-height, nor for either weight or height as a percentage of age standards. They also find no significance of women's education for all of these outcomes.

Mortality – Rosenzweig and Schultz have estimated reduced-form differential male-female child survival rates with rural district data from the 1961 Indian census in a well-known study. They argue that such survival rates reflect intra-household resource allocations, presumably including nutrients. They find that the relative survival rate is significantly responsive to expected differential labour force options by gender, which they represent by current adult gender employment rates. Therefore, they conclude that intra-household allocations are responsive to and reinforce market-determined relative returns by gender, rather than being compensating. Such results are provocative regarding the role of longer-run expected returns in intra-household allocation, though one might question the exact representation of those expected returns in this study (i.e., why employment rates and not expected wages?).